Death and the Textile Industry in Nigeria

This book draws upon thinking about the work of the dead in the context of deindustrialization—specifically, the decline of the textile industry in Kaduna, Nigeria—and its consequences for deceased workers' families.

The author shows how the dead work in various ways for Christians and Muslims who worked in KTL mill in Kaduna, not only for their families who still hope to receive termination remittances, but also as connections to extended family members in other parts of Nigeria and as claims to land and houses in Kaduna. Building upon their actions as a way of thinking about the ways that the dead work for the living, the author focuses on three major themes. The first considers the growth of the city of Kaduna as a colonial construct which, as the capital of the Protectorate of Northern Nigeria, was organized by neighborhoods, by public cemeteries, and by industrial areas. The second theme examines the establishment of textile mills in the industrial area and new ways of thinking about work and labor organization, time regimens, and health, particularly occupational ailments documented in mill clinic records. The third theme discusses the consequences of KTL mill workers' deaths for the lives of their widows and children.

This book will be of interest to scholars of African studies, development studies, anthropology of work, and the history of industrialization.

Elisha P. Renne is Professor Emerita in the Departments of Anthropology and of Afroamerican and African Studies, University of Michigan-Ann Arbor, USA.

Routledge Contemporary Africa Series

Corporate Social Responsibility and Law in Africa
Theories, Issues and Practices
Nojeem A. Amodu

Greening Industrialization in Sub-Saharan Africa
Ralph Luken and Edward Clarence-Smith

Health and Care in Old Age in Africa
Edited by Pranitha Maharaj

Rethinking African Agriculture
How Non-Agrarian Factors Shape Peasant Livelihoods
Edited by Goran Hyden, Kazuhiko Sugimura and Tadasu Tsuruta

Toward an Animist Reading of Postcolonial Trauma Literature
Reading Beyond the Single Subject
Jay Rajiva

Development-induced Displacement and Human Rights in Africa
The Kampala Convention
Romola Adeola

Death and the Textile Industry in Nigeria
Elisha P. Renne

Modern Representations of Sub-Saharan Africa
Edited by Lori Maguire, Susan Ball and Sébastien Lefait

For more information about this series, please visit: https://www.routledge.com/Routledge-Contemporary-Africa/book-series/RCAFR

Death and the Textile Industry in Nigeria

Elisha P. Renne

LONDON AND NEW YORK

First published 2021
by Routledge
2 Park Square, Milton Park, Abingdon, Oxon OX14 4RN

and by Routledge
52 Vanderbilt Avenue, New York, NY 10017

Routledge is an imprint of the Taylor & Francis Group, an informa business

© 2021 Elisha P. Renne

The right of Elisha P. Renne to be identified as author of this work has been asserted by her in accordance with sections 77 and 78 of the Copyright, Designs and Patents Act 1988.

All rights reserved. No part of this book may be reprinted or reproduced or utilised in any form or by any electronic, mechanical, or other means, now known or hereafter invented, including photocopying and recording, or in any information storage or retrieval system, without permission in writing from the publishers.

Trademark notice: Product or corporate names may be trademarks or registered trademarks, and are used only for identification and explanation without intent to infringe.

British Library Cataloguing-in-Publication Data
A catalogue record for this book is available from the British Library

Library of Congress Cataloging-in-Publication Data
A catalog record has been requested for this book

ISBN: 978-0-367-46552-0 (hbk)
ISBN: 978-1-003-05813-7 (ebk)

Typeset in Bembo
by Deanta Global Publishing Services, Chennai, India

KTL workers, their widows, and children

James 1:27: Religion that is pure and undefiled before God, the Father, is this: to care for orphans and widows in their distress, and to keep oneself unstained by the world.

The New Testament

The Women 4:36: Pay homage to God, and make none his compeer, and be good to your parents and relatives, the orphans and the needy and the neighbours who are your relatives, and the neighbours who are strangers and the friend by your side.

The Qur'ān

Late Kaduna Textiles Ltd workers' ID cards

Contents

List of illustrations viii
Acknowledgments xi

Introduction 1

1 The city of Kaduna as colonial construct 19

2 New work-time regimes: The rise and fall of Kaduna Textiles Ltd 37

3 Workers' health and deaths after the closure of Kaduna Textiles Ltd 58

4 Burying the dead: Hometowns, houses, and cemeteries 74

5 Widows' dilemmas and experiences of hardship 92

5 Interlude: Widows' portraits 106

6 Consequences for children, problems for families 115

Conclusion: Death, deindustrialization, and time 135

Index 153

Illustrations

Figures

	Late Kaduna Textiles Ltd workers' ID cards	v
I.1	Member wearing Coalition of Closed Unpaid Textile Workers Association Nigeria-Kaduna branch jacket, 26 January 2017, Kaduna (Photograph by E.P. Renne).	2
I.2	Letterhead of list compiled by the Coalition of Closed Unpaid Textiles Workers Association Nigeria of KTL textile workers who died, with names and dates of death (Photograph by E.P. Renne).	2
I.3	Map of Nigeria indicating Kaduna and Middle Belt states (Courtesy of the World Bank).	4
I.4	Oliver Bijip came from the village of Kauyemu, in Kachia Local Government, to work in the Weaving Department at the Kaduna Textiles Ltd in 1976. He died in 2003 and was buried in Kauyemu (Photograph of ID card by E.P. Renne, courtesy of Martina Oliver, Kaduna).	7
1.1	Lugard Hall, 1960s, Kaduna (Photograph courtesy of Nicholas Rutherford, Minchinhampton, UK).	22
1.2	The entry gate to the Kabala Cemetery, a small African Christian cemetery in Constitution Road, 9 May 2018, Kaduna (Photograph by E.P. Renne).	28
2.1	Drawing of Kaduna Textile Ltd, the first industrial textile mill in Kaduna, northern Nigeria, which was established in collaboration with the textile manufacturing firm, David Whitehead and Sons, Ltd, Rawtenstall, Lancashire, UK (Courtesy of David Whitehead and Sons, Ltd, Archives, Parbold, Lancashire, UK).	40
2.2	Kaduna Textiles Limited *Employee's Handbook* with motto: "WORK, HONESTY, OBEDIENCE," undated, Kaduna	

	(Photograph by E.P. Renne, 15 May 2018).	48
2.3	Weaving room workers at Kaduna Textile Ltd, note wristwatch worn by worker on the right (Courtesy of David Whitehead and Sons, Ltd, Archives, Parbold, Lancashire, UK).	49
3.1	Kaduna Textiles Ltd clinic for general mill workers, Kaduna, 2018 (Photograph by E.P. Renne).	62
3.2	List of workers attending the KTL clinic and health problem diagnoses, 26 March 2002 (Photograph by E.P. Renne).	63
3.3	Death certificate for Dauda Sani, form used by the Gwamna Awan Hospital, Kaduna (Photograph by E.P. Renne).	66
3.4	Death certificate for Abubakar Iliya, RTA (Road Traffic Accident), General Hospital, Kafanchan (Photograph by E.P. Renne).	70
4.1	Graves at Barnawa Muslim Cemetery. These two graves contrast with the more usual plain mounds of other graves, 7 May 2018, Kaduna (Photograph by E.P. Renne).	75
4.2	Coffin sold in stall near the Television Garage, 7 May 2018, Kaduna (Photograph by E.P. Renne).	81
4.3	Crucifix with Christ, detail of coffin cover, 7 May 2018, Kaduna (Photograph by E.P. Renne).	82
4.4	Funeral program for the late Daniel Anche, see also Chapter 5 Interlude, Widow Portrait 1 (Photograph by E.P. Renne).	83
4.5	Family members wearing white during the burial of the late Daniel Anche; see also Chapter 5 Interlude, Widow Portrait 1 (Photograph of photograph by E.P. Renne).	84
4.6	Grave for Ishaya Netsi Musa, inside the family compound in Anguwan Gika, with the new style of patterned tiles with a cross, 15 May 2018, Kaduna (Photograph by E.P. Renne).	86
6.1	Benedict Taru Yashim, who remembers his father's generosity, 23 July 2019, Kaduna (Photograph by E.P. Renne).	117
6.2	Former KTL worker, Taru Yashim, received a Certificate of Long Service after he had worked in the Weaving Department for 20 years, 15 May 2018, Kaduna (Photograph by E.P. Renne).	117
6.3	Kaduna State Bureau for Substance Abuse Prevention and Treatment (KADBUSA) signboard, which reads: "Message From: KADBUSA, Children and Adults, You Should Avoid Taking Drugs," 15 January 2020, Kaduna (Photograph by E.P. Renne).	127
C.1	Photograph of the former KTL worker, James Agene, who died in August 2009, Kaduna (Photograph of photograph by E.P. Renne).	145
C.2	Ezekiel Levinus was interviewed on 17 July 2019. He died in February 2020, a second generation of KTL deaths, 17 July	

2019, Kaduna (Photograph by E.P. Renne). 146
C.3 Television Cemetery, where James Agene and members of his family are buried, 9 May 2018, Kaduna (Photograph by E.P. Renne). 146

Table

4.1 KTL widows' ethnicity and place of husbands' burials 77

Acknowledgments

I would like to thank leaders of the Coalition of Closed Unpaid Textile Workers Association Nigeria, who generously took time to meet with me and to introduce me to many of the widows whose husbands had died after the Kaduna Textile Ltd mill closed, as well as to their children. Rahab Gajere and Adama David expertly organized our meetings, while Wordam Simdik and Ishar Iorngulum oversaw my participation in Coalition events. I am grateful to all of the widows and their children whom we interviewed and for their permission to use their materials and to take their photographs, which are included in this book. I am also grateful to former employees of Kaduna Textiles Ltd and David Whitehead & Sons who shared their experiences and insights of working at the mill during many helpful interviews, and to union officials at the National Union of Textile Garment and Tailoring Workers of Nigeria, Kaduna office. Special thanks go to Muhammed Buhari and Salihu Maiwada, Ahmadu Bello University; to Mohammadu Yahaya Waziri, Modibbo Adama University of Technology, Yola; to M.O. Umar (Director), Wuese Iorver, and Olusola Falaye of Kaduna Textiles Ltd; and to Gordon Hartley, Bernard Laverty, and Nich Rutherford, of David Whitehead & Sons, as well as to Jaclyn Kline, who facilitated connections with David Whitehead & Sons personnel. In Kano, Sa'idu Adhama and the late Abdulkadir DanAsabe provided insights regarding textile revival possibilities, while in Kaduna, Joseph Maigari, Kaduna State Bureau for Substance Abuse Prevention and Treatment explained the importance of rehabilitation. I also thank Musa Salih Muhammad, Arewa House, Kaduna; the staff of the Nigerian National Archives, Kaduna, and the Ministry of Information Office, Kaduna; and librarians at the University of Michigan-Ann Arbor. Garba Abubakar has continued to provide logistical support for my work in Kaduna. Finally, the Covid-19 pandemic is a reminder that we are all in this world together; those in Kaduna and Kano who have passed during the pandemic will be remembered.

While hardly an exhaustive list of all those who deserve thanks, I would like to acknowledge the special support of Ya'u Tanimu and Hassana Yusuf, who have helped me with my research in northern Nigeria since 1995. Together, they provided excellent counsel and information and patiently waited with me when I needed visa extensions. Hassana Yusuf continues to impress me with her willingness to pursue difficult leads as well as to accompany me through the many neighborhoods of Kaduna. As always, I owe her great thanks. I am likewise grateful to Leanne Hinves, Senior Editor, African and African Diaspora Studies, at Routledge, Sarah Silva at Deanta Global, as well as to the editorial and design staff and my copyeditor at the Press, all of whose kind but firm organization facilitated the publication process. Finally, project funding from the African Studies Center, the Department of Afroamerican and African Studies, and UROP, all of University of Michigan, Ann Arbor, and from the Pasold Foundation made initial stages of this project possible.

Introduction

> She tried to discover what kind of woof Old Time, that greatest and longest-established Spinner of all, would weave from the threads he had already spun into a woman. But his factory is a secret place, his work is noiseless, and his Hands are mutes.
>
> Charles Dickens, *Hard Times* (1854: 71)

During the period from 2002 to 2005, three of the four largest textile mills in city of Kaduna, the capital of Kaduna State, in northern Nigeria, had closed (Akinrinade and Ogen 2008; Maiwada and Renne 2013). The fourth mill closed in 2007 although it was reopened with reduced staff in 2010 (Babadoko 2007; Isuwa 2013a). None of the other mills has reopened, and as of 2020, remittances have only been paid to laid-off workers from one mill (and its affiliated mill), while those who worked at the other closed mills have not been paid their entitlements. In this volume, I examine the consequences of the closure of one of these mills, Kaduna Textiles Ltd, which ended production in December 2002 without paying workers their final remittances (Mudashir 2011a). The closure of this mill had significant consequences for the lives and subsequent deaths of many KTL textile workers, as well as for the lives of their widows and children.

This study builds upon research on the history of death in African societies (Lee and Vaughan 2008; Jindra and Noret 2011), particularly changing ideas about proper burial practices and colonial attempts to regulate graves and cemeteries in urban spaces. In Kaduna, these changes have contributed to writing the names of the dead on cement-covered graves and tombstones, on death certificates, in funeral programs, and in cemetery record books.[1] This naming of the dead reflects a shifting emphasis from the unnamed dead associated with an ancestral spiritual afterlife to more specific social, economic, and political relationships discussed by Thomas Laqueur (2015), in his volume, *The Work of the Dead*. Yet despite these changes in naming, burying, and counting the dead, Laqueur notes an overarching concern with showing respect for the dead through particular practices and rituals, some of which reflect earlier social and historical precedents, which are too important to be forgotten. This concern also reflects the continuing importance of the ways that the dead work for the living, maintaining connections to people, property, and position.

In *Death and the Textile Industry in Kaduna, Nigeria*, the dead work in a related but somewhat different way. In 2005, a group of unemployed textile mill workers and their wives, as well as the widows and children of deceased workers, met in Kaduna to establish the Coalition of Closed Unpaid Textile Workers Association Nigeria (Alimi 2018; Figure I.1, I.2). At this meeting, group leaders began their list of the names of workers who had died since the mills where they worked had closed (Coalition of Closed Unpaid Textiles Workers Association Nigeria 2017). According to the chairman of the Coalition and former textile mill worker, Comrade Wordam Simdik, "Medication is a luxury to us. Our children no longer go to school…We recorded more than 2000 deaths of our members and families." (Isuwa 2013c). He attributed these deaths to mill closures and to the non-payment of termination benefits (Adama 2014; Alabi 2011; Isuwa 2013a; Mudashir 2011a, b). By emphasizing the number of

Figure I.1 Member wearing Coalition of Closed Unpaid Textile Workers Association Nigeria-Kaduna branch jacket, 26 January 2017, Kaduna (Photograph by E.P. Renne).

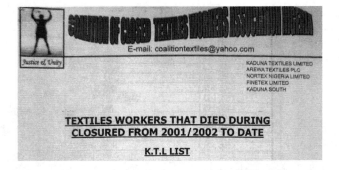

Figure I.2 Letterhead of list compiled by the Coalition of Closed Unpaid Textiles Workers Association Nigeria of KTL textile workers who died, with names and dates of death (Photograph by E.P. Renne).

worker deaths and publicizing their families' plight through the local press and protests, the Coalition sought to put pressure on government to pay laid-off workers' termination remittances. In this case, the dead are important to the living as a way of forcing government officials to provide unpaid remittances to workers (or their surviving widows) and to reopen these mills. The lists of their names, documented by the Coalition of Closed Unpaid Textile Workers Association Nigeria and publicized by these men's widows in demonstrations in Kaduna, both commemorate the dead and employ their names for the benefit of the living (Ahmadu-Suka 2017, 2019; Alabi 2011).

This volume considers the Coalition's actions as a way of thinking about death and the ways that the dead work for the living by focusing on three main themes. The first examines the growth of the city of Kaduna as a colonial construct which, as the capital of the Protectorate of Northern Nigeria, was organized by neighborhoods, by public cemeteries, and by industrial areas. The second theme examines the establishment of textile mills in the industrial area in the southern part of the city and new ways of thinking about work and labor organization, time regimes and money, and health, particularly occupational ailments documented in mill clinic records and by widows' descriptions of their husbands' illnesses. The third theme discusses the consequences of deindustrialization, focusing on KTL mill workers' deaths and the lives of their widows and children. Widows describe the burials of their husbands in Kaduna or in their hometowns—which reflect their ethnic and religious backgrounds—as well as their work to provide their children with education, housing, and food (Isuwa 2013c). Their children also have had various responses to their families' declining economic situation—some worked, some married, while some became involved in illegal activities and drug use. As such, deindustrialization in Kaduna, as elsewhere in the world, has contributed to unemployment, poverty, hunger, illness, and death (Minchin 2013), although within a particular historical context (Cowie and Heathcott 2003). While remittances for dismissed KTL workers remain unpaid, and the mill—as a source of employment and income for their children—has not reopened, the Coalition's listing of the names of the dead work continues, as a constant reminder of their society's injustice.

The city of Kaduna

This study is situated in the city of Kaduna, which was created during the colonial era when large tracts of land were set aside for administrative buildings, for cemeteries, and for an industrial area where the Kaduna Textiles Ltd mill later was constructed (David Whitehead & Sons 1973; Oyedele 1987). While initially the land was populated by the Gbagyi people (Gandu 2011), in 1917 the city was formally named as the capital of the Protectorate of Northern Nigeria (Simon 1992: 141) and the Governor, Frederick Lugard, had offices for colonial administrators and military personnel built there (Medugbon 1976). Subsequently, migrants from southwestern Nigeria came to work as clerks in government

4 *Introduction*

offices and traders from the southeast established shops in Kaduna's growing markets (Bununu et al. 2015). With the opening of the Kaduna Textile Ltd mill in 1957 in the Kakuri area of the city south of the Kaduna river, more migrants from the many small ethnic groups in southern Kaduna state as well as from Plateau, Benue, Nasarawa, and Kogi states (generically referred to as "the Middle Belt" of Nigeria) came to work in this and other mills (Figure I.3). Indeed, a majority of the workers at Kaduna Textiles Ltd interviewed in 1987 came to the mill from southern Kaduna (41%) and Middle Belt (39%) states, while 83% of KTL workers were Christian and 8% were Muslim (Andrae and Beckman 1999: 302). Through the missionary efforts of Catholic and Sudan Interior Mission churches in the Middle Belt area (Gaiya 2018; Ijagbemi 1986), those who had converted to Christianity also had some western education. Their ability to read and write as well as their familiarity with clock-based time-keeping made them attractive employees for the new mills. Additionally, many who settled in Kaduna in the areas surrounding the mills—such as Narayi and Sabon Tasha—established churches in their neighborhoods, which supported their Christian burial practices.

However, the large public cemeteries, which were established and overseen by colonial government officials, were related to their own concerns with health. Such cemeteries reflected colonial efforts to move the burial of the dead to areas separated from family houses, to control specific burial

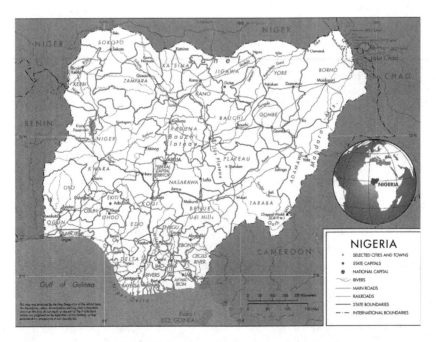

Figure I.3 Map of Nigeria indicating Kaduna and Middle Belt states (Courtesy of the World Bank).

procedures in Kaduna, and to register the names of the dead (Lee and Vaughan 2008). For example, Muslims were said to bury their dead in shallow graves as "The top soil is considered to be more blessed," according to John Carrow, the Resident of Kano Province. For health reasons, colonial health officials sought to enforce the burial of bodies at a depth of at least three feet (Nigerian National Archives-Kaduna, 1944–1957). Hence, the histories of the establishment of the large public cemeteries in Kaduna—distinguished by religion and often by race, ethnicity, and birthplace—reflect another aspect of the work of the dead. For, to some extent, these cemeteries reinforced distinctive identities of place associated with people.[2] However, not all labor migrants from the south followed government instructions, preferring burials next to their houses instead—as a way of maintaining a connection between the deceased, living family members, and ownership of their houses in Kaduna. Others travelled south with mill workers' bodies in order to maintain family connections and claims with the town or village from whence the deceased had come. When the mill was still operating, KTL helped families when a worker died although when it stopped production, this practice largely ended—yet another aspect of the impact of the mill's closure on family members.

Descriptions of the consequences of the absence of the dead for those who remain were elicited through extended interviews with widows and children whose husbands and fathers had worked at the Kaduna Textile Ltd mill. These interviews were conducted with the help of women leaders from the Coalition of Closed Unpaid Textile Workers Association Nigeria. Widows responded to questions about their relations with their husbands, their lives before and after the mill closed, and the situations—often illness—that led to their husbands' deaths. Some were able to provide their husbands' KTL mill ID cards, family photographs, death certificates, funeral programs, and even cloth caps; for those living in Kaduna, some assisted us in visits to their husbands' graves. Widows were then asked about their current situations and those of their children, the work they were involved in, housing, and food. Indeed, for some, hunger—"food poverty"—has been an ongoing concern (Charlton and Rose 2002; de Montclos et al. 2016),[3] and several women mentioned food when asked to relate a special memory of their husbands. After concluding these, at times, emotional interviews, I asked permission to take each woman's photograph, later printing copies which I gave to them. Many of these portraits convey a sense of the sorrow as well as the strength of these women, and are included as an important part of this study (see Chapter 5 Interlude: Widows' Portraits).

Following the deaths of their husbands, widows worked hard to support themselves and their families, often with little return and sometimes with unfortunate health consequences for themselves (Potash 1986). Many were unable to find funds for their children's continued education,[4] although extended family members sometimes helped out with school and examination fees. In some cases, older children helped their mothers as was the case with one older son who grows ginger on the family farm in order to help support his siblings. Not all mothers were so fortunate as some children, particularly sons, became involved in robberies and in the use of drugs such as Tramadol (Agha 2018; Ngbokai 2019).[5]

These three themes in which the dead work for the living in various ways are examined in more detail in the chapters that follow this introduction. The volume concludes with a discussion of the consequences of the deindustrialization of national textile manufacturing, youth unemployment, and the possibilities for reinventing the textile and clothing industry in Kaduna. Indeed, the deindustrialization of the textile industry in Kaduna may mark the end of an era and the beginning of a new one (Cowie and Heathcott 2003). Precisely what this new era will look like is unclear. Yet as one former KTL mill worker observed:

> Running a textile factory is like farming—because we have many millions of people in Nigeria who are looking for food to eat, [the demand is there]; the same thing applies to clothes to wear. So, the question is if textiles are to work in Nigeria, we need to stop imports from outside.
> (Interview: Sylvester Gankon, 24 May 2018, Kaduna)

He may be overly optimistic—for even if textile imports were halted, the mills' obsolete equipment needs to be replaced and electricity must be regularly supplied (Agbese et al. 2016; Onyeiwu 1997). But "it would be wonderful," as he observed, if these problems could be addressed in imaginative ways and if new forms of textile and cloth production could be initiated in Kaduna (Agabi 2019; Agbese and Alabi 2017; Aremu 2016).

The work of the dead for the living, the work of the living for the dead

Naming the dead

Aside from the list of names of deceased Kaduna Textile Ltd mill workers collected by the Coalition of Closed Unpaid Textile Workers Association Nigeria, the dead—through their graves—mark families' claims to houses and property and provide long-distance links between family members who travel to home villages to bury them and later return to commemorate them. As Robert Hertz famously noted in his volume, *Death and the Right Hand* (1960), while death is a biological event, how the dead are treated is framed by cultural beliefs and social practices, which may change over time but which may also continue in various ways. For the many men who migrated to Kaduna from agricultural areas in the south to work in the Kaduna textile mills and who subsequently died, their bodies were often taken back to be buried in family compounds in their home villages—rather than buried in cemeteries or near their houses in Kaduna.

Workers from southern Kaduna and Middle Belt states came from many small ethnic groups with their own burial practices. In the area around

Kafanchan, in southern Kaduna state, these ethnic groups include the Jaba [Ham], Kagoro, Atakar, and Kataf [Atyap] people.[6] 'Biyi Bandele-Thomas provides readers of his novel, *The Sympathetic Undertaker*, with a sense of these myriad ethnic groups and their respective languages:

> At that time, at the turn of the last century, what existed was a cluster of villages, each of which regarded itself as a sovereign state independent from the others. Even though they were all literally within a stone's throw of one another, their only common denominator was that they were all agricultural in economy; aside from that they each had a unique cultural identity, a separate language, a unique system of self-governance. They were the archetype of what one poet now calls our "*One kilometer is another language*" phenomenon. Our Tower of Babel.
>
> (Bandele-Thomas 1991: 34)

Oliver Bijip, who worked at Kaduna Textiles Ltd, and one of his widows, Martina Oliver, came from the area described by Bandele-Thomas, just northwest of the city of Kafanchan, in southern Kaduna state. Bijip was from the Atakar ethnic group, while his wife, Martina, was from the neighboring Kagoro group, from the village of Kwiya in Kagoro Local Government in southern Kaduna state. While Martina had some primary school education, her husband completed Primary 6; his ability to read and write made him an attractive hire as a weaving room worker at the KTL mill (Figure I.4). Oliver Bijip came to work at KTL in 1976 and worked there for 26 years. He died in 2003, shortly after the mill closed. He was buried in his family's compound in Kauyemu, Kachia Local Government.

Thus, despite the presence of church graveyards, as described by Bandele-Thomas (1991: 34): "The missionaries came and set up their churches and

Figure I.4 Oliver Bijip came from the village of Kauyemu, in Kachia Local Government, to work in the Weaving Department at Kaduna Textiles Ltd in 1976. He died in 2003 and was buried in Kauyemu (Photograph of ID card by E.P. Renne, courtesy of Martina Oliver, Kaduna).

schools—and cemeteries—among these villages," the Bijip family preferred to bury him in the family house, although they did write his name and date of death on his grave. However, Oliver Bijip's name is listed elsewhere, as number 134 on the list compiled by the Coalition of Closed Unpaid Textile Workers Association Nigeria.

Counting the dead: the Coalition of Closed Unpaid Textile Workers Association Nigeria

The Coalition of Closed Unpaid Textile Workers Association of Nigeria began to collect information on the deaths of mill workers at KTL, Arewa Textiles, Nortex, and Finetex textile mills in 2005 for the purposes of documenting the impact of textile mill dismissals and the non-payment of remittances on the lives of laid-off workers. According to the woman leader of the Coalition, Rahab Gajere:

> We didn't have anything to do, we started thinking that since our husbands lost their jobs, we started this organization in order to discuss what is disturbing us and to know how to solve our problems. Because since the company is closed and they have not paid our husbands…we started the organization to make the government realize our problems.
> (Interview: 18 January 2017, Kaduna)

They publicized the increasing numbers of mill workers' deaths at a demonstration in early September 2011 at the Kaduna Textiles Ltd mill, in the Kakuri (Kaduna South) area of Kaduna, as was reported in the northern Nigerian newspaper, *Daily Trust*:

> Widows and children of some of the workers, who died while waiting for their entitlements, also took part in the protest. They carried placards with inscriptions: 'Revive textile factories,' 'Namadi Sambo come and redeem your pledges,' 'Yakowa come to our rescue,' among others. Speaking to our correspondent, one of the widows, Rahmatu Adamu appealed to Northern governors to settle the entitlement of their late husbands.
> (Mudashir 2011a)

The Coalition's demonstration was heavily policed. However, a subsequent demonstration that was to begin in front of the Arewa Textiles mill in November 2011 was dispersed. Rahab Gajere told a *Daily Trust* reporter that this was their fourth attempt to demonstrate:

> "Every time, government will appeal to them to exercise patience. We have been patient enough. This time around, no more patience. Government should pay our husbands. If they pay us, they will not see us outside again. We are fighting for our husbands' money that they worked for and not

government's money." She called on the nineteen northern states to come to their rescue and ensure the payment of their husbands' gratuities and terminal benefits.

(Alabi 2011)

While the Coalition of Closed Unpaid Textile Workers Associations Nigeria sought to use mortality data to put pressure on the government, it is not a registered union. Thus, its activities are frowned upon, both by officials of the government's New Nigeria Development Corporation and of the National Union of Textile Garment and Tailoring Workers of Nigeria. The former was hoping to find buyers for the other closed mills; they did not want protests to disturb their plans (Interview: SH, 29 January 2017, Kaduna). The latter were negotiating with majority mill shareholders to come to an agreement to settle remittances owed and, indeed, these negotiations were successful for one mill and its affiliate.[7] However, leaders of the National Union of Textile Garment and Tailoring Workers of Nigeria were constrained in their efforts as one former mill manager explained:

About two or three years after the closure, the union took KTL management to court at Abuja. They asked them to calculate all the entitlements of workers and they did. And they said, "we are going to pay you." But you know, unfortunately, they didn't pay up until now—...And unfortunately, when the industry is not working, the union is weak. The union uses money to pursue any case—but since we're not working, the union does not have it.

(Interview: Sylvester Gankon, 24 May 2018, Kaduna)

Under these circumstances, the Coalition's collection of mortality data for laid-off workers has been a potentially beneficial means for asserting workers' rights by their families. Indeed, data on the adverse effects of textile manufacturing on the lives of workers is related to studies of mortality records of textile mill workers elsewhere in the world. One such study, conducted by Peter Kirby, beginning in 1982, documented the causes of death of British textile workers, who were members of the National Union of Dyers, Bleachers and Textile Workers for the period from 1976 to 1980.[8] Using union data and official death certificates, Kirby calculated the proportional mortality ratio that specified the types of illnesses which were related to mill workers' deaths. This method, however, would not be possible for Kaduna Textile Ltd workers as official death certificates were not available nor was data on workers' ages, types of mill work, and causes of death collected (Kirby 1984: 12). Nonetheless, this mortality data—namely, the listing of names and dates of death—was an important step for clarifying the socioeconomic impact of textile mill closures, deindustrialization, and unemployment (Sen 1998).

Kaduna Textile Ltd mill workers who died, their widows, and families

In 2012, I was told to contact Alhaji Shaibu Yusuf by a staff member of the Department of Industrial Design at Ahmadu Bello University, Zaria, because of his leadership position at the Kaduna Textile Ltd mill. I interviewed him in February 2012. He died two years later in 2014, which I learned when I interviewed his wife, Sofia Shaibu Yusuf, in May 2018. According to her, he was born in 1960 in Ankpa, in Ankpa LG, Kogi State, and moved to Kaduna as a young man. In Shaibu Yusuf's interview, he focused on his education and work. After receiving a Higher National Diploma (HND) in Textile Technology from Kaduna Polytechnic, he began work at Kaduna Textile Ltd as deputy manager in the Spinning Department. He was responsible for the work of 200 men, both in meeting production targets for certain sizes of yarn and for sizing thread to be used in weaving. As he observed in 2012, ten years after the closing of the KTL mill:

> When I started in Kaduna Textiles, the country was ok. The economy started falling back, as a result of government policies—such as the lifting of the ban on textile materials...Then another government policy that affected the textile industry was that power was not steady. When I started, it was perfect...[And] we were supposed to change out machinery, to meet modern challenges but it was not done. All these things, if they are addressed, [the industry] can start back, especially if there is oversight.
> (Interview: Shaibu Yusuf, 28 February 2012, Kaduna)

After his dismissal when the mill closed, Yusuf was "just managing" as a security guard for one company. The family's situation worsened in the years after his dismissal from KTL. By virtue of his work as a deputy manager in the Spinning Department, Shaibu Yusuf and his family were allocated housing in the junior managers' KTL Quarters, and his widow, Sofia, continues to live there. While there are a few other Muslim widows living in the Quarters, the majority of KTL widows living in the Quarters or in the Kakuri and southern areas of Kaduna are Christians, originally from the south.[9]

The KTL mill manager, Sylvester Gankon, who knew Shaibu Yusuf when they worked together at the mill, agreed with his assessment of the problems that led to its closure. He noted that the government has failed to organize proper planning for the replacement of outdated machinery, that there was insufficient control of textile imports by customs agents, and that the provision of regular electrical power was lacking (Interview: Sylvester Gankon, 28 February 2012, Kaduna). The views of these two men that government mismanaged the industry was seconded by one textile mill owner in Kano, who noted, "You know, the disaster in the textile industry, a lot of it was man-made, especially the northerners...Whoever is in textiles today can hardly forgive some of the Northern leaders, they surrendered it (Interview: S.D. Adhama, 23 January 2017, Kano; see Maiwada and Renne 2013: 184; also Odunlami et al. 2016).[10]

This failure of the Nigerian government to support the Kaduna textile industry and to maintain related infrastructure was also reflected in its failure to pay remittances to laid-off textile workers at the two mills, Arewa Textiles and Kaduna Textiles Ltd, with majority Northern Nigerian government ownership (through the New Nigeria Development Corporation). Thus, on 6 June 2013:

> The National Union of Textile Garment and Tailoring Workers of Nigeria (NUTGTWN) yesterday called on the 19 Northern States governors to pay N687 million to the staff of closed Kaduna Textile Limited (KTL). The union had in September 2005 obtained a court judgment for settlement of the entitlements of the workers amounting to N687,073,346.00 by its owners, 19 northern states. The governors have not adhered to the court orders in spite of appeals, prayers, rallies and protests by the workers and its unions.
>
> (Isuwa 2013b)

As Comrade Issa Aremu, General Secretary of NUTGTWN and Vice President of the Nigeria Labour Congress (NLC) wrote in a letter in 2013: "The union is disturbed by the continuous closure of Kaduna Textiles Limited since December 2002. Even more worrisome is the continuous delay in settlement of the entitlements of KTL workers by its owner-19 Northern States of the Federation. KTL workers are suffering untold hardship due to non-payment of their benefits" (Isuwa 2013b).

As of 2020, these payments had still not been made and plans for reopening the KTL mill have not been successful. For example, in early 2017, initial negotiations with the Turkish textile firm, SUR International Investments, were conducted (Interview: Wuese Iorver, 18 January 2017, Kaduna). A follow-up meeting in August 2017 in Kaduna led to the plans for a $15 million partnership for renovating KTL, which was to focus on the production of military and workers uniforms (Agbese and Alabi 2017).[11] Initially, the company was to refurbish the mill with updated equipment in order to produce uniforms, while it was expected that other garments would also be manufactured. According to Alhaji Ali Gombe, Chairman of the Restructuring Committee-KTL, "SUR will provide 35 percent of the total funds while the balance would be shared between the Federal Government and 19 Northern states" (Daily Trust 2017). However, one KTL mill worker was less optimistic:

> Last year people from Turkey said that they would come. Then from nowhere, quiet. They will tell us that they will soon open...They came but I think that the problem is, you see, it's the light problem. When they came, they discovered no light [electricity]. And these machines cannot

run on power from a generator, they will be running at a loss, to be frank. If NEPA did not stand up, there is no way. The machines use real power and not generator power.

(Interview: Haruna Joshua, 10 May 2018, Kaduna)

Aside from infrastructural obstacles, others explained Turkish abandonment of this project in terms of a failed economic incentive:

There is a snag in this arrangement as the company is insisting that the Federal Government invest 88 million USD in the project…but the Government is not investing in a privately-owned company…And the government funds are limited, they are not sufficient to take care of KTL.

(Interview: Wuese Iorver, 1 May 2018, Kaduna)

While the parties involved initially planned to move forward on this project, the SUR management's insistence that a large prepaid contract for uniforms from the Ministry of Defense be provided led to the abandonment of the project (Interview: Abdullahi Ali Gombe, 13 November 2017, Kaduna).

While there have been other possible investors—such as the Chinese Shandong Lue Group—who were interested in renovating the KTL mill, to date no substantial plans have been proposed. Nonetheless, the Central Bank of Nigeria has recently sponsored several schemes for supporting the revival of the textile industry through cotton-growing loans and restrictions on access to subsidized foreign exchange for textile importers (Agabi 2019; Aminu 2019). These efforts are important, yet the challenges of electricity, obsolete equipment, and unrestricted imported textiles persist. How successfully these challenges are met will help to address the problem of growing numbers of unemployed young people in Kaduna. For as Akin Ajayi, the director general and chief executive officer of the Institute of Directors, Nigeria, has noted, "The collapse of industries in the Northern part of Nigeria has done more damage to the region than the Boko Haram crisis" (Isuwa 2012; see also Abubakar 2016). In other words, the indirect violence, reflected in lack of income, food, access to health care, and housing (e.g., Aijmir and Abbink 2000; Bourgois 2009; Farmer 2004; Watts 1983),[12] which has affected former mill workers and their families, is comparable to or even exceeds the intermittent, overt violence associated with Boko Haram militants in northeastern Nigeria as well as with the political violence associated with federal elections, the introduction of Shari'a law, and recent kidnappings in Kaduna (Ahmadu-Suka 2019; Angerbrandt 2011; Harris 2013).

Conclusion

Like that man over there. The one in the lace babanriga…He's a carpenter. Specializes in coffins. Nothing but coffins. He calls himself an undertaker. That's

absolute rubbish. [But] that man is one of the richest people in Kafanchan. Through coffins. Nothing but coffins.
'Biyi Bandele-Thomas, *The Sympathetic Undertaker* (1991: 127)

When Taiwo Alimi interviewed members of the Coalition of Closed Unpaid Textile Workers Association Nigeria in November 2018, he was told that with the closure of the Kaduna textile mills and without final benefit payments, "they feel 'dead and buried'" (Alimi 2018). Indeed, many workers from the Kaduna Textiles Ltd mill have actually died, which members of the Coalition have documented through the listing of their names and dates of deaths. While their efforts had a specific goal—they were meant to put pressure on the government and textile mill management to live up to their agreement to pay workers' remittances, this naming of the dead reflects changing social relations in northern Nigerian society. For like the re-evaluation of the changing relationship between time and work—from farm work based on the seasonal succession of night and day and social relations to an impersonal time-money regime and the specialized work of the textile mills (Thompson 1967), making written lists of the names of the dead was part of another process of social transformation of people from farmers to mill workers. In the early 20th century, many rural Nigerians went by a single name—or several names, which reflected multiple social identities—family, ethnicity, town of origin, religious or political position. With the coming of Christian and Catholic missionaries to the areas now associated with southern Kaduna and Middle Belt states, converts acquired first and last names which were used in church and school attendance ledgers. This acquisition of lists of names was expanded to their use in hospital files as well as on birth certificates, tax records, census forms, and, at times, death certificates. With the opening of textile mills in the city of Kaduna, these names were compiled by company officials and health clinic personnel and were printed on ID cards. With the establishment of Nigeria as an independent state in 1960, these listings and forms of the names of the dead represented a particular social identity as citizens of Nigeria.[13] More recently, the naming of the dead—as deceased KTL mill-workers—underscores this identity as citizens, who deserve to have their negotiated rights recognized.

Alternatively, failure to name the dead implies their marginality and unimportance, as Laqueur (2015: 389) notes. The collapse of the textile industry and unemployment in Kaduna has contributed to growing inequality in Nigeria.[14] Yet a privileged few, some of whom have benefited from government positions and contracts, live ostentatiously in palatial compounds (Habila 2007; Oxfam 2017). Union officials, along with Coalition members who have insisted on making a list of names, are asserting the rights of the terminated textile workers—both the dead and the living—to their remittances and to a modicum of equality as human beings. The following chapters document the history of these efforts and lives, as well as their hopes and concerns for what lies ahead.

Notes

1 Few obituaries for mill workers have been published in northern Nigerian newspapers, which differs from their extensive publication by Yoruba families in southwestern Nigerian newspapers (Lawuyi 1989; see also Newell 2016).
2 In January 1947, the Secretary, Northern Provinces wrote to the Resident of Sokoto Province concerning the need to establish—"under section 37 of the Births, Deaths and Burials Ordinance Chapter 47"—a public cemetery in Gusau in order to bury the bodies of British colonial officials who had died there (Nigerian National Archives-Kaduna, 1944–1957).
3 In 2017, a young boy was shot and killed on the grounds of the Command Secondary School—Kaduna, when he and his mates were caught packing sand. "While others ran away, the boy pleaded to be allowed to pack the sand in order to get something to eat" (Alabi and Ahmadu-Suka 2017).
4 The government's failure to pay Kaduna Textiles Ltd mill workers' termination remittances has contributed to the "cumulative disadvantage" of their children (Case and Deaton 2017), whose impoverishment and interrupted education have led to unemployment, disrupted social relationships, and illness.
5 While Tramadol was banned in 2018 (*Daily Trust* 2018), some of the children of former textile workers have found ways to obtain this and other drugs (which is discussed in Chapter 6).
6 During the 19th century under Sokoto Caliphate rule, many of these ethnic groups received Hausa names, for example the Ham people became known as the Jaba, while the Atyap became known as the Kagoro, Atakar, and Kataf.
7 The relative strength of this union in Kaduna reflects its initial organization as well as Kaduna mill workers' sense of independence associated with their largely agricultural backgrounds (Andrae and Beckman 1996). The organization of unions in the Kano textile mills was somewhat different (Andrae and Beckman 1999; Lubeck 1986).
8 This study calculated proportional mortality ratios, namely ratios for 5-year age groups (from 15 to 64 years), using national figures for deaths for a particular age group (multiplied by the deaths observed for all causes of a particular group of mill workers—for each age group) to come up with an expected number of deaths for a specific cause of death (e.g., cancer) to determine the denominator, the "expected number of deaths for Cause 'X'." The numerator became the "observed deaths Cause 'X'" for the specific group of mill workers. By dividing the observed deaths by the expected deaths and multiplying by 100, the proportional mortality ratio was calculated (Kirby 1984; see also Shilling and Goodman 1951).
9 This was the case for Martina Oliver, Oliver Bijip's widow, who lives in a small, single room in the Romi neighborhood in the southern part of the city.
10 This man specifically mentioned the negotiations regarding the World Trade Organization agreement and the concession by the chairman of the Kantin Kwari textile market in Kano "to politicians" who benefited from the opening of this market to Chinese textiles and traders (see also Taylor 2007).
11 SUR International Investments is a private firm that invests in joint ventures with countries in Africa, with a focus on the integrated manufacture of military uniforms. In 2001, the Sur Military Clothing Factory was established, which produces uniforms for armed forces in the Middle East and North Africa (http://www.surinternational.com).
12 While Marc-Antoine de Montclos et al. (2016) focus on the politics of mortality and counting the dead associated with armed conflict, they do mention its effects on food production and consumption as well as employment opportunities and viable housing.
13 Some women publicize their new married names in lists of announcements published in local newspapers. Most of the women widows or wives of laid-off mill workers whom we interviewed took their husbands' first name as their last name.

14   The National Bureau of Statistics reported that "60.9% of Nigerians in 2010 were living in 'absolute poverty'—this figure had risen from 54.7% in 2004." This report also stated that in 2010, "almost 100 million people [are] living on less than a $1 (£0.63) a day" (BBC World News 2012).

References

Abubakar, Sanusi. "A Threat Worse than Boko Haram: Defusing the Unemployment Time-Bomb." *Daily Trust*, 28 June 2016. Accessed 28 June 2016. www.dailytrust.com.ng.

Adama, Dickson. "How Textiles Closure Cost Over 2,700 Lives in Kaduna." *Sunday. Trust*, 2 August 2014. Accessed 16 April 2017. www.dailytrust.com.ng.

Agabi, Chris. "CBN Moves to Revive Textiles, Bars Forex Access for Textile Imports." *Daily Trust*, 5 March 2019. Accessed 5 March 2019. https://www.dailytrust.com.ng/cbn-moves-to-revive-textiles-bars-forex-access-for-textile-imports.html.

Agbese, Andrew, and Christiana Alabi. "NNDC Raises Fresh Hope on Kaduna Textile Industry." *Daily Trust*, 3 September 2017. Accessed 19 September 2017. www.dailytrust.com.ng.

Agbese, Andrew, Christiana Alabi, Maryam Ahmadu-Suka, and Francis Iloani. "Why Textile Industry Remains Dormant Despite Fg's N100bn Bailout." *Daily Trust*, 3 July 2016. https://www.dailytrust.com.ng.

Agha, Eugene. "How Tramadol Codeine Are Smuggled into Nigeria." *Daily Trust*, 24 November 2018. Accessed 30 April 2019. https://www.dailytrust.com.ng/how-tramadol-codeine-are-smuggled-into-nigeria.html.

Ahmadu-Suka, Maryam. "Tears, as Workers of Closed Textile Coy Pray over Entitlements 15 Years On." *Daily Trust*, 4 November 2017, 14.

Ahmadu-Suka, Maryam. "JUST IN: Unidentified Gunmen Kidnap 5 in Kaduna." *Daily Trust*, 24 August 2019. Accessed 24 August 2019. https://www.dailytrust.com.ng/just-in-unidentified-gunmen-kidnap-5-in-kaduna.html.

Aijmir, Göran, and Jon Abbink, eds. *Meanings of Violence: A Cross Cultural Perspective*. Oxford: Berg, 2000.

Akinrinade, Sola, and Olukoya Ogen. "Globalization and De-Industrialization: South-South Neo-Liberalism and the Collapse of the Nigerian Textile Industry." *The Global South* 2, no. 2 (2008): 159–170.

Alabi, Christiana. "Widows of Kaduna Textile Workers Recount Their Plight." *Daily Trust*, 11 November 2011. Accessed 11 November 2011. www.dailytrust.com.ng.

Alabi, Christiana, and Maryam Ahmadu-Suka. "Army Probes Kaduna Shooting." *Daily Trust*, 10 June 2017. Accessed 10 June 2017. www.dailytrust.com.ng.

Alimi, Taiwo. "We Feel Dead and Buried." *Medium.com*, 2 November 2018. Accessed 22 May 2019. https://medium.com/@taiwo_alimi/we-feel-dead-and-buried-586142c0ada5.

Aminu, Habibu Umar. "CBN Moves to Revive Cotton Production." *Daily Trust*, 6 May 2019. Accessed 6 May 2019. https://www.dailytrust.com.ng/cbn-moves-to-revive-cotton-production.html.

Andrae, Gunilla, and Björn Beckman. "Bargaining for Survival: Unionized Workers in the Nigerian Textile Industry." Discussion paper No. 78. Geneva: UNRISD, 1996.

Andrae, Gunilla, and Björn Beckman. *Union Power in the Nigerian Textile Industry*. New Brunswick, NJ: Transaction Publishers, 1999.

Angerbrandt, Henrik. "Political Decentralisation and Conflict: The Sharia Crisis in Kaduna, Nigeria." *Journal of Contemporary African Studies* 29, no. 1 (2011): 15–31.

Aremu, Issa. "Return of Textile Industry?" *Daily Trust*, 17 October 2016. Accessed 17 October 2016. www.dailytrust.com.ng.

Babadoko, Sani. "Closure of Textiles Threat to Security in Kaduna—Yakowa." *Sunday Trust*, 4 November 2007. Accessed 25 December 2007. www.dailytrust.com.ng.

Bandele-Thomas, 'Biyi . *The Sympathetic Undertaker and Other Dreams*. Oxford: Heinemann, 1991.

BBC World News. "Nigerians Living in Poverty Rise to Nearly 61%." *BBC World News*, 13 February 2012. Accessed 13 February 2012. http://www.bbc.co.uk/news/world-africa-17015873.

Bourgois, Philippe. "Recognizing Invisible Violence: A Thirty Year Ethnographic Retrospective." In *Global Health in Times of Violence*, edited by B. Rylko-Bauer, L. Whiteford, and P. Farmer, 17–40. Santa Fe: School for Advanced Research Press, 2009.

Bununu, Y.A., A.N. Ludin, and Nafisa Hosni. "City Profile: Kaduna." *Cities* 49 (2015): 53–65.

Case, Anne, and Angus Deaton. "Mortality and Morbidity in the 21st Century, Conference Version." 17 March 2017. Brookings Papers on Economic Activity. Washington DC: Brookings Institute, 17 March 2017.

Charlton, Karen, and Donald Rose. "Prevalence of Household Food Poverty in South Africa: Results from a Large, Nationally Representative Survey." *Public Health Nutrition* 5, no. 3 (2002): 383–389.

Coalition of Closed Unpaid Textiles Workers Association Nigeria. "Textile Workers That Died During Closure from 2001/2002 to Date. K. T. L. List." Unpublished, 2017.

Cowie, Jefferson, and Joseph Heathcott. *Beyond the Ruins: The Meanings of Deindustrialization*. Ithaca, NY: ILR Press, 2003.

Daily Trust. "NNDC Moves to Resuscitate Kaduna Textile Company." *Daily Trust*, 14 August 2017. Accessed 14 August 2017. www.dailytrust.com.ng.

Daily Trust. "Why FG Banned Production, Importation of Syrups Containing Codeine." *Daily Trust*, 1 May 2018. Accessed 2 Dec 2018. https://www.dailytrust.com.ng/why-fg-banned-production-importation-of-syrups-containing-codeine.html.

David Whitehead & Sons. "Kaduna: The Largest Spinning and Weaving Operation South of the Sahara." *Textile Month*. Archives. Parbold, Lancashire: David Whitehead & Sons Ltd, June 1973.

de Montclos, Marc-Antoine Pérouse, Elizabeth Minor, and Samrat Sinha, eds. *Violence, Statistics, and the Politics of Accounting for the Dead*. Heidelberg: Springer International Publishing, 2016.

Dickens, Charles. *Hard Times*. Mineola, NY: Dover Publications, 1854 [2001].

Farmer, Paul. "An Anthropology of Structural Violence." *Current Anthropology* 45, no. 3 (2004): 305–325.

Gaiya, Musa A. "SIM's Hausa Mission: Ministering Among People on the Margin (*'Yan Babu*) Class in Northern Nigeria." In *Transforming Africa's Religious Landscapes: The Sudan Interior Mission (SIM). Past and Present*, edited by B. Cooper, G. Corwin, T. Eshete, M. Gaiya, T. Geysbeek, and S. Shankar, 121–144. Trenton, NJ: Africa World Press, 2018.

Gandu, Y. "Historical and Contemporary Basis for Sectarian Residential Settlement Patterns in Kaduna Metropolis of Northern Nigeria." *Mawazo: The Journal of the College of Humanities and Social Sciences. Makerere University* 10, no. 3 (2011): 72–91.

Habila, Helon. *Measuring Time*. Abuja: Cassava Republic Press, 2007.

Harris, Colette. "Violence in a Religiously Divided City: Kaduna, Nigeria—From the Shari'a Riots of 2000 to the Post-Election Clashes of 2011." *Space & Polity* 17, no. 3 (2013): 284–299.

Hertz, Robert. *Death and the Right Hand*, trans. by R. and C. Needham. Glencoe, IL. The Free Press, 1960.

Ijagbemi, E. Adeleye. *Christian Missionary Activity in Colonial Nigeria: The Work of the Sudan Interior Mission Among the Yoruba, 1908–1967*. Lagos: Nigeria Magazine, 1986.

Isuwa, Sunday. "Collapse of Industries Worse Than Boko Haram." *Daily Trust*, 20 February 2012. Accessed 20 February 2012. www.dailytrust.com.ng.

Isuwa, Sunday. "Has Fg's N100bn Textile Fund Gone Down the Drain?" *Daily Trust*, 14 April 2013a. Accessed 18 April 2013. www.dailytrust.com.ng.

Isuwa, Sunday. "Textile Workers Write Govs Over N687m Entitlement." *Daily Trust*, 7 June 2013b. Accessed 7 June 2013. www.dailytrust.com.ng.

Isuwa, Sunday. "Sacked Textile Workers Now Social Nuisance." *Daily Trust*, 19 July 2013c. Accessed 19 July 2013. www.dailytrust.com.ng.

Jindra, Michael, and Joel Noret, eds. *Funerals in Africa: Explorations of a Social Phenomenon*. New York: Berghahn Books, 2011.

Kirby, Peter. *Death in the Textile Industry: A Proportional Mortality Study of 952 Dyers, Bleachers and Textile Workers Who Died Between 1976–1980*. Bradford, West Yorkshire: Transport & General Workers Union, Textile Group, 1984.

Laqueur, Thomas. *The Work of the Dead: A Cultural History of Mortal Remains*. Princeton, NJ: Princeton University Press, 2015.

Lawuyi, Olatunde. "The Story About Life: Biography in Yoruba Obituaries." *Diogenes* 37, no. 148 (1989): 92–111.

Lee, Rebekah, and Megan Vaughan. "Death and Dying in the History of Africa Since 1800." *Journal of African History* 49, no. 3 (2008): 341–359.

Lubeck, Paul. *Islam and Urban Labor in Northern Nigeria: The Making of a Muslim Working Class*. Cambridge: Cambridge University Press, 1986.

Maiwada, Salihu, and Elisha Renne. "The Kaduna Textile Industry and the Decline of Textile Manufacturing in Northern Nigeria, 1955–2010." *Textile History* 44, no. 2 (2013): 171–196.

Medugbon, Andrew Kayode. "Kaduna, Nigeria: The Vicissitudes of a Capital City, 1917–1975." Unpublished PhD dissertation. Los Angeles, CA: University of California, 1976.

Minchin, Timothy. 2013. *Empty Mills: The Fight Against Imports and the Decline of the U.S. Textile Industry*. Lanham, MD: Rowman & Littlefield Publishers Inc.

Mudashir, Ismail. "Textile Workers Protest over Non-Payment of Entitlements." *Daily Trust*, 7 September 2011a. Accessed 7 September 2011. www.dailytrust.com.ng

Mudashir, Ismail. "Widows' Outburst." *Daily Trust*, 20 September 2011b. Accessed 20 September 2011. www.dailytrust.com.ng.

Newell, Stephanie. "From Corpse to Corpus: The Printing of Death in Colonial West Africa." In *African Print Cultures*, edited by D. Peterson, E. Hunter, and S. Newell, 389–424. Ann Arbor, MI: University of Michigan Press, 2016.

Ngbokai, Richard. "Police Arrest 54 Suspected Drug Dealers in Kano." *Daily Trust*, 6 March 2019. Accessed 6 March 2019. https://www.dailytrust.com.ng/police-arrest-54-suspected-drug-dealers-in-kano.html.

Nigerian National Archives-Kaduna. *Cemeteries*. Kadmin Health No. H021/81, Vol. I. Kaduna: Nigerian National Archives, 1944–1957.

Odunlami, Temitayo, Ibraheem Hamza, and Francis A. Iloani. "High Cost of Production Killed Kaduna Textile Industries – Dr. Bello." *Daily Trust*, 13 January 2016. Accessed 13 January 2016. www.dailytrust.com.ng.

Onyeiwu, Steve. "The Modern Textile Industry in Nigeria: History, Structural Change, and Recent Developments." *Textile History* 28, no. 2 (1997): 236–249.

Oxfam International. *Inequality in Nigeria: Exploring the Drivers*. Oxford: Oxfam, 2017.

Oyedele, Enoch O. "Colonial Urbanization in Northern Nigeria, Kaduna 1913–1960." Unpublished PhD dissertation. Zaria: Department of History, Ahmadu Bello University, 1987.

Potash, Betty, ed. *Widows in West African Societies*. Stanford: Stanford University Press, 1986.

Sen, Amartya. "Mortality as an Indicator of Economic Success or Failure." *Economic Journal* 108, no. 446 (1998): 1–25.

Shilling, R., and N. Goodman. "Cardiovascular Disease in Cotton Workers, Part 1." *British Journal of Industrial Medicine* 8, no. 2 (1951): 77–90.

Simon, Pius Bala. "The Spatio-Economic Impact of Informal Sector Activities on the Physical Development of Nigerian Cities: A Case Study of Kaduna." Unpublished PhD dissertation. Manchester, UK: University of Manchester, 1992.

Taylor, Ian. "China's Relations with Nigeria." *The Round Table: The Commonwealth Journal of International Affairs* 96, no. 392 (2007): 631–645.

Thompson, E.P. "Time, Work-Discipline, and Industrial Capitalism." *Past & Present* 36, no. 1 (1967): 56–97.

Watts, Michael. *Silent Violence: Food, Famine, and Peasantry in Northern Nigeria*. Berkeley, CA: University of California Press, 1983.

1 The city of Kaduna as colonial construct

A bus station in Kaduna is mentioned in Helon Habila's novel, *Measuring Time* (2007: 61):

> They stayed two weeks in Kaduna, sleeping with the street boys in rough shelters at the bus station at night, admiring the buildings and the cars and the incredible mass of people by day.

This station may have been the large area with taxis and buses travelling to all parts of Nigeria and beyond that is now known as Kawo Motor Park, located on the north part of the city of Kaduna, adjacent to the road that leads to Zaria and Kano. Initially, the Kawo area was a village adjacent to the Kaduna city limits, which like the Kakuri village to the south, was designated by colonial officials for the residence of northern Nigerian Muslim migrants (Medugbon 1976: 218). Alternately, Sabon Gari ("new town") was reserved for non-Muslim Nigerian migrants, while a European residential area known as the ERA (renamed GRA) was located near the administrative offices in the central part of the city. These early colonial plans for the city's residential areas changed to some extent as Kaduna's place as a government administrative center shifted, with the departure of most of the British colonial officials after Nigerian Independence in 1960. Indeed, with the growth of trade and the textile industry, many of the migrants from the Middle Belt states of Nigeria who came to Kaduna seeking employment in the 1960s settled in Kakuri and in nearby areas such as Television and Anguwan Romi, having obtained jobs in one of the textile mills. Once settled, they brought their wives—often new brides—along with junior family members to live with them in these more recently developed neighborhoods in the southern part of the city. KTL widows described their responses to the urban environment, which for most was very different from the agricultural villages from which they came.

Nonetheless, there were some similarities as these settlements eventually had churches, schools, and even street names associated with their hometowns, which distinguished them from the more northerly parts of Kaduna such as Tudun Wada and Kawo, whose residents were mainly Muslim. In this way, the preliminary 1913 plan of Sir Frederick Lugard, in which he sought to have

Kaduna organized in a grid-fashion, with separate residence areas populated by different groups distinguished by race, religion, and ethnicity, has continued to a certain degree. The cemeteries which were initially established by colonial officials in the 1920s and 1930s similarly were distinguished, with the Kaduna Civil Cemetery for British and expatriate burials, the Barnawa Cemetery for Christian Nigerians, and the Tudun Wada Cemetery for Muslim Nigerians. The number of cemeteries expanded with the growth of the city, even as some Kaduna residents continued to bury family members in or around their houses according to their hometown burial practices.

This chapter begins with a discussion of the establishment of Kaduna as the capital of the Protectorate of Northern Nigeria in 1917, and Frederick Lugard's 1913 preliminary plan for the city of Kaduna, along with the building of roads and the opening of the train station in 1927. Migrants from southern Nigeria traveled by new roads and train transportation to work in administrative positions and trade, which increased the population of the city to some extent (Medugbon 1976). However, it was in the late 1950s and early 1960s, with the opening of textile mills and other industries, that many migrants from the Middle Belt and Northern states were attracted to Kaduna and settled in the city. The first impressions of Kaduna expressed by KTL widows, who mainly came from Middle Belt villages, are then considered. Their initial experiences contrast with their subsequent situation after the mill's closure and their husbands' deaths. As migrants, their families' decisions about where their husbands were to be buried were influenced by several factors. While cemeteries in the Kaduna metropolis were initially established by colonial officials concerned about sanitation and health, many families' continued ties with their home villages led them to transport and bury deceased KTL workers in their hometowns, as will be discussed in Chapter Four.

Nonetheless, those who have resided in Kaduna for many years and who own houses have preferred to have deceased KTL workers buried adjacent to their family houses in Kaduna. This continued preference and practice suggests that despite the plans carried out for the layout of the city by colonial officials, Nigerians maintained some practices considered to be too important to be abandoned.[1] Thus while colonial concerns with what officials viewed as enlightened urban planning that included segregated residential areas, a grid-like pattern of roads, cemeteries, and a railway station, the implementation of their plans for Kaduna were not entirely successful. More recently, Nigerian government officials participating in the centenary celebrations for Kaduna held in 2017 noted both the improvements that colonial plans had contributed to residents' lives as well as the difficulties such as insecurity that residents have come to face (Agbese and Mustapha 2017; Ahmadu-Suka and Shuaibu 2017).

History of the city of Kaduna and the colonial city layout

The selection of Kaduna as the capital for the Protectorate of Northern Nigeria by Sir Frederick Lugard was based on several factors: its location in terms of access to water, roads, and the planned railway route between Lagos and Kano, as well as its appropriateness as a site for colonial administrative offices, military barracks, and mercantile business firms (Oyedele 1987: 150).[2] The area selected for the city was first surveyed in 1913 and in June of the same year, a preliminary plan for the development of Kaduna was written.[3] In 1915, Lugard, the Governor General of Nigeria, approved the plan and two years later, the enactment of the 1917 Township Ordinance provided the legislative framework for the implementation of the specific plans for the city. Plans for acreage, for government office buildings, for a European residential area, for the Royal West African Frontier Force (RWAFF) barracks, for African clerk quarters, and for a section "across the tracks" west of the railway for African laborers were described in detail. The layout for Kaduna was characterized not only by segregation by race and rank but by ethnicity and religion as well. For as Oyedele (1987: 154) astutely observed:

> This plan [for Kaduna] clearly…shows that settlement in the city was to be established on racial, ethnic and class lines. This pattern of residential segregation which partitions the urban social structure into separate worlds of space, standards and amenities each, guarded by occupation, education, place of origin and race was a major structural change on the pattern of organizing space in pre-colonial northern Nigeria. [The plan also] shows how the colonial government alienated large portions of land-area for their imperialist interest – governmental, residential and military.

While his plan emphasized the importance of British administrators and military support for the administration of its colonial regime, Lugard also stressed British interest in Nigeria as a source of raw materials through his insistence on the construction of a railway to northern Nigeria and his plan for the railway to pass along the western boundary of Kaduna. His concern was to provide railway service to the North as a means for the export of northern Nigerian agricultural raw materials such as cotton and the import of British manufactured textiles. Lugard succeeded in convincing the Colonial Office to provide funds for the railway which linked Kaduna in 1927 with Lagos and Ilorin, Zaria, and Kano. While the railway did serve the shipment of raw cotton to Lagos, from where it was sent to textile mills in Manchester, and provided easier access by Kano traders to textiles imported from England,[4] it also provided for the transport of colonial officials, Royal West African Frontier Force (RWAFF) soldiers, and Nigerian civilians. In other words, the administrative role of Kaduna was seen as its main function (Figure 1.1):

> The first plan of Kaduna by Lugard proposed the development of commercial activities such that the commercial and trading establishments operating were put away out of sight up in the North-West corner next to the railway. It was not unexpected therefore that the land use allocation (i.e., areas to be initially developed to accommodate the essential colonial

The city of Kaduna as colonial construct

Figure 1.1 Lugard Hall, 1960s, Kaduna (Photograph courtesy of Nicholas Rutherford, Minchinhampton, UK)

functions) by 1917 placed relatively little emphasis on commercial developments at this stage. The planning and development at these initial stages was obsessed with ensuring the instruments of administrative control were set in place.

(Simon 1992: 166)

Nonetheless, the central location of Kaduna, along with its access to water, rail and road transport, and developed infrastructure led to its subsequent growth as a center of trade and industry.

Growth of Kaduna, its expanded city layout, industrialization, and unplanned neighborhoods

The Nigerian population of Kaduna grew slowly in the first half of the 20th century and consisted mainly of laborers and office staff. In 1924, the total population of both Africans and Europeans was estimated at 5,206. According to government population statistics for 1929, "the Kaduna Township...in the space of 4 years (1924–1928) the total population has doubled itself and that within a five mile radius of the Township [which included its suburbs] the total nucleus of the population is now as high as 14,000" (Medugbon 1976: 111). By 1931, it was estimated that 1,391 Yoruba-speaking people (from both southern and northern Nigeria) and 1,272 Igbo-speaking people had settled in Kaduna Township proper (Medugbon 1976: 118). Indeed, compared with other northern Nigerian cities in 1931, Kaduna had the largest number of immigrants, which reflected the growing importance of trade in the city. Yet the consequences of the great depression and World War II limited growth in the city until the early 1950s. Thus, while the population of Kaduna Township and surrounding villages was estimated at 38,794 in 1952 (Medugbon 1976: 125), this number had expanded almost four-fold to 149,900 by 1963 (Medugbon 1976: 120; Lock and Partners 1967: 130). After World War II, the attraction of work opportunities in Kaduna contributed to the migration of more Igbo and Yoruba traders to Kaduna, who opened shops in the Sabon Gari area, which reflected the specialization in goods and services associated with these ethnic groups. For example, Igbo men worked as mechanics and sold auto parts in shops along Ahmadu Bello Way, while also selling foodstuffs such as stockfish in the market and running dry-cleaning shops. Yoruba traders specialized in textile sales in shops along Lagos Street and are known for their tailoring skills (Medugbon 1976: 162-63). Their presence also reflected the growth of Christianity as well as Yoruba Muslim groups associated with southwestern Nigeria (such as Ansar-ud-Deen) in the city.

This expanded migration to Kaduna reflected several factors. First, the number of people with houses increased considerably following the end of World War II when Nigerian soldiers who had enlisted in the Royal West African Frontier Force (RWAFF) in Kaduna returned from the war front were given land on which they built houses. Second, the opening of the Kaduna Textiles Ltd (KTL) mill in 1957, associated with the "Northernization Policy," resulted in "people, mainly males from all parts of the present ten Northern States, particularly from the Kabba [Kogi], Ilorin [Kwara], Benue, and Southern Zaria [Kaduna State] areas, coming to Kaduna by the thousands to seek employment" (Medugbon 1976: 142). Third, many migrants during this period also had primary school education which encouraged them to look for urban employment opportunities as most came from small agricultural villages; "less than 10% came from urban centers of more than 5,000 people" (Medugbon 1976: 142). This attraction continued after Nigerian Independence in 1960, when additional textile mills that required workers with primary school education opened in the southern part of the city, particularly around the Kakuri area.

The opening of textile mills in Kaduna

Although not initially the first choice for siting of a northern Nigerian textile mill,[5] Kaduna, the capital of the Protectorate of Northern Nigeria, was situated along the Kaduna River, with access to locally grown cotton and rail service. As will be discussed in the following chapter, the Kaduna Textiles Ltd mill was the first to be established in the city in 1957. As Lock and Partners (1967: 146) noted in the mid-1960s, with the "potential growth in the textile industry, there are expansion prospects for spinning, printing and the mass production of made up goods. It does not therefore seem unreasonable to reserve an area of up to 300 acres for the ultimate expansion of the textile industry in Kaduna." The growth of the textile industry in the southern part of the city, however, has resulted in "the sprawl of the many outer village settlements both inside and outside the present Capital Territory boundary," particularly in Kaduna South where there has been phenomenal growth (Lock and Partners 1967: 87). Indeed, many of the outlying, unplanned residential areas south of Kakuri, where the families of KTL mill workers now reside, were not named in the Lock and Partners 1965 to 1966 study. They include Television, Anguwan

Romi, Anguwan Narayi, Anguwan Makere, Anguwan Nasarawa, Anguwan Mission, Anguwan Sule, Anguwan Karatude, Anguwan Baje, Anguwan India, Sabon Tasha, Kurmin Garin, Kudenda, Juji, Trikania, and Gonin Gora. It was to some of these areas that the wives of former KTL mill workers came to live when they first moved to Kaduna.

Widows' first impressions of Kaduna

Many of the men who migrated to Kaduna to work in the textile mills came from the numerous small ethnic groups discussed by Bandele-Thomas (1991). Moving to areas south of the city, the majority were Christians. While many widows of workers at the Kaduna Textiles Ltd mill first came to Kaduna upon marriage to men from their hometowns who had moved to Kaduna to work, a few had come earlier with family members when they were quite young—in the early 1960s. These women met their husbands in Kaduna and subsequently married. But for those who came as new wives, they came mainly in the late 1970s and early 1980s, a time when the textile industry was still prospering. Their first impressions were generally, although not entirely, favorable. For example, one widow who came from the Angas-speaking area of Plateau state observed:

> I came to Kaduna in 1979. After we married, my husband brought me here. We started living in Television.[6] At that time, I really enjoyed Kaduna. Because at that time, there was the textile company and there were jobs and we didn't have a textile mill in our home village. I really enjoyed seeing the textile mill. But one thing that I didn't like about Kaduna, there were so many pigs in our area and I don't like pigs.
> (Interview: Maria Galau, 17 July 2019, Kaduna)

Others, however, mentioned being very impressed by the electric lights and trains:

> I came to Kaduna in 1970 when I married my husband. We started living in Kakuri. The first time I came to Kaduna, we stopped in Kakuri. I saw the electric lights. Then I said, "Ahhhh! Is that the way that towns look?" That was what I saw first and it impressed me.
> (Interview: Laraba Haruna, 25 July 2019, Kaduna)

> I have been in Kaduna for 35 years now [since 1984]. My husband got a job at KTL and he brought me to Kaduna. We started living in Television. Kaduna town was very beautiful, you could see cars, you could see trains passing, it was the train I took when I came with my husband.
> (Interview: Laraba Mallam, 23 July 2019, Kaduna)

Indeed, as one widow explained: "Everything was nice and beautiful in Kaduna then, I liked everything about Kaduna. Because I thought Kaduna town was another country—it was so different from my hometown" (Interview: Lami Iliya, 23 July 2019, Kaduna).

However, it was food that most impressed many of the widows when they first came to Kaduna, both the availability and low cost of many different types of food:

> Kaduna town impressed me at that time because we used to have good food. And there was no problem with my husband because he was working at KTL. But in our hometown, we only ate *fate* [a gruel made with millet or guinea corn flour], *tuwo* [porridge], and *kunu* [pap, a type of gruel]. But here in Kaduna, when we first came, we ate rice [*shinkafa*], with good soup that had meat and Maggi. If I were to say that there was something that I didn't like in Kaduna then, people would say that I am lying. Because I really enjoyed Kaduna at that time.
> (Interview: Laraba Paul, 25 July 2019, Kaduna)

Despite the advantages of inexpensive and easily accessed new types of food, along with electric light and pipeborne water (for some), and housing with metal roofs (for many), some widows initially missed the sociality of village life:

> When I first came to Kaduna town, I used to sit alone with no one to talk to. In my hometown, I would go to so many places and I especially remember when it was market day. I used to cry and wished I was there.
> (Interview: Laraba Haruna, 25 July 2019, Kaduna)

> I really enjoyed Kaduna at that time, the only thing was that I used to feel sad because I missed my family and could only write letters to them.
> (Interview: Hauwa Baba, 25 July 2019, Kaduna)

> What I didn't like about Kaduna the time that I first came, if you have any problems you have no one to talk to except your God.
> (Interview: Maryam Peter, 17 July 2019, Kaduna)

Eventually, though, as they raised families and attended churches, they became acquainted with other women, some from their own areas and ethnic groups. However, with the deaths of their husbands, along with the closing of the KTL mill and the difficulties they faced in obtaining ever more costly food, paying school fees and rent, along with outbreaks of political violence (Harris 2013), this situation led some to change their assessment of Kaduna:

> I don't like Kaduna now because the textile mills are not working because when the mills closed, everything spoiled in Kaduna. That's why I don't like Kaduna now.
> (Interview: Mary Taru, 25 July 2019, Kaduna)

> Before, I liked Kaduna very much but now I don't like Kaduna because there are so many difficulties here.
> (Interview: Laraba Mallam, 23 July 2019, Kaduna)

Nonetheless, while some widows have maintained hometown family ties, most say that they prefer to stay in Kaduna where some joined church women's groups and some have become active in ethnic associations.[7] These social ties later proved to be helpful after the deaths of their husbands, as members of these groups provided food served after funeral services and financial assistance for the burial of their husbands. For many of these men, their bodies were taken to their home villages where they were buried in (or near) family compounds.

Burial of the dead in Kaduna

Of the 85 KTL widows who were interviewed in 2018, the bodies of 41 of their husbands were taken back to their hometowns for burial in the family houses, despite the expense and the logistical difficulties of this practice. For those who owned houses in Kaduna, home burial was also common, which reflected both these families' property ownership and their preference for urban rather than rural life. As the son of one KTL worker remarked: "Even my father said that we should not take him to his hometown when he died, we should bury him in the house in Kaduna" (Interview: Bartholomew Samson, 23 July 2019, Kaduna). Thus, despite colonial officials' desire to establish cemeteries in different parts of Kaduna and to regulate the burial of bodies, for many of the families of KTL workers who died since the mill closed, their bodies were buried near their homes—either in their hometown or in Kaduna.

Yet the assumed dangers of this preference for home burials was raised by the Sanitation Inspector for Zaria Province in 1932, who sought to obtain government support for the establishment and use of cemeteries:

> It is observed that it is the custom for the dead to be buried in the compound. Although it is appreciated that this must be one of the older customs, it must be realized that a corpse is certain to foul the water supply, etc.

As Mabogunje (1992: 74) has noted, this perspective was "part of what Swanson (1977) had called 'the sanitation syndrome' of European colonialism, a syndrome influenced by public health theories of disease in the late 19th and early 20th century..." (see also Fourchard 2009: 191).[8] One official wrote that he had "discussed with Resident Emir and council, the latter state that it will be very hard to persuade the *talakawa* [working class people] to make any alteration. The Emir will discuss the matter further" (Nigerian National Archives-Kaduna 1944–1957).

However, some cemeteries were established during this period in Kaduna for Europeans and for Muslims. The Kaduna Civil Cemetery was reserved for UK soldiers who died as a consequence of World War I (three named graves) and World War II (ten named graves) (Commonwealth War Graves

Commission [GB]). The Muslim cemetery at Tudun Wada continues to be used for burials for area residents, as it was in 1932, as the District Head of Tudun Wada in Kaduna noted:

> They have gone where they may bury people in Tudun Wada. If they die, they went together with the white man who is in charge of the town to the place. The place—that is the place where they bury people who have died in the hospital. But because they don't bury them very well, the people [living nearby] were disturbed. Because of that, the white man who is in charge of the town said, "It is good to give them a place where they can bury them differently".
>
> (Colonial Office 1932–1952)

There was also some discussion about the need to pay farmers for the land that they had released for the cemetery.

It is unclear what the Tudun Wada District Head was referring to when he said that "people were disturbed." However, in May 1936, the Wambai [of Zaria Protectorate] noted the problem of hyenas digging up human remains in the Tudun Wada Cemetery. Colonial officials then discussed the provision of a barbed wire fence, although the required height of the fence was a topic of some debate ("Wombai [sic] informs me that hyenas DO jump. Will you find an estimate on a 4'6" basis?" 30 May 1936). It was subsequently decided to temporarily close the Tudun Wada Cemetery until the fence could be built and to encourage Muslim residents to bury their dead in the nearby Sabon Gari Muslim Cemetery. The Emir of Zaria agreed to this arrangement.

Other aspects of cemetery planning were also considered. Thus, in April 1956, the Director of Health Services, Northern Region, sent funds for the upkeep of cemeteries to provincial officials, while reminding them "to ensure that complete records are kept of all European Graves…especially those outside the Cemeteries and that they are looked after and cared for properly." One month later, the Medical Officer of Health-Kaduna sent a memo to the Kaduna Administrator, suggesting that a new site for a Muslim cemetery "to be far removed from the central part of Kaduna" be considered. "I inspected the present Cemetery recently. There is no immediate urgency. About two thirds of the area available for burials is still vacant. But I think that a new cemetery site should be reserved without undue delay" (Colonial Office 1956).

This suggestion that new cemetery sites be established had already been acted upon unofficially by Kaduna residents, as was observed in the report commissioned by the Government of Northern Nigeria written by Max Lock and Partners (1967: 201–202):

> There has come about a multiplicity of "pocket handkerchief" burial sites scattered all over the City and its villages…These tend to be not larger than 100 feet square or 200 feet square and many are unbeaconed, ungazetted

and unfenced. All these omissions should be rectified. Yes, as the town grows, there is a great need for a comprehensive and more far-seeing plan for bigger and better, but fewer, cemeteries...There is no reason why, within large areas of consecrated land, there should not be pleasant variety and intimacy, where informally planted groves of trees could be rounded off into intimate enclosures in which the graves from each family or local community could be grouped. Something of this intimate character is to be found in the small old African Christian cemetery in Constitution Road set amid trees and shrubs and possessing a simple dignity which gives food for thought for the planning of the future (Figure 1.2).

Yet Simon (1992: 158), who has considered the impact of the Max Lock and Partners report (prepared in 1965 to 1966), argues that various factors countered its effectiveness. For one thing, it was published in 1967, a time when the Nigerian Civil War began. Secondly, it recommended major expenditures that were impossible to accomplish at that time.[9] Furthermore, as its authors' recommendations for cemeteries suggest, the report had a European perspective that did not altogether correspond with Nigerian practices and beliefs. It is, nonetheless, a valuable document which provides a list of cemeteries—there were 26 cemeteries listed for the Kaduna Capital Territory in 1965. Many were unfenced and the authors suggest that the increasing numbers of cemeteries were related to the expansion of the outskirts of Kaduna where many KTL workers and their families came to live. Indeed, two of the major areas where Kaduna Textile Ltd workers' widows reside, Television and Anguwan Romi, were not mentioned in the report as they were barely populated at the time. As one widow noted, "I came to Kaduna in 1965 after we got married, we started living in Makera...At that time, Television was a bushy place, there was no settlement there" (Interview: Fatu Tom, 17 July 2019, Kaduna). Now both Television and Anguwan Romi have cemeteries. The Television Cemetery is quite large and six of the KTL workers who died since the mill's closure are buried there, as are some of their children

Figure 1.2 The entry gate to the Kabala Cemetery, a small African Christian cemetery in Constitution Road, 9 May 2018, Kaduna (Photograph by E.P. Renne).

(see Figure C.3). However, many smaller cemeteries have been established adjacent to some of the newer residential areas in Kaduna South. These cemeteries, like the residential areas they are associated with, are distinguished by religion, ethnicity, and race.[10]

Kaduna after 100 years

> The administration of Kaduna has succeeded in achieving the goal of an indivisible city and has at the same time been able to accommodate the tribal and cultural differences. The degree to which these immigrants are committed to urban life is a question on which further research is required.
>
> (Medugbon 1976: 166)

Much has happened since Medugbon conducted his research in Kaduna in the early 1970s. For one thing, its population has grown to the extent that it has become the fifth largest city in Nigeria.[11] It is an urban center with two universities (Kaduna Polytechnic and Kaduna State University), several hospitals, and a number of shopping malls. And in the 1970s, the textile mills—Kaduna Textiles Ltd, United Nigerian Textiles Ltd, Nortex, Norspin, and Arewa Textiles—were all functioning. However, a fall in oil prices in the early 1980s and subsequent economic constraints associated with the 1987 implementation of the IMF-sponsored Structural Adjustment Program led to the subsequent decline of the textile industry in Kaduna during the 1990s. As one KTL worker explained:

> The major problem was obsolete equipment. The problem started after SAP [Structural Adjustment Program] because the devalued naira made getting new machinery very expensive. So, they could not compete with the price of foreign imported textiles but also the quality.

There was also the problem of inadequate infrastructure, specifically the provision of electricity:

> They actually tried a private generator for power, but it was so expensive, their costs increased three-fold. The black oil/fuel that they used was too expensive.
>
> (Interview: Muhammed Buhari, 8 July 2010, Kaduna)

By December 2002, the Kaduna Textile Ltd mill had closed and the other mills followed.

The closure of these mills led to massive unemployment in the city. This situation, along with a declining infrastructure and the apparent growing wealth of government officials (and of those with access to government contracts), contributed to escalating violence in the city. Some blamed wealthy government officials, whose corrupt activities were thought to be responsible for KTL's decline—through their syphoning off of funds for mill renovation and infrastructural support, as well as by allowing for the entry of illegal imported textiles into the Nigeria market (Akinrinade and Ogen 2008). Indeed, unemployment and growing inequality have contributed to the uneasy relations among Christians and Muslims, evidenced by recurrent episodes of religious and ethnic conflict in Kaduna. The most widely known example, the violence surrounding debates about the possible implementation of Shari'a law in Kaduna, followed the return of democratic rule with the election of Olusegun Obasanjo, who was inaugurated as president on 29 May 1999. After the proposed establishment of Shari'a law in Kaduna State in early 2000, violence erupted between Christians and Muslim demonstrators at Government House in Kaduna (Angerbrandt 2011). It is estimated that between 2,000 and 5,000 people were killed (Harris 2013). Two years later, over 200 people were killed in Kaduna associated with violence surrounding the Miss World pageant which was scheduled to take place in Lagos, Nigeria, in November 2002. A controversial statement published in the Lagos newspaper, *ThisDay*, which was interpreted as blasphemous by Muslims, is believed to have been the spark that set off this outbreak of violence (BBC 2002). Nine years later, following the successful presidential campaign of Goodluck Jonathan, a Christian southerner from Rivers State, post-election violence in Kaduna again had serious consequences, with several hundred people killed (Human Rights Watch 2011). Nonetheless, opposition to Jonathan's proposed petrol price hike in January 2012 united the country during widespread "Occupy Nigeria" protests (Alhassan et al. 2012). The situation in Kaduna since 2012 has been relatively quiet (see SAIS 2017 for Kaduna State), partly as a result of the efforts of religious leaders and government officials to contain controversies and intermittent conflict (Harris 2016).

In December 2017, the city of Kaduna observed centenary celebrations, with parades, press conferences, and speeches by prominent politicians (Agbese and Mustapha 2017). On the final day of Kaduna's centenary celebrations, which were held at Murtala Mohammed Square, the spokesperson for President Muhammadu Buhari, Alhaji Muhammad Musa Bello, stated that "it is destiny that chose Kaduna to play a significant role in the formation and growth of Nigeria." He also expressed his optimism that the Kaduna State governor, Nasir El-Rufai "would solve the power problem bedeviling the nation, so that the industries in Kaduna and other states of the country that are down will begin to function" (Ahmadu-Suka and Shuaibu 2017).

This celebration, however, came after two difficult decades, which saw the closure of most of the textile mills in the city (2002–2007) and outbreaks of political and religious violence. Consequently, neighborhoods such as Tudun Wada, with mixed Christian and Muslim populations, became segregated along religious lines. Tudun Wada and most other areas north of the Kaduna River were largely inhabited by Muslims while the areas south of the river were largely Christian. Indeed, one Muslim taxi driver told me that he was advised not to wear a Hausa-style cap when driving in Kaduna South areas. The fear of post-election violence as well as kidnapping has affected people's feelings about living in Kaduna (Harris 2013; Ahmadu-Suka 2019).

This change was expressed by several KTL widows, whose situation is made worse by the loss of their husbands and the absence of textile mill final remittances. Several said that they no longer enjoy living in the city:

> Before I liked Kaduna very much but now I don't because there are so many problems—no peace, hunger, and other things. It is when I go to my hometown that they will help me with food if they have it.
> (Interview: Magdalene Daniel, 17 July 2019)

Others are farming in areas on the outskirts of the city: "There are so many difficulties now, that is why we are farming—just like in my hometown" (Interview: Monica Daniel, 25 July 2019, Kaduna). One former KTL worker, who was an assistant supervisor in the Weaving Department, has gone back to farming as well. And for those who do not own houses in Kaduna, some have moved out of the city altogether. One widow moved from rented housing in Television to an area even farther from Kaduna where she is now engaged in farming.

Whether this sort of reverse-migration continues remains to be seen, even though many widows and their children said that they intend to stay in Kaduna:

> Here in Kaduna we are doing small-small business so I want to stay in Kaduna. By the grace of God, I will never go back to my hometown. Because I have nothing to do there and because I have my life in Kaduna... When we go to my village, we would see how difficult it was to live there. It is not easy when we saw how they lived.
> (Interview: Ruth Galau, 17 July 2019, Kaduna)

Conclusion

The city of Kaduna reflects the legacy of colonial origins as an administrative and military center for the Protectorate of Northern Nigeria. Its spatial layout of distinctive residential areas, its roads (some named for political figures as well as for places of origin), the Kaduna Bridge, linking Sabon Gari (in Kaduna North) and Birnawa (in Kaduna South), its railway station, and its cemeteries all refer back to Kaduna's planned urban beginnings. The post-World War II increase in trade and industrialization—particularly the opening of the first textile mill, Kaduna Textiles Ltd in the Kakuri industrial area—occurred in preparation for Nigerian independence. The influx of workers from many different parts of Nigeria—from both the north and south—resulted in the initially mixed populations, by ethnicity and religion, of some neighborhoods (such as Tudun Wada) and the growth of many areas adjacent to Kaduna. This situation countered the earlier expectations of British colonial administrators such as Henry Bell and Frederick Lugard who sought to establish residential areas distinguished by race, class, ethnicity, and religion.

While the infrastructural inadequacy that reflected varied service in different parts of Kaduna in terms of roads, water, and electricity continued in the 1990s, the frequent shut-downs and stoppages of the textile industry contributed to increasing tension in the city. The 2000 riots following the proposed establishment of Shari'a law in Kaduna State, after which Christians moved from Tudun Wada and Muslims moved from neighborhoods in the southern part of the city (Harris 2013), led to a return to the distinctive religious and ethnic identities of different areas of Kaduna. This segregation may also be seen in the many Kaduna cemeteries—with their distinctive religious identities—associated with several residential areas of the city.

The closure of the main Kaduna textile mills after 2002 with the subsequent unemployment, poverty, and increasing inequality seen in different residential areas underscores this throwback to the colonial period when the GRA had large houses, good roads, and working infrastructure. The infrastructure of other residential areas such as Sabon Gari, Tudun Wada, Kabala, and Kawo, along with the newer residential areas along the edges of the city, has fallen into disrepair. The inadequate maintenance of these areas, while not necessarily the intention of colonial officials or later, northern Nigerian political leaders, reflects the economic inequality that has become more pervasive with the closing of most of the Kaduna textile mills.

Both national and state political leaders have emphasized the need to revive the textile industry and some have implemented plans, unsuccessfully to date, to do so. Yet Max Lock and Partners made a prescient observation concerning the textile industry in their 1960s report:

> There could also be undesirable risks for Kaduna in relying too heavily on textile production alone to provide manufacturing employment. Kaduna will never be a "one industry" town. The diversification provided by Government and distributive employment will make sure of this. But to allow the industrial arm to become too dependent on textiles could be the weak link in Kaduna's future prosperity although there would seem to be no prospect within sight of a recession in textile demand.
> (Lock and Partners 1967: 134)

Rather than depending solely on the revival of the big textile mills in Kaduna, smaller industries producing a range of goods—from clothing to ginger products—could be opened that take Lock and Partners' (1967: 134) advice into account:

> The criterion of industrial development in Kaduna should surely be to see that every pound invested creates as many new "basic" jobs as possible and not vice-versa [i.e., to save labor costs]. Only in this way will there be a spread of work over as many people as possible and with it a wider

opportunity for practical experience and training. The efficiency of an industry should not be judged in isolation but against the whole economy into which it is to go.

Perhaps renovation of the city's infrastructure—particularly provision of electricity and pipeborne water, the implementation of progressive taxation, as well as the revival and support of some medium-sized textile mills and other smaller industries in the city would address unemployment and inequality. In this way, some of the city's 21st century problems could be remedied (Oxfam 2017; Usman 2019). As a consequence, Kaduna could be able to return to the vision of the city described by Medugbon in 1976: "The administration of Kaduna has succeeded in achieving the goal of an indivisible city and has at the same time been able to accommodate the tribal and cultural differences." For as the Secretary to the State Government, Balarabe Abbas Lawal, "recalled the good old days of the city where the people lived together in peace," during preparations for the centenary celebration for Kaduna city, he also hoped that "the event will bring back its lost glory" (Ahmadu-Suka and Shuaibu 2017). This daunting situation contrasts with the ebullience and hope that marked the opening ceremonies for the Kaduna Textiles Ltd mill in 1957, which anticipated Nigeria's independence from Great Britain in 1960. The beginnings of KTL and workers' experiences there as well as its subsequent decline are examined in the next chapter.

Notes

1 See Ranger (2004) for a discussion of how burial practices in the city of Bulawayo, Zimbabwe [formerly Rhodesia], also a colonial constructed city, reflected a European insistence on cemetery burials. Ndebele people have never buried the bodies of family members in or around their houses, thus the move to cemetery burial was widely accepted. However, the one-year memorial ceremony known as *umbuyiso*, which transformed the dead into ancestors, was prohibited by European missionaries. Since many Ndebele had converted to Christianity, they reluctantly observed this prohibition until African cultural nationalists began to practice a Christian form of *umbuyiso* in the African Presbyterian Church in Bulawayo in 1955.
2 After the amalgamation of the southern and northern Protectorates of Nigeria in 1914, Lugard had hoped to locate the capital of Nigeria in Kaduna. However, due to the location of Lagos on the coast and its extensive trade and administrative history, it continued as the national capital until 1976, when it was moved to Abuja.
3 See Simon (1992: 152) for a discussion of the initial movement of Royal West African Frontier Force soldiers from Zungeru in February 1913 to the area of Kaduna now known as Birnawa.
4 Cotton exports never fulfilled British expectations (Johnson 1974: 184): "The average annual export of raw cotton [in 1926] from Northern Nigeria was still only a little over 5,000 bales of 400 lb. each... in the north, the bulk of the crop was retained for the local manufacture of native Kano cloths." However, the export of groundnuts (peanuts) by rail exceeded expectations: "It was because it enabled the farming season to be extended that groundnuts proved such a popular crop, exploiting the possibilities opened up by the railway" (Johnson 1974: 184; see also Hogendorn 1978, 1995).
5 According to Oyedele (1987: 479), three sites were suggested by Stanhope White (a British colonial official who was the Director for Commerce and Industry in the

Northern Region until 1954): one near Kaduna town, one at Jebba on the Niger River, and one at Makurdi near the Benue River. Kano was also considered, based its history as a major textile production center with an experienced management and labor force. However, Kaduna, as the regional administrative capital, located near cotton-growing regions, the Kaduna River, and rail service led to its choice as the site of the first major mill in northern Nigeria (Paden 1986: 264).

6 The neighborhood known as Television was named for the old television station building located there, which was subsequently relocated along the Kaduna-Abuja Road.
7 Some ethnic associations and clubs focused on political activities although many had social and economic functions such as support for burials. They also "served to perpetuate traditional community ties, social practices and cultural ideals…[and] helped to maintain links with the home area (Oyedele 1987: 440).
8 Laqueur (2015: 235) discusses "the public health argument" that led to burial boards that enforced a shift from burials in churchyards to cemeteries in 19th century England.
9 At the beginning of 2020, Nabilah Umar (2020) notes that an urban renewal project for improving and increasing a network of roads in Kaduna reflects the earlier plans developed by Max Lock & Partners.
10 The establishment of cemeteries in Kaduna differs from the process described by Laqueur (2015: 271-288) in England where churchyard burial grounds were eventually replaced by mostly privately owned and managed cemeteries. Indeed, government-owned cemeteries that were established during the colonial period in Kaduna have been followed by public cemeteries associated with neighborhoods and distinguished by religion. And the preference for home burials—either in their hometowns or in the home compounds in Kaduna—by Christian families continues.
11 "Today, Kaduna is considered Nigeria's fifth largest and most populous city after Lagos with 10,578,000 people, Kano with 3,395,000 people, Ibadan with 2,837,000 people and Abuja with 1,995,000 people" (Bununu et al. 2015: 57).

References

Agbese, Andrew, and Hafsat Mustapha. "Kaduna's Role in Nigeria Chosen by Destiny – Buhari." *Daily Trust*, 16 December 2017. Accessed 16 December 2017. www.dailytrust.com.ng.

Ahmadu-Suka, Maryam. "JUST IN: Unidentified Gunmen Kidnap 5 in Kaduna." *Daily Trust*, 24 August 2019. Accessed 24 August 2019. https://www.dailytrust.com.ng/just-in-unidentified-gunmen-kidnap-5-in-kaduna.html.

Ahmadu-Suka, Maryam, and Faruk Shuaibu. "Centenary Celebration Will Bring Back Kaduna's Lost Glory." *Daily Trust*, 3 December 2017. Accessed 3 December 2017. www.dailytrust.com.ng.

Akinrinade, Sola, and Olukoya Ogen. "Globalization and De-Industrialization: South-South Neo-Liberalism and the Collapse of the Nigerian Textile Industry." *Global South* 2, no. 2 (2008): 159–170.

Alhassan, Amina, Mulkat Mukaila, Imaobong Esu, Hamisu Mohammed, Francis Okeke, Ismail Mudashir, Rukaiya Aliyu, Halima Musa, and Rakiya Mohammed. "Why 'Occupy Nigeria' Protests Are Spreading." *Weekly Trust*, 7 January 2012. Accessed 7 January 2012. www.dailytrust.com.ng.

Angerbrandt, Henrik. "Political Decentralisation and Conflict: The Sharia Crisis in Kaduna, Nigeria." *Journal of Contemporary African Studies* 29, no. 1 (2011): 15–31.

Bandele-Thomas, 'Biyi . *The Sympathetic Undertaker and Other Dreams*. Oxford: Heinemann, 1991.

BBC. "Nigeria Buries Its Dead." *BBC World News*, 25 November 2002. Accessed 11 May 2017. http://news.bbc.co.uk/2/hi/africa/2510743.stm.
Bununu, Y.A., A.N.M. Ludin, and Nafisa Hosni. "City Profile: Kaduna." *Cities* 49 (2015): 53–65.
Colonial Office. *Burials in Native Towns, 1932–1952*, ZARPROF (Fed) 7/1 File 428. Kaduna: National Archives Nigeria-Kaduna, 1932–1952.
Colonial Office. *Cemeteries*, KADMIN Health No. HO21/81/Vol. I. *Kaduna*. Kaduna: National Archives of Nigeria, 1956.
Fourchard, L. "Dealing with 'Strangers': Allocating Urban Space to Migrants in Nigeria and French West Africa, End of the Nineteenth Century to 1960." In *African Cities: Competing Claims on Urban Spaces*, edited by F. Locatelli, and P. Nugent, 187–218. Leiden: Brill, 2009.
Habila, Helon. *Measuring Time*. Abuja: Cassava Republic Press, 2007.
Harris, Colette. "Violence in a Religiously Divided City: Kaduna, Nigeria—From the Shari'a Riots of 2000 to the Post-Election Clashes of 2011." *Space & Polity* 17, no. 3 (2013): 284–299.
Harris, Colette. "Masculinities, New Forms of Religion, and the Production of Social Order in Kaduna City, Nigeria." *Journal of Religion in Africa* 46, no. 2–3 (2016): 251–287.
Hogendorn. *Nigerian Groundnut Exports; Origins and Early Development*. Zaria: Ahmadu Bello Press, January 1978.
Hogendorn. "The Cotton Campaign in Northern Nigeria, 1902–1914: An Early Example of a Public/Private Planning Failure in Agriculture." In *Cotton: Colonialism, and Social History in Sub-Saharan Africa*, edited by A. Isaacman, and R. Roberts, 50–70. Portsmouth, NH: Heinemann, January 1995.
Human Rights Watch (HRW). "Nigeria: Post-Election Violence Killed 800." *Human Rights Watch*, 2011. Accessed 7 July 2013. http://www.hrw.org/news/2011/05/16/nigeria-post-election-violence-killed-800.
Johnson, Marion. "Cotton Imperialism in West Africa." *African Affairs* 73, no. 291 (1974): 178–187.
Laqueur, Thomas. *The Work of the Dead: A Cultural History of Mortal Remains*. Princeton, NJ: Princeton University Press, 2015.
Lock, Max, and Partners. *Kaduna 1917 1967 2017: A Survey and Plan of the Capital Territory for the Government of Northern Nigeria*. New York: Praeger, 1967.
Mabogunje, Akin. "New Initiatives in Urban Planning and Management in Nigeria." *Habitat International*. 16, no. 2 (1992): 73–88.
Medugbon, A.K. "Kaduna, Nigeria: The Vicissitudes of a Capital City, 1917–1975." Unpublished PhD dissertation. Los Angeles, CA: University of California, 1976.
Nigerian National Archives–Kaduna. "Births, Deaths and Burials Ordinance, Chapter 47, Section 37." Kaduna: Nigerian National Archives, 1944–1957.
Oxfam International. *Inequality in Nigeria: Exploring the Drivers*. Oxford: Oxfam, 2017.
Oyedele, E.O. "Colonial Urbanisation in Northern Nigeria: Kaduna 1913–1960." Unpublished PhD dissertation. Zaria: Department of History, Ahmadu Bello University, 1987.
Paden, John. *Ahmadu Bello: Sardauna of Sokoto*. Zaria: Huda Huda Press, 1986.
Ranger, Terence. "Dignifying Death: The Politics of Burial in Bulawayo." *Journal of Religion in Africa* 34, no. 1/2 (2004): 110–144.
Simon, Pius Bala. "The Spatio-Economic Impact of Informal Sector Activities on the Physical Development of Nigerian Cities: A Case Study of Kaduna." Unpublished PhD dissertation. Manchester, UK: University of Manchester, 1992.

Swanson, M. "The Sanitation Syndrome: Bubonic Plague and Urban Native Policy in the Cape Colony, 1900-1909." *Journal of African History* 18, no. 3 (1977): 387–410.

Umar, Nabilah Hassan. "Putting Kaduna in Nigeria's Mega-City Top League." *Daily Trust*, 16 January 2020, 10.

Usman, Umar. "How Govt Can Get Youths into Productive Employment." *Daily Trust*, 18 November 2019. Accessed 19 November 2019. https://www.dailytrust.com.ng/how-govt-can-get-youths-into-productive-employment.html.

2 New work-time regimes
The rise and fall of Kaduna Textiles Ltd

> We want good workers, because Kaduna Textiles is a place where people are expected to work hard. We make no apology for that, in fact we are proud of it, but do see to it that conditions are good and that there is a proper reward for work done. We want that reward to be as high as possible.
>
> Kaduna Textiles Ltd *Employee's Handbook*

The opening of the Kaduna Textiles Ltd (KTL) mill on 22 November 1957 was a significant event as it reflected beginning efforts to industrialize the North and hence was received with much fanfare (Andrae and Beckman 1999; David Whitehead & Sons 1973).[1] This mill represented the combined efforts of northern Nigerian political leaders, including Sir Ahmadu Bello, the Sardauna of Sokoto, and the Premier of the Northern Region, along with officials from the Ministry of Trade and Industry and the Northern Region Development Corporation, as well as the management of the British textile manufacturing firm, David Whitehead & Sons, and British colonial administrators (Maiwada and Renne 2013; Onyeiwu 1997; Waziri et al. 2020).

Yet by December 2002, Kaduna Textile Ltd had closed. There were several reasons for its closure. However, the chapter begins with the optimism displayed at its opening, for the Kaduna Textiles Ltd (KTL) mill served as a model for future industrial development of northern Nigeria. It first describes the establishment and growth of textile manufacturing at KTL—under the administrative leadership of the Northern Region Development Corporation and David Whitehead & Sons officials. It continues with a discussion of labor migration to Kaduna and specifically, how family and ethnic connections as well as the "push" of western education associated with their religious backgrounds led many KTL workers to seek employment at the mill (Andrae and Beckman 1999; Hinchliffe 1973; Medugbon 1976). It then considers the hiring process, training, and incentives of KTL mill workers as described by former KTL workers, who emphasized mill officials' attention to hard work and punctuality. This attitude toward time and work is explained in the Kaduna Textile Ltd *Employee's Handbook*, which those who were hired received:

> The Company therefore aims at recruiting, training and retaining a body of employees who are efficient in their work and enabling each employee to make to this joint effort the fullest contribution of which he is capable.

Interviews with former KTL mill workers further clarify management strategies through their experiences of the promotion process and pay levels. Once hired, mill officials were concerned with retaining workers through a range of incentives such as access to the mill clinics and "certificates of long service," described in the KTL *Employee's Handbook* and by former mill employees.

The selection of workers with some western education and their retention through various incentives relates to the other part of the worker-management equation, namely that KTL was "a place where people are expected to work hard." This hard work reflected a shift to industrial production and to a particular equation of time and money, noted by E.P. Thompson (1967: 61):

> Those who are employed experience a distinction between their employer's time and their "own" time. And the employer must *use* the time of his labour, and see it is not wasted: not the task but the value of time when reduced to money is dominant. Time is now currency: it is not passed but spent.

Thus, new workers at KTL were trained for the specific work at the mill—for example, as operators of looms, and of cotton carding and spinning machines—but also in attending to time and to schedules of work. While most workers had been exposed through primary school attendance to a different configuration of time as compared to agricultural work in their villages, which relied on the sun and the seasons to organize labor, mill routines were even more standardized. The presence of clocks, the sounding of sirens, and the use of punch-cards reinforced the textile mill's particular work-time regime.

However, despite the dedication of many mill workers and their adherence to mill rules, when the KTL mill ended operations in 2002, they were not paid their negotiated gratuities. The final section of the chapter considers the reasons for the Kaduna Textiles Ltd mill's closing and its effect on workers' time. Kaduna Textiles Ltd had several problems associated with production, which the KTL management attempted to address through various means of cost reduction. These included cutting back its labor force, union negotiations, and accommodation to workers' informal resistance, which enabled the mill to continue operations until it could no longer do so. Workers' experience of time after the mill closed changed as their urban experience of time was no longer equated with money and abundant food, but rather with futility, poverty, and hunger. Yet the mill's decline and this new regime of time could hardly have been foreseen during the optimistic days of its opening and workers' pride in their achievement as employees of KTL.

The beginnings of the textile industry in Kaduna

The political context of the mill's opening in the final years of colonial rule in Nigeria reflected a major shift in British manufacturers' and colonial officials' views on manufacturing in the country. Prior to the mill's opening, there were no large modern textile mills set up in Nigeria, reflecting the British colonial policy of extracting raw materials from its colony to be used in manufacturing in the UK, with the subsequent textiles to be sold by agents of British trading firms in Nigeria (Johnson 1974). However, by the 1950s, British textile manufacturers began to see the advantages of manufacturing closer to the source of its raw materials—cotton, and its customers—Nigerian consumers. Also, new shipping and rail services to Kaduna made the transport of equipment and building materials feasible. Thus, in 1954, following Nigerian inquiries, Mr. J. C. Whittaker, the co-director of David Whitehead & Sons, established the David Whitehead & Sons Overseas Liaison Office to accommodate these goals (Hartley 2012; Maiwada and Renne 2013; Onyeiwu 1997).

Yet the earlier anti-manufacturing policy had consequences for the building and running of a large textile mill; Nigerian officials and workers had no experience or training in the operation of such an enterprise.[2] Thus, on the Nigerian side, Northern Nigerian officials were interested in partnering with a textile manufacturing firm that could provide textile technology and expertise. Sir Ahmadu Bello, who was the Premier of the Northern Region, was a major force behind industrial development in northern Nigeria (Paden 1986: 265). He became interested in the British manufacturing firm, David Whitehead & Sons Ltd, possibly as a consequence of a visit to southern Rhodesia (now Zimbabwe) where he had seen the David Whitehead & Sons mill, which the company had built there—its first in Africa (Interview: N. Rutherford, 2 March 2012, Minchinhampton). In March 1955, the Northern Regional Government invited David Whitehead officials to establish a textile mill in Kaduna, in collaboration with the Northern Region Marketing Board and the Northern Region Development Corporation. Officials at David Whitehead & Sons also saw the advantages of citing a mill in Kaduna. In April 1955, Ahmadu Bello, officials from the NRDC, the Northern Region Marketing Board, and David Whitehead & Sons met in Rawtenstall, Lancashire, UK, to discuss the details of becoming partners in a textile manufacturing plant in Northern Nigeria (Maiwada and Renne 2013: 175). An agreement was subsequently negotiated to provide construction plans and equipment, as well as training staff, which was signed in Rawtenstall on 7 September 1955, with Ahmadu Bello and Alhaji Aliyu, Turakin Zazzau (the Minister of Trade and Industry, later Director of the Northern Region Development Corporation), other NRMB and NRDC board members, and officials of David Whitehead & Sons in attendance.

Construction of the steel and concrete mill began in early 1956, under contract with the UK firm, Taylor Woodrow (West Africa) Ltd, with prefabricated steel parts that were shipped from the UK (David Whitehead & Sons 1973).

On 7 March 1956, Ahmadu Bello laid the foundation stone in a ceremony attended by David Whitehead & Sons personnel (Maiwada and Renne 2013). Construction continued while reconditioned spinning equipment (13,608 spinning spindles), new Barber Colman winding and beaming equipment, and 288 new S-type Northrop automatic looms were shipped from the UK, and were later installed (David Whitehead & Sons 1973). By November 1957, the No. 1 Kaduna Textiles Ltd mill was ready to begin production following the mill's official opening.

The mill's opening ceremony

Many dignitaries attended the mill's opening on 22 November 1957. Colonial government officials as well as personnel from David Whitehead & Sons and the Premier's Office spent much time in preparing for this event (Kaduna Textiles Ltd 1957). A special brochure was commissioned from the British public relations firm, H. & B. Rose, in August 1957, which included a forward by Sir Ahmadu Bello and a brief history of David Whitehead & Sons' involvement in the construction of the mill, along with many illustrations (Maiwada and Renne 2013: 176). The opening, which Mary, Princess Royal and Countess of Harewood, was scheduled to attend, was carefully managed by British colonial officials in the Ministry of Trade and Industry. These officials developed scheduling, parking, and lists of invitees, many of whom were from the major foreign mercantile firms (e.g., John Holt, UAC, and Paterson Zochonis) working in Nigeria. Guests were taken around the offices and mill and were given brief explanations of the textile manufacturing processes (Kaduna Textiles Ltd 1957; Figure 2.1).

The mill began operation in November 1957, producing unfinished baft of the sort that had been earlier manufactured in Manchester for the Nigerian market (David Whitehead & Sons 1973). Gordon Hartley, a former employee of David

Figure 2.1 Drawing of Kaduna Textile Ltd, the first industrial textile mill in Kaduna, northern Nigeria, which was established in collaboration with the textile manufacturing firm, David Whitehead and Sons, Ltd, Rawtenstall, Lancashire, UK (Courtesy of David Whitehead and Sons, Ltd, Archives, Parbold, Lancashire, UK).

Whitehead & Sons, described the experimental process whereby the right combination of weave and starch led to the desired result (Maiwada and Renne 2013: 176). Mill management and workers successfully produced increasing quantities of quality baft cotton cloth, which was attractive not only to agents from major textile firms operating in Nigeria but especially to Nigerian customers.

The early success of Kaduna Textiles Ltd was highlighted in the Kaduna Exhibition—"Made in Nigeria," which opened in May 1959. British colonial officials were also anxious to show the positive efforts toward self-governance, modernization, and development which KTL represented, in anticipation of Nigerian Independence in 1960. This approach, which attempted to negate earlier British opposition to industrialization, was reflected in the showcasing of Kaduna Textiles Ltd. Nigerian and British political figures, which included Ahmadu Bello and Harold Macmillan, as well as many Kaduna residents, walked through the exhibit which featured a series of exhibit booths with accompanying explanatory panels that illustrated the textile production process from cotton field to cotton bales and finally to bales of woven baft cloth (Maiwada and Renne 2013: 177).

Another change which occurred at this time was a shift from the distribution of Kaduna Textiles products through trading firm offices in the UK to sales through their Nigerian offices, although the control of distribution remained in European mercantile hands. However, with Nigerian Independence in 1960, Kaduna Textile Ltd officials sought to sell bales to independent Nigerian traders and merchant houses such as the Kano Merchants Trading Company (DanAsabe 2020), which had their own distribution networks (Hartley 2012). Kaduna Textiles' sales to Nigerian traders grew as increased production of new products, such as bleached starched shirting, were manufactured in the new No. 2 mill which was built in 1960–1961 (Interview: N. Rutherford, 2 March 2012, Minchinhampton).

In 1974, the owner of the Northern Nigerian Textile Mill—which specialized in printed cotton textiles—was leaving the country. Through a special arrangement, control of the company was transferred to Kaduna Textiles Ltd (Maiwada and Renne 2013: 178). Subsequently, two more mills were constructed in order to produce additional bleached cotton cloth that was used in the adjacent Northern Nigerian Textile Mill, with the printed textiles marketed under the KTL name. This increased production of KTL cloth meant that the mill needed additional employees—to work in the spinning, weaving, printing, and finishing departments as well as in clerical services and management. These job openings were filled by men who travelled to Kaduna, having heard through word of mouth and by radio of employment opportunities there.

Looking for employment at the Kaduna textile mills: labor migration from southern Kaduna and the Middle Belt states

In 1962, when the second mill was opened in order to provide bleached cotton shirting material for the market, over 2,600 workers were employed (nd: 4). These numbers increased so that by 1980, it was estimated that KTL had over 4,000 employees who worked in the mill's three shifts (Andrae and Beckman 1999: 301). And, as has been mentioned, many—but not all—of the workers who came to work at KTL were from towns and villages to the south of Kaduna whose families had converted to Christianity in early part of the 20th century. Indeed, three former KTL mill employees who subsequently had management positions, Sylvester Gankon, Haruna Joshua, and the late Shaibu Yusuf, all came from different areas and different ethnic groups south of Kaduna. Gankon, a Manchok man, came from a town in Kaura Local Government in southern Kaduna State, and Joshua, an Ngas man, came from Kamke Local Government in Plateau State—are both Christians. Yusuf, an Igala man, who came from Ankpa, a town in Ankpa Local Government in Kogi State, was Muslim. All three came to KTL with some secondary school education.

Having a secondary school education was relatively unusual during the 1950s; approximately one in five of the men who came from the south to work at Kaduna Textiles Ltd had such an education. However, many workers—about 60%—had attended primary school and thus had elementary reading and writing skills (Andrae and Beckman 1999: 302). These men (or their fathers) had acquired basic literacy through the work of evangelist missionaries, particularly those of the Sudan Interior Mission (SIM) who fostered the building of churches in small villages in southern Kaduna and Plateau states. Initially, SIM evangelists were particularly active in Kogi and Niger states, with the first SIM station established in Pategi (a Nupe-speaking area in Niger state; Ijagbemi 1986). They later continued their proselytizing in villages in areas in southern Kaduna state and Plateau state, where they preached in newly-built churches where reading and writing were also taught. These "Classes for Religious Instruction" were an important part of SIM evangelism as the mission's education policy made clear:

> The education policy of the Mission in the main recognizes no greater responsibility than teaching an illiterate population to read and write so that they can use the Holy Scripture for themselves and teach intensively those Scriptures. Because the greater bulk of the people in the Central Sudan are illiterate, teaching must of necessity go hand-in-hand with evangelism.
>
> (Gaiya 2018: 126)

Nonetheless, this emphasis on literacy's importance for SIM evangelism did not extend to "subjects such as English, Mathematics, Commercial Arts…and other worldly arts and sciences…[as] they become a source of temptation to the pupil to enter Government service," as the SIM evangelist, Dr. Andrew Stirrett observed (Gaiya 2018: 126). However, rather than government service, this literacy provided men with preparation for work at the Kaduna Textile Ltd mill and hence many moved to Kaduna, where many have remained. For these men, the possibility of employment in the textile mills in Kaduna was an attractive option compared with the tedium of farm work.

The junior mill manager, Haruna Joshua, came to Kaduna in 1966 from Plateau State, as he explains:

> I met my townsmen to join textile mill work in 1967, when I was very young, I was 15 years old. It was the year which was the beginning of the Nigerian Civil War. I really liked to work in textiles because they were weaving some good cloth and I had interest to see the cloth and wondered how weaving worked. At that time, it was the British who ran Kaduna Textiles.
>
> We had three shifts A, B, and C, 12 midnight to 8 in the morning, 8am to 4pm, then 4pm–12 midnight. I was in the B shift, from 8am–4pm. We had a uniform, each shift was a different color so when you saw a colleague, you knew that this man was from a certain shift. The shift goes together with the uniform. But not completely, for some men were identified by their specific jobs, such as maintenance workers who wore black uniforms. (Most of them were on early morning duty.)
>
> As a weaver, you have to come early, at least ten minutes to the time, i.e., the closing time for the earlier shift so that other men going out will handover whatever they left off. So, you will take over from where they stopped, then you'd carry on. We had clocking cards to keep track of our time and we were wearing wristwatches then, in order to know the time. I bought it when I started the work.
>
> During that time, the machines were very good, they were working very well so that when a thread broke, the loom would stop automatically so that one man could control 20 looms. Then you have a spare workman, in case you wanted to go to the toilet, then the spare man will take over, otherwise the two of you will be together with 20 machines.
>
> (Interview: Haruna Joshua, 10 May 2018, Kaduna)

There are several themes embedded in Haruna Joshua's description of his work at Kaduna Textiles Ltd in 1967 that underscore the particularities of his experience of the transition from agricultural work to industrial capitalism in Kaduna. First of all, he found his way to the KTL mill through his connections with other Ngas men who preceded him at the mill (LaPin 1983).[3] Second, he began work in the mill in 1967, the year that marked the beginning of the Nigerian civil war, when many older mill workers left to join the Federal army. This situation, combined with the increasing demand for textiles by the government, enabled him to join the Kaduna Textiles Ltd work force when he was only 15 years old. Third, 1967 was also the year that Ahmadu Bello was assassinated in his home in Kaduna by Igbo military officers, who objected to what they saw as his political-religious agenda. For not only was Ahmadu Bello an advocate for the industrial and educational development of northern Nigeria, he was also, as the Sardauna of Sokoto, a member of the Sokoto royal family and as such, sought to support the predominance of Islam in northern Nigeria. Indeed, during the early 1960s, he led what has been referred to as "conversion tours," in which he travelled to villages in southern Kaduna in order to counter the work of Christian missionaries and to support conversion to Islam (Abba 1981). He viewed the establishment of textile mills in northern Nigeria as a way of providing Muslim men with increased economic opportunities, just as his support for the first university in northern Nigeria, Ahmadu Bello University, was meant to strengthen northern Nigerians' opportunities for higher education (Paden 1986). Thus, while the Kaduna Textiles Ltd *Handbook* explicitly states that, "It is not the Company's intention to interfere with the individual employee's religious practices," various concessions to Muslim workers there were made. For example, "Moslem workers are assured that these [meal] breaks and shift change times have been agreed by both religious and Government Authorities who accept that they are so timed as to permit a Moslem to perform his obligatory prayers" (Kaduna Textiles Ltd nd).

However, the majority of the workers at KTL were Christians, although there were some Muslim mill workers. Alhaji Shaibu Yusuf, a Muslim originally from Kogi State, served as a deputy manager at KTL, having attended Kaduna Polytechnic where he received a Higher National Diploma in Textile Technology and also in Public Administration. But many Muslim young men were more likely to receive Islamic, rather than Western, education.[4] While this situation changed with the opening of Islamic primary and secondary schools that taught both Islamic and Western education, at that time young men taught to read and write in mission schools to the south had an advantage. For reading and writing were essential prerequisites for employment at the KTL mill. As one man put it, "KTL at that time, it was a nice textile mill, everyone liked to work at KTL," but not everyone was hired.[5]

Getting a job at Kaduna Textiles Ltd

Men working as farmers in villages throughout southern Kaduna State and the Middle Belt region heard about work opportunities at the textile mills in Kaduna by various means. Some were encouraged to come by family members or fellow villagers already working at one of the mills. Others heard about job openings at the Kaduna textile mills through radio broadcasts. Some, having completed their primary education in the village, came to seek employment in the big city on their own initiative:

> I finished my school in 1968 and came to Kaduna. I heard that they were looking for people who can work in Kaduna. Most companies used to advertise that they needed workers. Some of the news we heard on the

radio and some we heard from people who came back to their village. When they came back, they said we could find a job either sweeping or working in an office. That was how I came to Kaduna and I stayed with my brother.

(Interview: Wuyah Adze, 24 July 2019, Kaduna)

Once in Kaduna, they sought out work, often with the assistance of family members already living in the city. The first step in seeking employment at textile mills such as KTL was to apply for work at the government labor office:

At the labor office, we had to make a queue…From there, they selected me to go to KTL. When I got there, they sent me to the Weaving Department, that department was good for me. That was how I was appointed to KTL. When I went to the KTL factory, they interviewed us. We went to their office one by one for the interview. That time the personnel manager was the senior brother of the Governor of Plateau state, J.D. Gowon. He was the one who interviewed me. First of all, he looked at your hands and if they are rough, he will say you cannot work because you will be working with cotton. The man was very intelligent.

(Interview: Haruna Joshua, 16 July 2019, Kaduna)

There was also an effort made to equitably hire workers by ethnicity and by their cultural embeddedness, as Haruna Joshua explained:

The Idoma were the greatest number among the 30 people there, they were 18 out of the 30. The personnel manager told his personal assistant to move the chairs out of the room. Then he said that all the Idoma should come. He told them to dance the way that they danced in their hometowns. One of them was singing their song and the rest answered. They were asked to go one way in a line—those who were not living in their hometowns but were living in Kaduna town [*barriki*], they could not do the dance, so they were knocking into each other. The manager then said, "Those who could not dance among them, they could not do the work in the factory so they should go."

That was how he selected the Idoma. He then turned to us—those who were not Idoma—and asked us to bring our primary school certificates. He saw where I came from. His father was a tax collector in my own village, AmKyar, we called him Mr. Achi. The personnel manager said he knew my father. I was happy that he knew my father because I knew I would be hired. He asked me a question, he said, "If you are going to Jos and you drop one person at Saminaka, two stop at another place, etc.—I answered correctly…So that is how he employed me. Because he realized that I answered the question correctly and that my hands were clean and soft.

> We who were selected, they gave us some forms, the rules and regulations of the factory were written on it. Some things written on the form: "If you fight with each other you will be sacked; if you steal from the company you will be sacked; if you are absent for 3 days, you will also be sacked." We were asked to sign the form that we agreed with the rules and regulations of the factory and that we will obey them.
>
> (Interview: Haruna Joshua, 16 July 2019, Kaduna)

However, one Idoma man, Godwin Okwoli, had a somewhat different experience:

> The employment was conducted by province with your certificate at that time. The procedure was that the KTL personnel manager would look at your school certificate. At the front gate they would call us by province and through that province, they kept some, then after Lokoja Province, then Benue Province, then to Kaduna. So, after that, based on the number of people that they needed they would recruit almost 20. Not all 20 from Benue alone, they selected 3 or 4 from Benue. They selected workers based on your certificate, they then removed you from the major line and put you in another line. There were some who didn't finish primary 7, they weren't selected.
>
> (Interview: 24 July 2019, Kaduna)

Once a worker had been approved to work at KTL by the personnel manager, he was sent to the clinic for a health check-up. If he passed muster, he was sent to a particular department to begin work, as Bulus Ayuba explained:

> I was employed and sent to the Operations Department. There was a trial period of about 2 months to see if you will be able to do the job. Then they will give you a permanent position and they gave me my name tag—and they would also give you a number. I still remember my number, it was 1068 at that time.
>
> (Interview: Bulus Ayuba, 24 July 2019, Kaduna)

This trial period was varied based on the workers' abilities and the company's needs. Depending on the position and type of work, workers were sent for further training at the workshop in the mill itself and others were sent to Kaduna Polytechnic and other schools in the Kaduna area. Depending on the course of training, some workers attended school for a year, others for several years, as Samson Okwoli explained: "Then they sent me to Kaduna Polytechnic where I spent five years, learning textile science and management, I have the certificate."

As Thompson (1967: 84) has noted, schools contributed to new ways of thinking about time regimes:

> One other non-industrial institution lay to hand which might be used to inculcate "time-thrift": the school. Clayton complained that the streets of

Manchester were full of "idle ragged children; who are not only losing their Time, but learning habits of gaming", etc. He praised charity schools for teaching Industry, Frugality, Order and Regularity: "the Scholars here are obliged to rise betimes and to observe Hours, with great Punctuality."

In some ways, discipline in the Methodist schools—both in Nigeria and England—conditioned children, some of whom became textile mill workers, to follow school rules, to be obedient, and to be "on time": "Once within the school gates, the child entered the new universe of disciplined time…The first rule to be learned by the scholars was: 'I am to be present at the School…a few minutes before half-past nine o'clock'" (Thompson 1967: 84).[6]

By the early 1900s, these ways of thinking about time were well inculcated in the minds and behavior of British missionaries who came to Nigeria to teach children in SIM and Methodist schools, and were learned by children who attended them. These ways of thinking about time and work—that one must work hard, be punctual, and not waste time—also framed the company requirements and were accepted by those who were hired to work at the Kaduna Textiles Ltd mill.

Kaduna Textiles Ltd: new regimes of work and time

> The Company therefore aims at recruiting, training and retaining a body of employees who are efficient in their work and enabling each employee to make to this joint effort the fullest contribution of which he is capable.
>
> Kaduna Textile Ltd *Employee's Handbook*

In order to operate the mill equipment efficiently, workers and section heads needed training that was provided through various methods of instruction—at the KTL mill itself, through attendance at local schools, and through on-the-job training. They also needed to be efficient with their use of time for, as Godwin Okwoli observed, "Those days, time was very scarce."

As with other workers, Okwoli became familiar with the mill's regimen of time, which included the use of sirens that marked shift changes, the wearing of wristwatches, and the use of clocking cards, as one KTL junior mill manager, Haruna Joshua, explained: "We were given clocking cards—so if you were late, it would show the time you clocked in so it was better that you came to clock in earlier than to be late." Wuyah Adze described his own beginning work experience of mill time:

> You know when you are newly employed, they will put you in the morning section. Sometimes we used to start work at 7 am. I used to know the time when the rooster crowed. Honestly, I would get up because I had to trek from Tudun Nupawa and I would follow long the Kaduna Bridge to come to work. Early in the morning we would trek to come to the mill and go back later. When we were close to the mill, we could hear the siren

but later they introduced clocking cards—so you would clock in and clock out. That was how we knew the time.

(Interview: 24 July 2019, Kaduna)

These comments exemplify what E.P. Thompson has observed about new conceptions of time as money associated with industrial capitalism.

The specifics of time and work requirements were provided in the KTL *Employee's Handbook* regarding "Hours and Conditions of Work," for shift and non-shift workers (Figure 2.2). As Haruna Joshua, recalled, there were incentives and alarms to encourage workers to keep to time:

> In the olden days, when you resume by 12 noon they will be showing films in the Welfare Centre so you will come early and you won't be late…We enjoyed the films before lunch-time, then when it was ten minutes to lunch time, they would blow the alarm and the whole of Kakuri will hear the alarm, that it's now 10 minutes to 12 noon. So even if you are asleep, you will wake up and wash your face and come at that time, ten minutes to twelve to take over for the out-going person.
>
> (Interview: 10 May 2018, Kaduna)

Nonetheless, some workers did come late. They were required to get permission from their supervisor to begin work and unless "permission is given or a good cause shown, disciplinary action may be taken by the employer" (Kaduna Textiles Ltd nd).

Men were proud to keep to time by wall clocks, alarms clocks, and even wristwatches (Figure 2.3). When asked when he first had a wristwatch, Wuzah Adze exclaimed:

> I couldn't afford a watch then [in the village], we were even using salt sacks to make short pants for school. How could I wear a wristwatch at that time?

Figure 2.2 Kaduna Textiles Limited *Employee's Handbook* with motto: "WORK, HONESTY, OBEDIENCE," undated, Kaduna (Photograph by E.P. Renne, 15 May 2018).

New work–time regimes and Kaduna Textiles Ltd 49

Figure 2.3 Weaving room workers at Kaduna Textile Ltd, note wristwatch worn by worker on the right (Courtesy of David Whitehead and Sons, Ltd, Archives, Parbold, Lancashire, UK).

> I started wearing a wristwatch in 1970 when I was working at KTL. Then I would say that I was an "*oga*" when I started wearing that wristwatch.[7]
> (Interview: 24 July 2019, Kaduna)

When Godwin Okwoli first started to work at KTL in 1963, wristwatches were not common. However, they became readily available by the 1970s in Kaduna with traders selling them in front of the KTL entry gate, as Reuben Yakubu explained: "Those wristwatches, some fellows, they used to sell them on credit to us. When we got our pay, we would give them their money, N20 or N30, for some of them" (Interview: 24 July 2019, Kaduna).

Some workers also had purchased wall clocks in order to arrive at the mill on time:

> We had a wall clock and set the alarm in our house. They—the managers didn't give them to us, we bought them. We'd set the alarm and come to work. At the time of closing, the company would tell us.
> (Interview: Godwin Okwoli, 24 July 2019, Kaduna)

These means of keeping to time differed from village time-keeping, as Samson Okwoli, a former KTL worker, observed:

> Initially I started work at KTL at 8pm. Since I knew that I would resume work at 8pm, I would have to get there earlier. My alarm clock would tell me the time and they have an alarm clock here at the mill. I had a wristwatch then too. But in the village, we used to farm. Everyday we would get up, we would use the sun to know the time, whether it is rising or it is setting—then they would know it was evening, after doing a day of farming.
>
> (Interview: Samson Okwoli, 24 July 2019, Kaduna)

Yet some men who came from villages in southern Kaduna State were quite familiar with clocks from their attendance at school, as Bulus Ayuba said:

> In our own village, you know, many people had already gone to school and had an education so they had wall clocks. Because at that time, we had already grown up, education had gone on. But our people in the olden days, they kept local time by the light [sun]. So when they said it was 10 o'clock and you looked at the wall clock, it said 10 o'clock exactly. So early in the morning they would say it was time to go to school. When it is morning time, they would know it's almost 6 o'clock, 7 o'clock and then you will know it's 10-11am as that was the time the Fulani people are selling *fura* and grazing their animals because they know the time.
>
> (Interview: 24 July 2019, Kaduna)

This shift from assessing time based on the sun—daytime—or its absence—nighttime, as well as time based on tasks—selling *fura*—to time based on timepieces—such as wall clocks, wristwatches, and alarm clocks—was reinforced by KTL managers, who devised a system of incentives to motivate superior workers who kept to time.

KTL work incentives

There were several incentives which encouraged employees to work hard and to stay with the company. Several workers received certificates of long service for 10, 15, 20, 25, 30, 35, and even 40 years of service. While cloth wrappers (six-yard pieces of KTL fabric) and, for some, money, were given along with the certificates, the ten-year long service award was particularly special, as Godwin Okwoli explained:

> They sent your name to the Department, after ten years they give you wrappers and a wall clock, 10 year service award, after 15 years and then 20 years award. They didn't give me money—but rather cloth and a wall

clock but the clock only once. The wrapper number depended on your grade, the last one I collected 6 pieces of wrapper cloth for 20 years of service.

(Interview: 24 July 2019, Kaduna)

According to Haruna Joshua, "I was given a certificate after 10 years, after 25 years, and 30 years… They gave us six cloth wrappers and money—we enjoyed ourselves!" Cloth wrappers (six-yard pieces) were also given at special holidays such as Christmas and Ramadan.[8] There was also a company clinic (as will be discussed in the Chapter 3) which attended to workers' and their immediate family members' health problems. If the problem was serious, the worker was transferred to a local hospital with expenses covered by the company. In addition, a canteen located at the mill provided subsidized meals prepared by local women, while films were regularly shown at the Welfare Centre located on the KTL site. KTL also provided housing in the Barnawa [Birnawa] area for junior staff members, some of whose widows continue to live there.

> In all these ways—by the division of labour, the supervision of labour; fines; bells and clocks; money incentives; preachings and schooling; the suppression of fairs and sports – new labour habits were formed, and a new time-discipline was imposed.
>
> (Thompson 1967: 90)

For those who were hired, many stayed on despite increasing difficulties for workers, union organizers, and management alike (Andrae and Beckman 1999: 106).

Signs of distress and the mill's closure

> What needs to be said is not that one way of life is better than the other, but that this is a place of the most far-reaching conflict; that the historical record is not a simple one of neutral and inevitable/technological change, but is also one of exploitation and of resistance to exploitation; and that values stand to be lost as well as gained.
>
> (Thompson 1967: 93–94)

The textile mills in Kaduna were still operating in the 1990s although they were operating with obsolete equipment, without the capital to obtain spare parts, and without a regular source of electricity. In 1997, the Kaduna Textiles Ltd mill was "on the verge of collapse" (Onyeiwu 1997: 244). The subsequent closing of Kaduna Textiles Ltd and other textile mills in Kaduna partly reflected the fall in international oil prices in the early 1980s (Andrae and Beckman 1999: 38). This situation contributed to a reduction of government support for textile manufacturing in northern Nigeria. The IMF Structural

Adjustment Program (SAP), signed by former President Ibrahim Babangida in 1986 and implemented in 1987, led to the subsequent currency devaluation which contributed to the process of decline for the Kaduna Textiles Ltd mill. One oft-cited reason for the mills' decline was that outdated textile equipment was neither repaired nor replaced because the foreign exchange needed to purchase spare parts and new equipment was not available. Yet even if spinning machines, winders, and looms had been replaced, they became prohibitively expensive to operate due to the irregular supply of electricity and the need to use "black oil" as a source of power for textile mills in Kaduna. This situation was one of the main reasons for mill closures cited in the literature, in newspaper articles, and by textile workers alike. The economic constraints on textile mill production due to the lack of electricity in Kaduna had a variety of consequences for textile mill workers.

At the Kaduna Textiles Ltd mill, the lack of working equipment led to temporary shut-downs and stoppages (Onyeiwu 1997: 244–245). These shut-downs and production stoppages affected mill managers' ability to pay workers in a timely fashion and led to periods of compulsory leave. In January 1984, KTL workers were given the option of closing the mill altogether or taking a 50% reduction in pay, a situation which led to a labor protest (Andrae and Beckman 1999: 15–17). After a settlement agreement the following month that reinstated all workers with a 25% pay reduction, the mill continued operations although the work force was reduced, not by dismissals but by attrition. After 1984, a new manager was put in place who streamlined production by closing the third and fourth mills, by refurbishing equipment through salvaging spare parts from decommissioned machinery, and by putting fewer workers in charge of more machines (Andrae and Beckman 1999: 104). While these actions improved production and even led to a slight profit in 1986, inefficiencies of production and relatively high prices of KTL products led to their lack of competitiveness, in part reflecting industrial attrition associated with Abacha regime corruption (Andrae and Beckman 1999: 286).[9]

New and different regimes of time

By 2002, the KTL mill had closed. After the closure of this mill and other mills in Kaduna, the equation of "time is money" associated with industrial capitalism collapsed as former KTL workers, dismissed without gratuity payments, had abundant but purposeless time. Several widows mentioned their husbands' frustration with their failure to receive their benefits and their worries about supporting their families. For example, Audu Kuru, who worked in the KTL Spinning Department, was consumed with worries about obtaining his gratuity payment, which his widow believed led to his death:

> The problem he faced, he was always thinking—he didn't receive his gratuity. Whenever he was eating, you would see him moving his head and

his eyes would become red. Besides that, he came to discover that he had *ciwo suga* [diabetes] before he died.

(Interview: Asabe Audu, 9 May 2018, Kaduna)

Other former KTL workers became disoriented and, as one widow put it, her husband, Ayuba Dandume, "lost his mind":

> After he lost his job, he started work as a security man…There was a time he spent two days—we didn't see him, he was just walking around Abuja Road. We found him and brought him back home. He was suffering from that time until the time when he couldn't speak or move…Even his food, I had to feed him because he could not feed himself—because he could not lift his arms. He suffered for three years. We took him to St. Gerard's Hospital and [after he died], we buried him in this house.
>
> (Interview: Cecilia Ayuba, 9 May 2018, Kaduna)

For many KTL workers who abided by the company's rules about being "on time"—coming early, clocking in and out using clocking cards, and promptly resuming work after breaks, time *was* money. And even though pay for most workers was not great, food prices were low in Kaduna in the 1960s and 1970s so that the money they earned was associated with abundant food. "We even threw food away," as one widow recalled. However, after the KTL mill closed and workers were discharged without their gratuities and could not find other jobs, they not only had "time on their hands," but many were unable to buy sufficient food for their families. While several former workers (and their wives) resorted to farming, in many cases returning to one's hometown was not a realistic option. For it was not only workers, and later, their widows, who had come to Kaduna and had become accustomed to urban life, which was the case for many of their children who were born in the city. It was also the fracturing of extended family ties, reinforced by the regimented hours and regular income associated with industrial employment, as opposed to the hours which fluctuated with the seasons; the hard, physical labor associated with farming; and the intimate sociality of village life. This disjunction of family connections was reflected in the experiences of some widows and their children on returning to their hometown after their husbands' and fathers' deaths, as one daughter explained:

> We didn't find it easy when my father died…We went back to our hometown, but the way they have been there, it's not easy because my mother was staying with the wives of my father's brother—they were gossiping about her and insulting her. So my mother said that she couldn't stay there and brought us back here to Kaduna. I don't think that we will go back home in the future although we used to go from time to time. But there has been no help from our relatives, not even N5 up until now.
>
> (Interview: R. Galau, 17 July 2019, Kaduna)

This lack of social or financial support, faced by some but not all KTL widows and their children, underscores their very different experience of post-capitalist industrial time in Kaduna, Nigeria.

Conclusion

Kaduna Textiles Ltd provides a particular example of the growth of industrial capitalism in a specific sociocultural, economic, and political context; the KTL mill was opened as a government initiative, with assistance from a private foreign textile firm. Through the opening of the Kaduna Textiles Ltd mill Ahmadu Bello, the Premier of the Northern Region, was determined to develop the economy of the North and, furthermore, to increase Muslim conversion in southern Kaduna and Middle Belt states. Yet as one Middle Belt mill worker, Pa Afolabi, observed: "we were always saying that [the] late Sardauna was a Northerner by origin but a Nigerian by action because all he did was for the benefit of all irrespective of place of origin" (Mudashir 2010). While the particular history that preceded this situation—particularly the 19th century control of much of northern Nigeria by Muslim rulers associated with the Sokoto Caliphate and the subsequent imposition of British colonial rule in the early 20th century—is beyond the scope of this volume,[10] this history affected the political inclination of those belonging to the many small ethnic groups in southern Kaduna and Middle Belt states. Their distasteful memories of northern emirate rule and the associated practice of slavery contributed to their acceptance of the British and Christian missionaries who taught them to read the Bible, which inadvertently contributed to labor migration to Kaduna and affected who was hired by Kaduna Textiles Ltd managers.

Thus, while the outcome of this industrialization process reflects the particularities of northern Nigerian history and culture, one might also say that the deindustrialization of the textile mills in Kaduna is also specific to the Nigerian context. For example, unlike Nigeria, most of the cotton textile mills in the UK ended production in the late 20th century (BBC National Films 2014; Blackburn 1993; Famie and Jeremy 2004), largely due to insufficient labor. But, as in Nigeria, their demise was also due to reduced production capacity and foreign competition.[11] As Blackburn (1993: 256–257) observed regarding the cotton textile industry in the UK:

> At the end of 1991, there were a derisory 460,000 spindles in place (compared with 9 million in 1961) and 8,700 looms (as against 168,000 in 1961)…On the evidence of the capacity figures mentioned it is not an exaggeration to say that the UK no longer has a cotton textile industry of any consequence.

This decline in spinning and weaving capacity reflected the closing of many cotton textile mills in Lancashire, Manchester, and Blackburn, as is noted in the BBC National Film production, "From Boom to Bust: The Decline of the Cotton Industry":

> During the 1960s and 70s, mills were closed across Lancashire at a rate of almost one a week. By the 1980s the textile industry of the North West had all but vanished. Only the empty factories and northern towns which sprung up as a result, were left—a legacy of an industry that was once the pride of Britain.

This situation has been difficult for many former UK textile mill workers. Yet other employment opportunities, particularly for those with higher education, along with government programs that provided unemployment support and health care lessened the impact of this transition in the UK.

While the Kaduna Textiles Ltd mill was built and equipped by a British textile manufacturing firm, David Whitehead & Sons Ltd, Nigerian textile mill workers experienced a different situation after the KTL mill had closed in Kaduna as compared to that of British textile mill workers. With the ownership of KTL continuing to be held in trust by the 19 northern state governments, an agreement on final remittance payments has not been reached despite union, coalition, and worker efforts, nor has health care been provided by KTL or the state government. Thus, despite KTL workers' acceptance of the new work and time regime, this particular form of industrial state-owned, "public capitalism," has led to their forced acceptance of either a return to agricultural labor with its time-regimen based on the seasons or of "free time," during which they are unemployed but hardly at their leisure. For those preferring to remain in the city, the difficulties of living there without regular income and access to affordable health care has contributed to the many health problems experienced by former KTL workers and the subsequent deaths of many. The health problems associated with their work at the KTL mill and their deaths after the mill's closure are explored in the following chapter.

Notes

1 The opening of Kaduna Textiles Ltd was reported in newspapers from three continents: the *Chicago Defender, Gaskiya Ta Fi Kwabo*, the *Manchester Guardian, The Times (London)*, and the *Washington Afro-American*.
2 Following World War II, the Department of Development and Welfare established Textile Training Centres to encourage floor loom handweaving in Nigeria and to provide employment for returning soldiers However, knowledge of handweaving was hardly preparation for using industrial looms and associated carding, spinning, dyeing, and finishing equipment nor were most veterans interested in handweaving as an occupation (Renne 1997).
3 This connection resembles the "sibling chain of assistance," described by demographers in explaining family strategies that enabled the education of younger children through the work of older, educated children (Caldwell 1977: 20).
4 Of the 100 KTL mill workers interviewed by Andrae and Beckman in 1987, only 8% were Muslim, and of these men, 6% had Islamic education alone (Andrae and Beckman 1999: 302).

5 This man later went to work at Arewa Textiles, another textile mill in Kaduna (Interview: Johannes Kukah, 28 February 2012, Kaduna).
6 Thompson (1967: 86) cites the remark of a Gloucester UK hemp and flax [spinning] thread manufacturer in 1786 regarding the effects of schools on his workers: "They… become more tractable and obedient, and less quarrelsome and revengeful."
7 As Thompson (1967: 69) notes, during the 1800s in England: "The small instrument which regulated the new rhythms of industrial life was at the same time one of the more urgent of the new needs which industrial capitalism called forth to energize its advance. A clock or a watch was not only useful; it conferred prestige upon its owner, and a man might be willing to stretch his resources to get one."
8 One widow mentioned that her husband would sell the KTL cloths and purchase more costly cloths for her with the proceeds (Interview: Saidi Ishaya, 15 May 2018, Kaduna).
9 Funds for the textile industry and other government programs were syphoned off by the Abacha family and deposited in overseas accounts. In 2005, $752 million dollars (US) were recovered from a Swiss bank account, as was $322.5 million dollars (US) in 2017. An agreement for the release of an additional $308 million dollars (US) held in an Isle of Jersey account has recently been settled. In the past, recovered funds have been used for infrastructure and cash transfers to the poor (Azu 2019). The $308 million dollar settlement will be used for road and rail projects (Odeyemi 2020).
10 There are several sources that document the history of the Sokoto Caliphate and Emirate rule in northern Nigeria and the Middle Belt states which include: Kani and Gandi (1990); Last (1967); Lovejoy (1978); and Philips (1992).
11 The British wool textile industry also followed a downward trajectory: "Despite the efforts made by the industry, trade unions and government,…by the end of 1978 there were only 54,755 wool textile workers left in Britain. The industry was never to recover" (Price 2014: 44; see also Jenkins 1972).

References

Abba, Isa Alkali. "Sir Ahmadu Bello: The Sardauna of Sokoto's Conversion Campaign 1964–1965 in Adamawa Division and Northern Sardauna Province." *Kano Studies* 2, no. 2 (1981): 53–60.

Andrae, Gunilla, and Björn Beckman. 1999. *Union Power in the Nigerian Textile Industry*. New Brunswick, NJ: Transaction Publishers.

Azu, John Chuks. "What We're Doing About Abacha's $300m, by FG." *Daily Trust*, 6 June 2019. Accessed 6 June 2019. https://www.dailytrust.com.ng/what-were-doing-about-abachas-300m-by-fg.html.

BBC National Films. *Boom to Bust—The Decline of the Cotton Industry*, 2014. Accessed 15 September 2019. http://www.bbc.co.uk/nationonfilm/topics/textiles/background_decline.shtml.

Blackburn, John A. "The British Cotton Textile Industry Since World War II: The Search for a Strategy." *Textile History* 24, no. 2 (1993): 235–238.

Caldwell, J.C. "The Economic Rationality of High Fertility." *Population Studies* 31, no. 1 (1977): 5–27.

DanAsabe, Abdulkadir. "The Kano Textile Trade and Industry During the Independence Era." In *Textile Ascendancies: Aesthetics, Production, and Trade in Northern Nigeria*, edited by E. Renne, and S. Maiwada, 115–134. Ann Arbor, MI: University of Michigan Press, 2020.

David Whitehead & Sons. "Kaduna: The Largest Spinning and Weaving Operation South of the Sahara." *Textile Month*. Archives. Parbold, Lancashire: David Whitehead & Sons Ltd, June 1973.

Famie, D.A., and David J. Jeremy. *The Fibre That Changed the World: The Cotton Industry in International Perspective, 1600–1990s*. Oxford: Oxford University Press, 2004.

Gaiya, Musa A. "SIM's Hausa Mission: Ministering Among People on the Margin (*'Yan Babu*) Class in Northern Nigeria." In *Transforming Africa's Religious Landscapes: The Sudan Interior Mission (SIM). Past and Present*, edited by B. Cooper, G. Corwin, T. Eshete, M. Gaiya, T. Geysbeek, and S. Shankar, 121–144. Trenton: Africa World Press, 2018.

Hartley, Gordon W. "Former Commercial Manager, Kaduna Textiles Limited." Unpublished Report, 18 February 2012, in author's possession.

Hinchliffe, Keith. "The Kaduna Textile Workers: Characteristics of an African Industrial Labour Force." *Savanna* 2 (1973): 27–37.

Ijagbemi, E. Adeleye. *Christian Missionary Activity in Colonial Nigeria: The Work of the Sudan Interior Mission Among the Yoruba, 1908–1967*. Lagos: Nigeria Magazine, 1986.

Johnson, Marion. "Cotton Imperialism in West Africa." *African Affairs* 73, no. 291 (1974): 178–187.

Kaduna Textiles Ltd. *KTL Employee's Handbook*. Kaduna: Kaduna Textiles Ltd, nd.

Kaduna Textiles Ltd. "Opening Ceremony." Kadmin-Tra-Ind 10/1, file no. I.59E 79 A21. 1957.

Kani, Ahmad M., and Kabir A. Gandi, eds. *State and Society in the Sokoto Caliphate*. Sokoto: Usman Danfodiyo University, 1990.

Jenkins, J. Geraint, ed. *The Wool Industry in Great Britain*. London, Boston, MA: Routledge and K. Paul, 1972.

LaPin, Deirdre. *Sons of the Moon: The Ngas of Central Nigeria*. Philadelphia, PA: ISHI, 1983.

Last, Murray. *The Sokoto Caliphate*. London: Longman, 1967.

Lovejoy, Paul. "Plantations in the Economy of the Sokoto Caliphate." *Journal of African History* 19, no. 3 (1978): 341–368.

Maiwada, Salihu, and Elisha Renne. "The Kaduna Textile Industry and the Decline of Textile Manufacturing in Northern Nigeria, 1955–2010." *Textile History* 44, no. 2 (2013): 171–196.

Medugbon, A.K. "Kaduna, Nigeria: The Vicissitudes of a Capital City, 1917–1975." Unpublished PhD dissertation. Los Angeles, CA: University of California, 1976.

Mudashir, Ismail. "Heydays of Kaduna Textiles, by Pa Afolabi." *Daily Trust*, 1 October 2010. Accessed 29 November 2010. www.dailytrust.com.ng.

Odeyemi, Joshua. "US, Nigeria Sign Agreement on Abacha Loot Return." *Daily Trust*, 4 February 2020. Accessed 4 February 2020. https://www.dailytrust.com.ng/us-nigeria-sign-agreement-on-abacha-loot-return.html.

Onyeiwu, Steve. "The Modern Textile Industry in Nigeria: History, Structural Change, and Recent Developments." *Textile History* 28, no. 2 (1997): 234–249.

Paden, John. *Ahmadu Bello: Sardauna of Sokoto*. Zaria: Huda Huda Press, 1986.

Philips, J.E. "Ribats in the Sokoto Caliphate: Selected Studies 1804–1903." Unpublished PhD dissertation. Los Angeles, CA: University of California, 1992.

Price, Laura. "Immigrants and Apprentices: Solutions to the Post-War Labour Shortage in the West Yorkshire Wool Textile Industry, 1945–1980." *Textile History* 45, no. 1 (2014): 32–48.

Renne, Elisha. "'Traditional Modernity' and the Economics of Handwoven Cloth Production in Southwestern Nigeria." *Economic Development & Cultural Change* 45, no. 4 (1997): 773–792.

Thompson, E.P. "Time, Work-Discipline, and Industrial Capitalism." *Past & Present* 36, no. 1 (1967): 56–97.

Waziri, M., S. Maiwada, and E. Renne. "Kaduna Textile Industry, Trade, and the Coming of Chinese Textiles." In *Textile Ascendancies: Aesthetics, Production, and Trade in Northern Nigeria*, edited by E. Renne, and S. Maiwada, 87–114. Ann Arbor, MI: University of Michigan Press, 2020.

3 Workers' health and deaths after the closure of Kaduna Textiles Ltd

'What do you weave with wool so white?'
'I weave the shoes of Sorrow;
Soundless shall be the footfall light
In all men's ears of Sorrow,
Sudden and light.'

> William Butler Yeats, "The Cloak, the Boat, and the Shoes" (1885)

Death is a difficult subject to discuss, and the difficulties of documenting and maintaining mortality records for adults in sub-Saharan Africa are well known (Kaufman et al. 1997; Timaeus 1993). For those who die in their homes in rural villages, official documents are rarely obtained, while written records for those dying in cities such as death certificates are not uniform, with information on the cause of death sometimes omitted. How rigorous and standardized such information is depends on government oversight of vital statistics.[1] Yet some mortality data is available, even if it is variable and insufficient for demographic analysis.[2]

In the case of the workers who lost their jobs after the Kaduna Textiles Ltd (KTL) mill closed in December 2002 without being paid their remittances, the listing of the names of workers who died by the Coalition of Closed Unpaid Textile Workers Association Nigeria provides an indirect source of information about the dates of their deaths. Many of the widows whom we were able to contact also kept KTL mill identification cards, hospital records, and death certificates, hoping that these materials would provide proof of employment in the event that KTL management were to pay their deceased husbands' entitlements. However, even when written documentation of their husbands' deaths was not available, their verbal autopsies of these men's deaths after the mill closed suggest the importance of mortality data as evidence of the declining quality of their husbands' lives and the difficulties of survival for them. The non-payment of their remittances was a major factor that contributed to this situation and several widows described their husbands' continuous trips to the KTL mill to learn if remittances were paid. For some men, this money would have been used to relocate their families to their home villages, while for others, they could have used it to start businesses in Kaduna, to cover their children's school fees, to repair houses or pay rent, and to pay for hospital visits.

Yet even before the mill closed, the wages that most workers received were not high, as one man explained:

> You see, KTL, they didn't work on Sunday but their salary was good. But it also depends on your level. When you serve 30 years and you've not been promoted, your money will not be high, it will be low. Like me, I was deputy manager so my own would be high. And when you put the workers together, those who were paid like me, there were not more than five in the factory.
>
> (Interview: Haruna Joshua, 16 July 2019, Kaduna)

Nonetheless, the mill did provide social services for its workers, such as the operation of the mill's two health clinics, the provision of free drugs and hospital care, and subsidized canteen meals. Indeed, many widows mentioned the ready availability of inexpensive food as one of the most alluring aspects of living in Kaduna when they first moved to the city. In contrast, the difficulty in obtaining sufficient food characterized their experience of life after the mill closed. As Amartya Sen (1998: 8–9) has noted, organized social services for the provision of health care and food are two major factors that contribute to the quality of life and longevity, regardless of the amount of one's earnings. KTL workers who received only basic wages thus could support their families—with food, clothes, education, and health care, in part through the social services provided by the company. However, when the mill closed, these services were no longer available nor were there government programs in place to provide food subsidies, health care, and educational stipends for unemployed workers and their families. With neither their salaries, subsequent remittances, free health care, subsidized food, nor holiday bonuses (of KTL textiles), the quality of life of KTL workers and their families dramatically declined. For some workers, this decline also contributed to their deaths, as their widows have explained.

The chapter begins with a discussion of the KTL Board of Directors' plans in 1957 and 1958 for the provision of health care at the mill. Two clinics were established and by 1959, a system for clinic attendance was devised. The clinics not only attracted men (and some women) to work at the Kaduna Textiles Ltd mill, particularly when other mills had opened in the 1960s, but also were used as part of the hiring process as several former workers noted.

While most of the clinic records are no longer available, attendance records and related materials for 2002, the last year of the mill's operation, were found in the KTL mill workers' clinic. The second section of the chapter discusses these attendance lists, which include workers' departments, names, health problems presented, and whether they were treated. The most common illnesses as well as drugs ordered by the clinic personnel for the treatment of workers are discussed. The experiences of former workers who attended the KTL Clinic and of one medical doctor who treated those who attended the clinic are presented, along with a discussion of the symptoms of byssinosis ("brown lung" disease), a condition associated with cotton textile manufacturing globally (Lai and Christiani 2013).[3]

While the KTL Clinic lists of worker attendance do not mention worker deaths, the list compiled by the Coalition of Closed Unpaid Textile Workers Association Nigeria included the name of just one man who died before the mill closed when the clinic was still operating. In subsequent years, however, the number of former KTL workers included in the Coalition of Closed Unpaid Textile Workers Association Nigeria list who died increased. The verbal autopsies provided by widows suggest that cardiovascular and pulmonary diseases were the most frequent reasons for their husbands' deaths. These verbal autopsies are compared with information on the death certificates which some of the widows retained. In addition to heart, lung, and liver-related diseases, a small number of former KTL workers died from road transport accidents (which were similarly documented in the KTL Clinic attendance lists). The details of these incidents provided by some widows, which are missing from death certificates and clinic lists, underscore the importance of open-ended, qualitative interviews in assessing the impact of road-related deaths in Nigeria (World Health Organization 2018).

The chapter concludes with a return to the discussion of the difficulties of assessing adult mortality data without standardized and detailed death registration data. Nonetheless, the descriptions of their husbands' deaths, corroborated by death certificates, along with the observations of KTL medical personnel and former KTL workers, when available, provide a sense of the consequences when basic social services as well as monetary remittances are not provided. While moving to a thriving urban center—Kaduna—was initially seen as beneficial by many widows, the closing of the Kaduna Textiles Ltd mill and their subsequent experience of the illnesses and deaths of their husbands have led some to question the benefits of modern, urban living, and for some, to maintain their ties with rural extended families and to reconsider farming as work.

Health as amenity, health care as incentive: health clinics at Kaduna Textiles Ltd

When Kaduna Textiles Ltd was opened in November 1957, the large manufacturing complex included several buildings that provided services for workers. Early on in the development phase of KTL's operation, the Board of Directors discussed health care provision for mill workers. In its 4 May 1957 meeting, the board discussed the possibility of medical attention for African workers:

It was reported that a Medical Officer had offered his services to the company at 1 hour a day to attend to African employees at a fee in the region of 20 guineas a month. It was <u>Resolved</u> that this offer should be accepted.
(Kaduna Textiles Ltd, Minutes of the Meeting of Directors, 4 May 1957, Kaduna)

The following year, however, the board set up a sub-committee to consider the expanding medical services with the opening of a clinic on the mill site in order to provide regular health care for workers:

The Chairman expressed the view that as by next year we expected to employ about 1,100 Northerners and 40/50 Europeans, the Company should consider having its own doctor. The time lost by workers in attending the Government doctor was a material factor. A sub-committee consisting of Messrs. R.A. Berrif and R.F. Miles, Mallam Rafih and a member of U.A.C. to be co-opted to study the possibility of employing a company's doctor in conjunction with other firms, and to report to the November meeting of the Board.
(Kaduna Textiles Ltd, Minutes of the Meeting of Directors, 12 June 1958, Kaduna)

At the November 1958 meeting, it was reported that U.A.C. (the United Africa Company—a British trading firm, a subsidiary of Unilever) did not want to share the costs of a clinic at that time. Thus:

IT WAS RESOLVED to employ a suitable qualified Northerner on a one year contract on trial at a salary of in the region of £360 per annum and that the Management should provide reasonably improved facilities for the clinic, and that the cost of his house on the grounds would be £400 or so. He would be at call day and night.
(Kaduna Textiles Ltd, Minutes of the Meeting of Directors, 13 November 1958, Kaduna)

Yet as of its May 1959 meeting, the board had been unable to find a Northern Dispensary Attendant, although it was noted that the board would continue its search. In the meantime: "The new Clinic had been opened and was a great improvement in every way on the previous one, and the introduction of a ticket system had cut down the number attending the Clinic considerably by discouraging malingering" (Kaduna Textiles Ltd, Minutes of the Meeting of Directors, 13 May 1959, Kaduna). In November 1959, it was reported that a qualified man had been found to take charge of the clinic, although it was noted that the number of workers attending the clinic continued to decline (Kaduna Textiles Ltd, Minutes of the Meeting of Directors, 9 November 1959, Kaduna). It is unclear why attendance declined—whether there was insufficient or unqualified staff or that the "ticket system" was unsatisfactory.

However, in the May 1960 report, the Chairman and board agreed to employ "a [part time] doctor…[to] attend the Mill for an hour-daily on a retainer basis" (Kaduna Textiles Ltd, Minutes of the Meeting of Directors, 5 November 1960, Kaduna). KTL subsequently had two clinics, one for general mill workers (Figure 3.1) and another for managerial staff, both of which were attended to by a doctor, nurses, and dispensary attendants (Interview: Samson Asuga, 19 January 2017, Kaduna).

The clinic, along with a canteen (which provided a subsidized daily meal) and housing for some staff, provided incentives for workers to apply to Kaduna Textiles Ltd for employment. The clinic was also part of the hiring process: "There was a medical check-up too, you have to go to the KTL Clinic and they did serious tests. I'm not a medical person but I know they took my blood and they checked my body" (Interview: Samson Okwoli, 24 July 2019, Kaduna). Assuming the applicant passed this health inspection and other requirements, he or she would be hired to work at KTL.

KTL clinic attendance and morbidity records

The opportunity to attend the KTL clinic was appreciated by many workers, as one KTL manager who went to the clinic when needed said:

> Yes, I used to go there…At that time, KTL had money, we had qualified doctors who were well-paid, we had qualified nurses, we were given all the drugs except if the sickness was up to a certain level that the clinic could not handle, they would send you to an outside hospital. St. Gerard's Catholic Hospital, yes, we had about three hospitals outside.
> (Interview: Sylvester Gankon, 24 May 2018, Kaduna)

The clinic was well-attended, attested to by the extensive attendance lists compiled in the year just prior to the mill's closing. For example, during the month of March 2002, 657 visits to the clinic were made by workers with various jobs

Figure 3.1 Kaduna Textiles Ltd clinic for general mill workers, Kaduna, 2018 (Photograph by E.P. Renne).

in the mill (weavers, electricians, poly, printing and finishing, spinning, and engineering, among others) for diagnoses and treatment. The details of health problems presented by workers based on attendance data confirm the finding of other studies of cardiovascular disease in Africa (Mbewu and Mbanya 2006). Thus, in March 2002, hypertension (high blood pressure) was the most commonly diagnosed health problem at the KTL clinic, with 24% of workers listed as having this condition (Figure 3.2). Other more common health problems documented included coryza [cold], cough, diabetes, enteritis, and plasma (blood disorders). Hypertension (18% of workers) was also the most common condition listed in the health clinic entries for October 2002, two months before the mill's closure. Other conditions listed that month included aches/pains, coryza, and coughs.

When these health problems could be treated with drugs or bandages, the worker would be treated and then released. The clinic staff regularly ordered drugs for treating workers who attended the clinic. The most commonly treated condition, hypertension, was treated with four different drugs (Adalat, Aldactone, Brinerdin, and Moduretic), while a range of painkillers (Baralgin, Novolgin, Optalido, and Paracetamol) were used. Specific drugs for coryza [cold symptoms] (Stelbid), ulcers (Tagamet), malaria (Chloroquine), and anxiety disorders (Libruim) were also given.

If the condition could not be treated at the clinic, the worker was transferred to a local hospital. One man who attended the clinic was diagnosed with

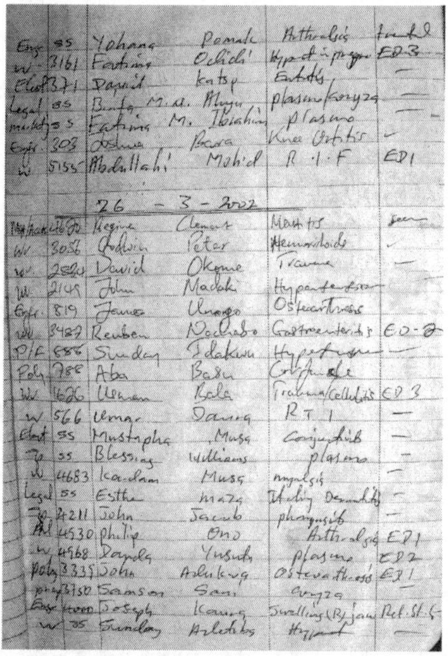

Figure 3.2 List of workers attending the KTL clinic and health problem diagnoses, 26 March 2002 (Photograph by E.P. Renne).

a hernia and underwent an operation (Interview: Wuyah Adze, 24 June 2019, Kaduna), while another worker, Reuben Yakuba, had a more serious, though not uncommon, illness:

> When the company was about to close, I fell sick. The company took me to one of the hospitals in town—Al-Barka Hospital. For any major sickness, the company would take you to that hospital. At that time, I didn't realize that I was so sick. But when I closed from work and reached home, I began to feel cold entering my body and my stomach swelled up. They rushed me to our clinic here, where they said it was beyond their power so they rushed me to that hospital. I was put on scanning machine for seven days before they detected what the problem was. So they had to operate on me, some doctors from ABUTH, that was in 2002. I spent three months in the hospital, I didn't even know what was the afternoon, what was night. They just told me it was typhoid, they operated and were successful, they didn't tell me at the time, only after I was discharged. If it were not for KTL, maybe I would be forgotten now.
> (Interview: 24 July 2019, Kaduna)

Dr. Olusola Olukayode Falaye, one of the medical doctors who worked at the KTL Clinic, observed that the most commonly seen diseases at the KTL Clinic were typhoid and malaria, although many workers exhibited hypertension which could lead to chronic heart disease (Mbewu and Mbanya 2006). He also remembered cases of ischaemia (blockage of the arteries to the heart) and cor pulmonale (high blood pressure in the arteries of the lungs), although he noted that none of these conditions is necessarily linked to cotton textile mill work *per se*, but could also reflect other risk factors such as stress, ageing, diet, and lifestyle. Furthermore, he pointed out that clinic doctors were unable to diagnose byssinosis ("brown lung" disease associated with textile mills) without lab tests. While the main symptom of byssinosis is coughing, this could also be a symptom of TB or asthma. Since the clinic did not have facilities for lab tests for byssinosis, it was not included on KTL Health Clinic lists (Interview: Olusola Falaye, 3 June 2018, Kaduna). Yet the number of workers who were seen in the clinic with a range of symptoms related to byssinosis (dry cough, muscle and joint pain, fever, and shivering), suggests that this disease was probably the case for some. In the KTL Clinic lists for both March and October 2002 ($n_{total} = 1{,}307$), for example, there were 55 worker visits for coughs, 101 worker visits for aches/pains, and 28 worker visits for fever. While KTL management was aware of the health problems associated with breathing cotton dust and distributed face masks to workers, not everyone wore them, as one KTL manager explained: "Those who were in cotton ginning and the spinning departments, they were given masks that would protect them. But many were removing their masks because they couldn't breathe properly" (Interview: Haruna Joshua, 16 July 2019, Kaduna).

Causes of death: KTL workers after the mill's closure

As the political and economic situation in Nigeria worsened following the implementation of the Structural Adjustment Program and the devaluation of its currency in 1987, KTL management implemented workers' compulsory leave, shortened work weeks, and half-pay, if their salaries were paid at all in the 1990s (Andrae and Beckman 1999). It is not surprising that many KTL workers attending the company clinic in the 2001 to 2002 period were diagnosed with hypertension and stress:

> My husband died before the factory closed and he was the 9th person to die in 2001. He was sick for three days, he told me he had a headache and fever…So we went to the KTL clinic, they said that we should go to one of the hospitals. And because he was smoking, the people in the hospital said it might be from that. But I didn't believe that. I thought that someone had done something to him…He died on a Sunday and we took him to his hometown on Thursday. KTL gave us a vehicle to take him to his hometown (Kureta) and N20,000.
> (Interview: Laraba Paul, 24 May 2018, Kaduna)

While smoking is a contributing risk factor for pulmonary-cardiovascular related diseases, this widow believed "that someone had done something" to her husband, meaning witchcraft. Although not literally the case, her assessment may not be entirely amiss, considering the deteriorating conditions at the mill and the unregulated mask use as protection against cotton dust that were the likely causes of his illness and death.

Yet many of the widows of KTL workers who had taken their husbands to the clinic accepted the clinic doctors' diagnoses. While not all verbal autopsies provided by widows whom we interviewed were sufficiently detailed to determine the possible reasons for their husbands' deaths, some were quite specific and also utilized diagnostic terms that reflected their interactions with health workers at the KTL clinic and later at hospitals they attended, mainly in Kaduna.[4]

KTL widows' verbal autopsies and KTL workers' death certificates

Of the 20 KTL widows who had death certificates for their husbands that they showed to me, half had death certificates from two of the main hospitals in Kaduna, Gwamna Awan Hospital and St. Gerard's Catholic Hospital. Other hospitals outside of Kaduna (in Kafanchan and Benin City) and government offices (Kaduna State, Nigeria; Ministry of Health-Kaduna State; and National Population Commission, Nigeria) also provided death certificates. These documents varied in the amount of detail provided, with the two main Kaduna hospitals providing the most information, both on the cause of death and on contributing factors. For example, the doctor who filled out the death certificate issued by the Gwamna Awan Hospital for Dauda Sani wrote that he died from cardiovascular arrest that was due to shock and to gastroenteritis (Figure 3.3). His widow, Jummai Dauda, described the sequence of death as follows:

> [After the mill closed], it was the problems that caused him to have high blood pressure. He had no work, no food, and he had children…He used to trek down to go to Gwamna Awan Hospital, he would go in the morning and stay until evening without eating. Whenever he came back, he would talk about his benefits, his money from KTL. When they gave him his benefits, he would say, his children would be enjoying. He was planning these things all his life and whenever they would call a meeting at KTL, he would always go with the hope that he would hear good news. And he used to trek to KTL but he would come back with no good news.
>
> Because of this, he was not happy and it was the cause of his high blood pressure. He was sick Tuesday and he died Friday. He died in the house because we thought that it was just a fever and that it was nothing serious. He had even gone to see the doctor on Thursday. When he went to see the doctor and the doctor have him medicine, he couldn't swallow the medicine. It was Friday night when I realized that his condition was very serious and I didn't have money to take him to the hospital. I called his brothers and told them that they should come and take him to the hospital. They were about to come that night, but before they came, he died.
> (Interview: 14 May 2018, Kaduna)

Other widows' verbal autopsies were less descriptive and more like the summaries of death described on their husbands' death certificates:

Figure 3.3 Death certificate for Dauda Sani, form used by the Gwamna Awan Hospital, Kaduna (Photograph by E.P. Renne).

He was doing *kabu kabu* [little things] after the mill closed. He had diabetes and we took him to his hometown, near Benin City where he died on 5 October 2008.
(Interview: Theresa Godwin, 29 May 2018, Kaduna)

Godwin Oseghale. Primary cause: Neuroglycopenia [low glucose blood level to the brain]
Secondary cause: Diabetes mellitus.
(Death certificate, Faith Medical Centers, Benin City).

In this case, the cause of death given by his wife and the doctor at the medical center in Benin City was diabetes. Such parallel prognoses were also true of several men whose deaths were attributed to cardiovascular-pulmonary disease or cardiac arrest, both by hospital personnel and their wives:

When the factory closed in 2002, we faced a problem because we didn't have food…sometimes we would only drink water…He died when he was doing farming, and the farm wasn't our own, we used to pay 2,000 or N3,000 to farm there. And the farm was far away from our house, we had to trek quite a distance before reaching the place. He had *hawan jini* (high blood pressure) then. We went to several hospitals, after we went to Gwamna Awan Hospital, then we went to another hospital in Chikun Gari, he was admitted there. From there we went to Yusuf DanTsoho Hospital in Tudun Wada, then to another hospital. We used to go to one hospital to another, he really suffered, he suffered for eight years. We have his death certificate.
(Interview: Esther Audu, 15 May 2018, Kaduna)

The cause of death listed on her husband's death certificate from the Ministry of Health, Kaduna is CVA, cardiovascular arrest.

While the number of death certificates listing causes of death is limited to 20, they tend to agree with the verbal autopsies of the widows who have kept them. There are several reasons which may explain this situation. Widows who went from hospital to hospital with their husbands could hear the diagnoses which doctors gave to their husbands. While not necessarily knowing complicated medical terms, such as neuroglycopenia, many would have heard of diabetes (locally known as *ciwo suga*, literally sugar disease in Hausa). Similarly, they were familiar with high blood pressure (*hawan jini*)—hypertension—from KTL Clinic visits. Other diagnoses such as branchogenic carcinoma (a type of lung cancer) were less well known:

My husband faced a lot of problems after the mill closed. He started farming to get food. But he had cancer, he spent two months at ABUTH-Kaduna. When we were at the hospital for the two months, they operated on so many places and removed "water" and growths. After he was discharged from the hospital he fell ill again. We were on the way to take him to the ABUTH-Kaduna Hospital when he died.

(Interview: Fatu Tom, 30 April 2018, Kaduna)

Nonetheless, having a death certificate was not always informative, as three certificates did not list a cause at all, while one listed the cause of death as "illness." The lack of uniformity and detailed information on some, but not all, certificates underscore the difficulties in determining the causes of death among adults in northern Nigeria (Kaufman et al. 1997; Randall and Coast 2016).

Road-related accidents

This lack of information was also the case for road-related deaths and injuries. Among the KTL workers who attended the company clinic in March 2002, nine men suffered from injuries and two suffered from trauma related to road and pedestrian accidents,[5] although the details of their injuries and treatments are not given.

Nigeria is currently considered by the World Health Organization to be a middle-income country with road-related deaths that reflect road conditions, high speed driving, and minimal traffic regulation (World Health Organization 2018).[6] Like cardiovascular diseases, which have increased in countries such as Nigeria due to changes in diet and exercise, road-related deaths have also increased with more cars on the road and congested city streets.

Four widows described such road-related deaths of their husbands after the KTL mill closed, when they had taken up new, lower-paying jobs, in Kaduna and in outlying areas. One was hit by a vehicle when walking to work, another while riding his bicycle to work, and another was hit by a motorcycle—all on streets in Kaduna. While each of these three men was taken to St. Gerard's Catholic Hospital with the hope of saving his life, none lived more than a week after these accidents. The details of the fourth man who died in a road accident is less clear, although he was traveling frequently to gather cow bones as part of his bone collection business. He apparently had two road-related accidents, although it is unclear exactly what happened, as his wife explained:

> He was doing business with the money he got from selling plots he had bought in Kaduna. He started a business, buying *kashi* [bones] from the cows, he bought and sold them. He went to different places to buy and sell them. He was facing problems but he didn't tell me…It was the month he was to die he told me all these things—all the problems he faced. There was a time, one Thursday, that he went to his hometown and came back that very day. Then Friday, the next day, he said he would go back again. I asked him why he wanted to go back because he had just come back the day before. He said that someone had cow bones that he wanted to buy.

He said he would go and buy them and then sell them in Abuja…The day he was going to our hometown, he came back four times, he kept saying that he forgot something. The fourth time he came back, he asked his children and the children of a woman in the house renting us a room to escort him. When the children were about to go, he gave them money and told them to go home, and that he would come back from Abuja on Sunday.

Later, he called me and the last thing he said to me, that he would not be going to Abuja, that he saw someone else with bones which he wanted to burn. He said he would come back on Sunday. On Sunday, I waited for him to come back—but he didn't come back. I called his cell phone, it was switched off. I thought it was a network problem because sometimes our village at home has that problem. On that Sunday, I went to church with my children—he still had not returned. Monday, I waited for him to come back but he didn't show up. But that Monday, I felt something in my body, I wasn't comfortable. That Monday I started forgetting what his face looked like—I was unable to see his face.

It was that evening that I received a call, that my husband had had an accident and that I should come to our hometown. But I didn't have money that day. But they said…I should send my first son and my fourth son before I came. I got the money and gave it to them and they went there. It was that day, there was a relative who never came to our house. That day, he came. He was asking me, "Where is your husband?" I said to him that he had travelled to our hometown the day before yesterday and that I was told that he'd had an accident, that he was in the hospital. He gave me transport money and told me to go the next day. He knew my husband was dead but he didn't tell me.

(Interview: Lami Iliya, 14 May 2018, Kaduna)

While Lami Iliya did not have detailed knowledge of his husband's road accident, she did have a death certificate. However, it did not provide detailed information for the cause of death was simply written as "R.T.A."—Road Traffic Accident (Figure 3.4).

Conclusion

As the myriad sources of death data for former KTL workers indicate, the difficulties of addressing their husbands' health problems and preventing their deaths has been a continual challenge for KTL widows. While many have kept records of their husbands' attendance at hospital and clinics and some have their husbands' death certificates, the paper trail of these deaths is not always sufficiently detailed or uniform to provide a clear picture of the causes of adult workers' mortality in Kaduna. Much as economic data on workers' income do not provide an adequate representation of workers' well-being and quality of life, as Sen has observed (1998), neither does simply noting the mortality

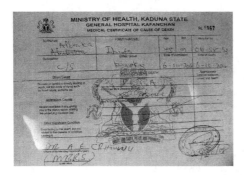

Figure 3.4 Death certificate for Abubakar Iliya, RTA (Road Traffic Accident), General Hospital, Kafanchan (Photograph by E.P. Renne).

data from death certificates and morbidity data from clinic records provide a sense of the experiences of workers who benefited from the mill's social and health services. Even in the last years before the mill closed and medical treatment was supported by KTL management, some workers received and were grateful for company health care, as was noted by Reuben Yakuba, who was hospitalized and was operated on: "If it were not for KTL, maybe I would be forgotten now." However, after the KTL mill closed, workers and their wives suffered as the quality of their lives declined. Without the verbal autopsies of their widows, their movements from hospital to hospital seeking treatment for hypertension and other illnesses would be obscured, nor would the dangerous difficulties of road travel to collect cow bones for sale after the mill closed be recorded.

Another aspect of the deaths of former KTL mill workers relates to the consequences of rural-urban migration when the benefits of urban employment and the life-styles it supported no longer existed. Yet it was precisely some of these benefits that, even had the mill remained open, contributed to workers' problems. Many widows mentioned that food was one of the things that differed from their home villages and how much they liked their new diet of rice and meat, seasoned with salty Maggi bouillon cubes. Yet their increased consumption of beef may have been a contributory factor to increased "obesity, hypertension, and diabetes" (Livingston 2019: 35). Some women, such as Laraba Haruna, also mentioned being introduced to palm oil in Kaduna, as did Martina Oliver: "In Kaduna you can eat food with palm oil but in our hometown, they only cook without palm oil" (Interview: 25 July 2019, Kaduna).[7]

It is likely that such a diet, which is high in saturated fat, has contributed to increased risk for stroke, cardiovascular mortality, and colorectal cancer (Wolk 2017). Additionally, white rice, which has less fiber than whole grain millet, and sorghum porridge (*tuwo dawa*) may have contributed to an increase in type 2 diabetes (Aune et al. 2013). While several researchers note the need for further study of the health consequences of these foods, diet along with increased stress may indeed have contributed to the large number of cases of hypertension seen in the KTL Clinic attendance lists.

On the one hand, the disadvantages to the health of workers and their families from diets with more red meat and refined grains were reinforced by textile mill manufacturing, where those working in spinning and weaving sections were exposed to cotton dust and related pulmonary health problems. Furthermore, these problems were compounded by the increasing number of cars and the expansion of roads which have contributed to road-related traffic accidents and deaths. These difficulties underscore the dangers of unregulated textile manufacturing and roadways, as well as unhealthy diets—all seen as beneficial for the development of a modern economy yet also may be fatally harmful. These dilemmas raise the question of how reopening the textile mills may exacerbate these problems. On the other hand, the unemployment of Kaduna youth has contributed to drug use (to be discussed in Chapter 6), social inequality, ethnic conflict, and insecurity. By addressing these issues, the reopening the mill, along with providing education about health for mill workers and better control of the health conditions of textile mills in Kaduna, may improve the situation in Kaduna to some extent.

One consequence of the closure of the KTL mill, the end of company health and social services, and the failure of the company to pay worker remittances has been the return of some workers and their families to their hometowns and villages to live and farm. Others have returned to farming just outside of Kaduna, while some have started new businesses there in the city. For not all widows and their children wish to return to a rural way of life, which one widow suggested had changed for the worse. According to Helen Dauda, "In this modern time, nobody will help you" (Interview: 8 May 2018, Kaduna). Yet this situation has not been the experience for all widows when it came to family assistance in helping with the burial of their husbands.

Notes

1 As Foucault (1991: 6) observed in his discussion in *The Birth of the Clinic*, "Disease is perceived fundamentally in a space of projection without depth, of coincidence without development." In other words, the disease is identified through symptoms and laboratory tests while the historical causes of these symptoms are not involved.
2 Kaufman et al. (1997: 390) suggest that longitudinal studies using population-based surveys are "the best alternative for determining cause-specific estimates."
3 According to Lai and Christiani (2013: 153): "Early stage byssinosis in many respects fulfills the criteria for the diagnosis of asthma: reversible airflow obstruction and airway hyper-responsiveness." They also note: "There are no studies currently in textile workers that document whether bronchial hyper-reactivity persists after worker retirement; thus it is unclear if textile workers develop an exposure related asthma-like syndrome vs. the persistent airway hyper-reactivity that is present in asthma despite exposure cessation" (Lai and Christiani 2013: 154).
4 Sen (1998: 20) suggests that "Our observational analyses from particular 'positions' can be 'objective' enough from that position, and yet very far from what we could know had

we been differently placed." The benefits of "positional objectivity" appears to be the case for urban widows who accompanied their husbands to the KTL clinic and hospitals in Kaduna, although having greater knowledge of their husbands' health problems did not necessarily translate into extending their lives when government support for health care was lacking.

5 For the month of October 2002, only two workers came to the clinic following road traffic accidents. It is unclear why there were more such accidents in March 2002; possibly the period before crops were harvested engendered irregular driving.

6 The 2018 World Health Organization Report does not provide a breakdown by type of road user category for Nigeria (WHO 2018: 205), as it is included in the group of "countries without eligible death registration data" (WHO 2018: 293).

7 Palm oil, while high in fatty acids, also has a "high concentration of antioxidants such as β-carotene, tocotrienols, tocopherols and vitamin E," which counter diseases associated with oxidative stress (Oguntibeju et al. 2009). And according to WebMD, palm oil has many benefits: "preventing vitamin A deficiency, cancer, brain disease, and aging. It is also used to treat malaria, high blood pressure, high cholesterol, dementia, and cyanide poisoning." (https://www.webmd.com/vitamins/ai/ingredientmono-1139/palm-oil).

References

Andrae, Gunilla, and Björn Beckman. 1999. *Union Power in the Nigerian Textile Industry*. New Brunswick, NJ: Transaction Publishers.

Aune, D., T. Norat, P. Romundstad, and L. J. Vatten. "Whole Grain and Refined Grain Consumption and the Risk of Type 2 Diabetes: A Systematic Review and Dose-Response Meta-Analysis of Cohort Studies." *European Journal of Epidemiology* 3, no. 28 (11) (2013): 845–858.

Foucault, Michel. *The Birth of the Clinic: An Archaeology of Medical Perception*, trans. A. M. Sheridan Smith. London: Routledge, 1991.

Kaduna Textiles Ltd. "Minutes of the Meeting of Directors." Unpublished documents. Archives. Parbold, Lancashire: David Whitehead & Son, 1957–1960.

Kaufman, J., M. Asuzu, C. Rotimi, O. Johnson, E. Owoaje, and R. Cooper. "The Absence of Adult Mortality Data for Sub-Saharan Africa: A Practical Solution." *Bulletin of the World Health Organization* 75, no. 5 (1997): 389–395.

Lai, Peggy, and David Christiani. "Long Term Respiratory Health Effects in Textile Workers." *Current Opinion in Pulmonary Medicine* 19, no. 2 (2013): 152–157.

Livingston, Julie. *Self-Devouring Growth: A Planetary Parable as Told from Southern Africa*. Durham: Duke University Press, 2019.

Mbewu, Anthony, and Jean-Claude Mbanya. "Cardiovascular Disease." In *Disease and Mortality in Sub-Saharan Africa*, edited by R. Feachem, and D. Jamison, 305–328. Washington, DC: The World Bank, 2006.

Oguntibeju, O., A. Esterhuyse, and E. Truter. "Red Palm Oil: Nutritional, Physiological and Therapeutic Roles in Improving Human Wellbeing and Quality of Life." *British Journal of Biomedical Science* 66, no. 4 (2009): 216–222.

Randall, Sara, and Ernestina Coast. "The Quality of Demographic Data on Older Africans." *Demographic Research* 34 (2016): 143–174.

Sen, Amartya. "Mortality as an Indicator of Economic Success or Failure." *Economic Journal* 108, no. 446 (1998): 1–25.

Timaeus, I.M. "Adult Mortality." In *Demographic Change in Sub-Saharan Africa*, edited by K.A. Foote, K.H. Hill, and L.G. Martin, 218–255. Washington, DC: National Academy Press, 1993.

Wolk, A. "Potential Health Hazards of Eating Red Meat." *Journal of Internal Medicine* 281, no. 2 (2017): 106–122.

World Health Organization. *Global Status Report on Road Safety*. Geneva: World Health Organization, 2018.

Yeats, William Butler. "The Cloak, the Boat, and the Shoes." *Selected Poems of William Butler Yeats*, selected by M.L. Rosenthal, 3. Franklin Center, Pennsylvania: The Franklin Library, 1885 [1979].

4 Burying the dead
Hometowns, houses, and cemeteries

> We were once like you, tomorrow you might be like us. Repent.
> Written over front gate, Kabala Cemetery, Kaduna

After their husbands' deaths, KTL widows, their children, and their husbands' extended family members made preparations for these men's burials. Where and how they were buried, however, reflected their religion, ethnic background, and place of birth, although some men gave particular instructions to their wives and children as to where they were to be buried. Yet many KTL workers—almost half—have been buried in their hometowns, either in or near family compounds or in local cemeteries in order to maintain relationships with their families, claims to family land, and connections with their hometown. For some, this continuity has enabled families living in Kaduna to return to farming after the KTL mill had closed and other employment options in Kaduna had dwindled. This approach, a sort of socioeconomic "safety net," did not appeal to those who had built houses in Kaduna and who had become accustomed to urban living. There, almost a third of these families preferred to bury deceased KTL men adjacent to their Kaduna houses—partly in order to maintain their claim to their property but also to assert their sense of being urban citizens of Kaduna. This sense of being modern urbanites was certainly the case for many of these men's children, as will be discussed in Chapter 6. However, along with house burial in Kaduna, there are a number of cemeteries in the city (as discussed in Chapter 2), where some men were buried, reflecting religious practice—Muslim men were buried wrapped in white cloth shrouds shortly after their deaths; economic constraints—some Christian men's families did not have sufficient means to transport their bodies to their home villages or did not own houses in Kaduna; and ethnicity. Specifically, while almost all families from ethnic groups in southern Kaduna and Middle Belt states brought the bodies of deceased KTL workers to their hometowns for burial, none of the Christian families from one ethnic group—the Bajju—did so.[1] Yet only 18 of the 85 Christian or Muslim KTL widows interviewed buried deceased KTL worker-husbands in cemeteries in Kaduna (Figure 4.1). These particular aspects of the work of the dead, reflected in

Figure 4.1 Graves at Barnawa Muslim Cemetery. These two graves contrast with the more usual plain mounds of other graves, 7 May 2018, Kaduna (Photograph by E.P. Renne).

different practices, underlying beliefs, and motivations associated with burial which distinguished people by sociocultural and economic factors, are the subject of this chapter.

The chapter begins with a discussion of women's memories of the preparations for their husbands' burials, who was involved, how bodies were managed and transported, and the production of funeral posters and programs, as well as the support of family, friends, church groups, and ethnic associations for funeral activities. It continues with an examination of specific burial objects and practices such as the purchase of coffins (by Christians), the printing of funeral programs, and the making of different types of cemetery and home grave markers—which include cement covering, tiled cement slabs, and gravestones that may or may not include the names and dates of the dead. The implications and consequences of these distinctive forms of burial practices are then considered. For while the social ideal for many Christian families coming from small ethnic groups to the south of Kaduna was burial within or adjacent to one's house (even as British colonial officials sought to instill a cemetery culture), home burials were not always possible in practice. Furthermore, the kinship connections that many families living in Kaduna sometimes sought to maintain were not always reciprocated by their hometown relations. The number of former KTL workers whose bodies were buried in Kaduna suggests a contraction of extended family relationships, just as the slowing of rural-urban migration reflects the closure of the textile mills. In their hometowns, as one daughter observed, "We have no relatives who will help us. [In the village], everyone gathers for themselves. They don't care about their relatives" (Interview: Ruth Galau, 17 July 2019, Kaduna). The chapter concludes with a discussion of burials as "the work of the dead" as ideally maintaining connections between immediate family members and place, in representing socioeconomic status, as well as in reinforcing religious identities and new ways of thinking about time. The persistence of home burials also suggests the "the work of the dead" in maintaining traditions from the past.

Widows' preparations for the burial of their textile worker husbands

Upon the deaths of their husbands—whether at home or in hospitals, widows were assisted by family members, friends, and association members in organizing their burial. These burials reflected religion, ethnicity, family connections, finances, and status within the mill. As has been mentioned, 83% of KTL workers interviewed in 1987 were Christian, while only 8% identified themselves as Muslim (Andrae and Beckman 1999). Of the Muslim workers who died, most were buried in Muslim cemeteries in Kaduna, although a few were buried in Muslim cemeteries in their hometowns. Alternatively, Christian KTL workers who died were buried in several places: either in their family compounds in their hometowns; in or near their houses in Kaduna; in Christian cemeteries in Kaduna; or, infrequently, in churchyards in their hometowns (Table 4.1).

Religious practices associated with Muslim burial were somewhat uniform as bodies, wrapped in white cloth, are required to be buried by male relatives and friends within 24 hours of death. Thus, even for one Muslim man who died in Kaduna in the evening, he was taken to his hometown and buried the next day:

> My husband, one day he left the house and went to his Igala ethnic association meeting. It was at that place that he fainted and died. When he died, he was attending a meeting from his mother's side, so they were the ones who took responsibility to take him home. They paid for the transport and everything. He died around 7:30 pm and early the next morning, we took him to Ankpa [in Kogi State]. The day that we arrived, we buried him in the Muslim cemetery in our village…I stayed there for ten days and then came back to Kaduna. After we came back, people from our Igala ethnic association came to greet us and offer their condolences. It was in Kaduna that I finished my 40-day seclusion.
>
> (Interview: Sofia Shaibu Yusuf, 10 May 2018, Kaduna)

For other Muslim workers who died, they were buried in Muslim cemeteries in the city. Alhaji Husseini Adamu was buried in Tudun Wada Cemetery on

Table 4.1 KTL widows' ethnicity and place of husbands' burials

Ethnicity	House Burial-Kaduna	House Burial-Home village	Cemetery-Kaduna	Cemetery-Home Village	Data Missing	Total
Jaba	4	8	2	–	–	14
Kagoro/Atakar	3	3	2	–	–	8
Zango-Kataf	3	1	2	–	–	6
Bajju	3	–	2	–	–	5
Hausa-Fulani	–	–	5	–	–	5
Idoma	–	5	–	–	–	5
Koro [Berom]	2	3	–	–	–	5
Gbagyi	2	2	–	–	–	4
Kadara/Fako	2	–	1	–	–	3
Limzo	1	2	–	–	1	4
Ebira	–	–	3	–	–	3
Angas/Ngas	–	2	–	–	–	2
Igo	–	2	–	–	–	2
Kagomo	–	2	–	–	–	2
Pero	–	2	–	–	–	2
Agatu	1	–	–	–	–	1
Bandikat	–	1	–	–	–	1
Eshan	–	1	–	–	–	1
Fier	–	1	–	–	–	1
Gumei	–	1	–	–	–	1
Igala	–	–	–	1	–	1
Katugal	–	–	–	–	1	1
Kauyemu	–	1	–	–	–	1
Kenyi	–	1	–	–	–	1
Kilba	–	–	–	1	–	1
Kulo	–	1	–	–	–	1
Lantan	–	1	–	–	–	1
Maju	–	–	1	–	–	1
Shimaninzi	1	–	–	–	–	1
Taro	–	1	–	–	–	1
TOTAL	22	41	18	2	2	85

the same day he died and a sign was put by his grave. The burial was followed by mourning and condolences. Many people came to Alhaji Husseini's house to pray and offer their sympathy for almost a month. Some returned for the final prayers performed after four months and ten days, after which the belief is that one's soul is established in eternal Paradise (see Chapter 5 Interlude, Widow Portrait 2-Ramatu Husseini Adamu).

The time frame for the burial of Christian workers' burials varied considerably, depending on where they were buried, the distance from Kaduna, and the need to wait for participation of extended family members. Thus, Gona Bagudu was buried three days after he died: "We waited 3 days after he died because he was a big man in his church and we had to wait for his brother to come" to Kaduna:

> We buried him in Gonin Gora cemetery, near his uncle because he said that when he died, they should bury him near his uncle. It was a Christian burial, the relatives bought the coffin. I don't remember how much it cost. It was from the church they took him to the burial ground in Gonin Gora. We didn't pay for transport because anyone who had a car or machine [motorcycle], they could get to the burial ground. We cemented the grave and we wrote his name, his age, and the day he died. But we didn't tile the grave because at that time, they weren't using tile.
> (Interview: Hannatu Gona, 10 May 2018, Kaduna)

Others buried their deceased husbands in Kaduna cemeteries for lack of funds:

> He was knocked down by a car—because of that he had a problem with his legs. We went to Gwamna Awan Hospital, he had this problem for a year and then he died. It was a carpenter who made the coffin for N15,000. We didn't pay the mortuary because he died at home, but he stayed for two days at home before they buried him. It was relatives who paid for the coffin. We buried him near our house—in Gonin Gora Cemetery—because we didn't have money. They cemented the grave and wrote his name and the day he died. KTL people didn't attend the funeral or give us anything. The Church didn't give us anything. The ethnic association paid for food for the funeral and they did *fate*[2] and gave it to people who came.
> (Interview: Cecelia Peter, 15 May 2018, Kaduna)

However, if one owned a house in Kaduna, family members often buried the deceased within the house compound or just outside of it, although like Christian cemetery burials in Kaduna, most were located in the southern part of the city. For such burials, relatives and friends of the deceased would gather at the house in Kaduna, as one widow explained:

> We didn't go to our hometown, my husband was buried here in Kaduna. It was his relations who bought the coffin. They bought it for N45,000. He died on Wednesday, we buried him on Saturday. He was taken to the church, we had a funeral in the church—and wake keeping there. He was buried in his house in Kaduna. They tiled the grave but didn't write his name (see Fig. 4.6). KTL didn't attend the funeral and didn't give us anything. It was the women's church association who gave us something. I was a member of the group and we have an arrangement, if you are

paying they will give you something. They gave me N6,800, it depends on the money you contribute.³ Our Jaba ethnic association also gave me N7,000.

(Interview: Saidi Ishaya, 15 May 2018, Kaduna)

Burial in one's house had several advantages as it meant that widows did not need to travel and arrangements for feeding funeral attendees could be more easily arranged. Thus, even with cemeteries located in several parts of Kaduna, Christian widows with houses in the city preferred to bury husbands near their houses as they would in their home villages. Cemeteries were seen as places to bury husbands if one did not own a house in Kaduna or to bury family children, unlike other cities in Nigeria where Christian churchyards were adjacent to particular churches or where city regulations encouraged cemetery burial (Adeboye 2016: 9). While new aspects of burial—such as the use of coffins, marked graves, and funeral programs—were accepted by KTL Christian families, cemetery burial for senior family members was seen as marking a family's second-class status in Kaduna, rather than seen as being modern and urbane.

Hometown burials

Yet despite the social prestige of burying one's husband in one's house in Kaduna, many family members preferred to take the bodies of the deceased to their hometowns for burial, which, nonetheless, often necessitated elaborate arrangements. There were also considerable expenses associated with transport, coffin purchase, mortuary stays, and printed funeral announcements:

We took my husband to his hometown, Anku (Jaba LG, Kaduna State), they buried him in the family house It was his friends and neighbors who paid for the coffin, because he was the eldest and his juniors didn't have money (he was even helping them). They paid N40,000 for the coffin. The transport cost N50,000, the mortuary cost N10,000 for 5 days. Because the people contributed money—both Muslim and Christian—to go to our hometown, we used the money to cook food here in Kaduna and brought it to our village. We spent five days there before coming back to Kaduna. We took the body to the church in the village, then we brought it back to the house and buried him there. They took his poster to KTL but no one came and KTL didn't give us anything. The women's association only followed us to our hometown and the church gave us N20,000.

(Interview: Rahila Goro, 28 May 2018, Kaduna)

Often adult children, family members, and friends took care of these arrangements and organized payments, although widows were usually involved in food arrangement for funeral attendees, described by one widow, Helen Dauda:

> My husband was buried at his hometown [Kagoma, in southern Kaduna State], it is their tradition to bury anyone who died in their home. Even the children wanted to bury him here [in Kaduna] but his family said, "No, we have a place to bury him here." We didn't do much—posters and we bought the coffin in Kaduna. I don't know the cost of the coffin, the son-in-law bought it and the relatives took care of the transport. I don't know how much they spent because I can't ask them.
>
> They buried him and covered the grave with tiles and included his name and the day he died. KTL didn't come to our hometown, they only came to the KTL Quarters but our neighbors came with us. We spent two days in Kaduna, then we took three days to take him to his hometown and buried him there. We didn't get anything from KTL or the Coalition but the church and the ethnic association rotating credit group (*adashi*) gave money for the funeral and burial.
>
> (Interview: 8 May 2018, Kaduna)

Most of the KTL widows interviewed whose husbands were buried in their hometowns said that only house burials were carried out in these places. One widow mentioned that there was a cemetery in the village located by the church hospital near the ECWA church, but it was mainly used to bury pastors: "Most people in our town bury their family members at the back of their houses" (Interview: Jummai Daniel, 25 July 2019, Kaduna). Another said: "Every family buries their family members near their house in the family burial ground. We don't have any special burial except Christian burial but there are some who are still doing traditional religious burial in our town" (Interview: Magdeleine Daniel, 17 July 2019, Kaduna). In other words, while all people in these villages bury family members in their houses, some perform Christian burials while others perform traditional religious burial rites. None of the families of deceased KTL workers interviewed in Kaduna performed traditional burial practices.

However, one widow, Elizabeth Kefas, whose husband was from Jimeta, Thabu Hong LG in Adamawa State, said that cemetery burial was commonplace in this village. Yet for most of the towns from which KTL workers and their wives came that did have cemeteries, they were used mainly to bury Christian pastors (as Jummai Daniel noted), and younger people as Laraba Haruna observed:

> There is a cemetery in our hometown, Kasuwa Magani [in Kaduna State]. But we don't bury old people in the cemetery, we bury them in our houses. But the younger ones (20-30 years old or younger), we bury them

in the cemetery. Before they used to do traditional burial but only men attended because there used to be *dodo* [masquerades].[4] But now they don't do it because of Christianity. They only do Christian burial.

(Interview: Laraba Haruna, 25 July 2019, Kaduna)

Thus, most families of deceased KTL workers performed what they viewed as Christian burials—going to church for wake-keeping and having the pastor or priest come to their family compounds for prayers offered during interment. While the religious leaders of village churches performed Christian burials, hence distinguishing the family of deceased KTL workers as Christians rather than followers of traditional religion, almost all villagers were buried in their family compounds rather than in church graveyards. This combination of Christian funeral practices and traditional home burial practice represents these families' merging of the old and the new. Similarly, most of the widows who went to their husbands' home villages to perform proper burial rituals did not remain in their husbands' villages, as they would have done in the past. Rather, they returned to Kaduna, which for many had come to feel like home.

Material aspects of burial and graves

Burying deceased family members in coffins has been part of the process of conversion to Christianity for many families from southern Kaduna and Middle Belt states (Adeboye 2016: 6). On the road that runs past the Arewa Textiles mill on the way to Television Garage, just across the railroad tracks in the Television section of Kaduna South, there are between five and ten sheds with coffins for sale (Figure 4.2). In Kaduna, Christian family members who are preparing to bury the bodies of deceased KTL workers often come to these sheds to select a coffin, which range from N20,000 to N50,000 or more in price depending on size and style. For example, a white coffin with gold-plate

Figure 4.2 Coffin sold in stall near the Television Garage, 7 May 2018, Kaduna (Photograph by E.P. Renne).

Figure 4.3 Crucifix with Christ, detail of coffin cover, 7 May 2018, Kaduna (Photograph by E.P. Renne).

handles and ornamentation, that has a two-part cover that allows the face of the deceased to be viewed, sold for N45,000 (Figure 4.3; Interview: 27 May 2018, Kaduna).[5] Nonetheless, there are other sources of coffins as several widows mentioned. Naomi Bulus's son who was learning carpentry made the coffin for his father, while another widow's family had a coffin made by a local carpenter. Depending on the resources of family and friends, elaborate or simple coffins were purchased for burying the dead. However, because Muslim families prepared their deceased family members by wrapping them in white cloth shrouds (Halevi 2007), they did not need coffins but rather used stretchers (*makara*) to transport their bodies to local cemeteries.

Similarly, because the bodies of deceased Muslims are required to be buried within 24 hours of death, family members did not need to keep them in hospital mortuaries in Kaduna. For Christian families, however, in addition to coffin expenses and often expenses to transport them to their hometowns, the bodies of deceased KTL workers, particularly those who died in hospitals, were kept in mortuaries until families had made final funeral arrangements. Some Christian families circumvented this expense by keeping corpses in their houses until moving them to their hometowns. However, for KTL workers who died either before or soon after the mill closed, the company assisted with transport expenses and sometimes provided a vehicle for taking deceased workers to their hometowns.

Once the arrangements for burial had been confirmed, some Christian families prepared posters announcing the death of these men and providing information about funeral proceedings, while some had more elaborate funeral programs printed. In keeping with the literate, urban status of deceased KTL workers, these programs stated the schedule of events, including dates, places, and times. Thus, the front cover of the funeral service program for the late Elder Daniel Anche included the dates of his birth and death, the date and time of wake-keeping on 4 August 2017, "by 4:00 pm," and the burial service on 5 August by 10:00am. The program also included pages with Christian

Figure 4.4 Funeral program for the late Daniel Anche, see also Chapter 5 Interlude, Widow Portrait 1 (Photograph by E.P. Renne).

prayers—written in Hausa, a short biography—written in English, and children's tributes (Figure 4.4). Several other funeral programs followed a similar format, with the time of wake-keeping and burial clearly stated on the program cover. As was the case during their working lives, their printed names and photographs on ID cards, as well as the imposition of a particular time regime were part of the lives of deceased KTL workers.

Dressing the dead, feeding the living

Muslim men were buried in white cloth shrouds, while Christian men were buried in coffins, often wearing their Sunday clothes, while some wore traditional ethnic dress.[6] For Christian men who had titled positions within their communities or associations, they were buried in special clothing that marked their office. As one widow explained: "My husband was the section head in Television. When he died and was buried, he wore his *mai anguwan*'s cloth with a red cap and turban" (Interview: Margaret Isah, 17 July 2019, Kaduna). During the burial services, wives and children of the deceased were distinguished from others attending by the white clothing that they wore (Figure 4.5).

Depending on the widow and her family's resources as well as contributions from friends, neighbors, and members of ethnic associations and church groups, funerals attendees were given food and water, as the widow, Rifkatu Gona, a member of the Cherubim & Seraphim Church, explained:

> I don't know if KTL attended the funeral but they didn't give us anything. The Church gave us corn (*massara*) and guinea corn (*dawa*). We used it to cook *tuwo* porridge and *kulu* (beans) for those people attending the funeral. It was the Church Women's Association who helped cook the food.
>
> (Interview: Rifkatu Gona, 14 May 2018, Kaduna)

Figure 4.5 Family members wearing white during the burial of the late Daniel Anche; see also Chapter 5 Interlude, Widow Portrait 1 (Photograph of photograph by E.P. Renne).

Indeed, the main sources of support for Christian widows, aside from family and friends, were churches, women's church associations, and ethnic associations.

For Muslim widows, this situation was slightly different, as ideally, they are secluded for 40 days in their houses. Consequently, people brought food and water for guests but they also brought food for widows:

> We buried my husband in Tudun Wada Cemetery…and we did seven days of mourning. Our neighbors and other people brought food to us. After seven days, the women who don't have food can go out but me, my father helped me so I didn't need to go out.
> (Interview: Saudi Abubakar, 9 May 2019, Kaduna)

After the KTL mill closed in December 2002, families rarely received funeral help—funds or transport—from the company. Nor did they receive financial assistance from the Coalition of Closed Unpaid Textile Workers Association Nigeria, which began public protests in 2005. However, the Coalition has continued protests with the demand that the widows of deceased KTL workers should receive their husbands' remittances. Indeed, during a recent protest held on 18 July 2019, Coalition leaders made use of the funeral metaphor to publicize the plight of widows. Coalition widows, seated next to open wooden coffins, spoke with reporters:

> Mrs. Juliana Segun Williams, who is now a widow, said that since her husband died she has been battling to cater for the family. She said she had resorted to selling sachet water which does not bring enough money to meet the needs of the family…She called on government and other relevant authorities to look into their plight.
> (Ahmadu-Suka 2019)

According to one of the Coalition leaders, they covered various things with cloth to give the appearance that there were corpses in the coffins.

Graves and naming the dead

The treatment of the graves of the KTL workers buried in Kaduna and in their hometowns depended on their families' means and also on when they were buried. Some graves were covered with sand, either in anticipation of future finishing or simply left to mark the ephemeralness of life on earth. The latter treatment may be seen in Muslim cemeteries in Kaduna, such as the Tudun Wada and Barnawa cemeteries, where there are mainly rows of mounds and few grave markers. Indeed, these mainly unmarked mounds, which eventually disappear, underscore the transience of earthly existence, as one widow noted:

> Before the children used to go to the cemetery [Tudun Wada Cemetery], they knew the grave but now, it's been a long time because water [wiped away] the place and they've even buried someone else there.
> (Interview: Saudi Abubakar, 9 May 2018, Kaduna)

However, the graves of Christian KTL workers have been marked in various ways. Some graves in workers' hometowns were only covered with sand, as one widow explained: "We buried him in our family cemetery because every house in our village has its family cemetery because we have land. We only put sand and a cross on the grave because we don't have money" (Interview: Naomi Bulus, 29 May 2018, Kaduna). Yet it was more common for hometown graves—both near family homes and in cemeteries—to be covered with cement, with the deceased's name and date of death written on them. Some widows explained cement grave-coverings as being the old fashioned; more recent graves have been covered with white tiles:[7]

> We buried him in his father's compound and we wrote his name on his grave. But the cement was not good. The cement broke up and settled into the ground. So, we went back and put tiles like the modern grave but we didn't write his name.
> (Interview: Monika Thomas, 30 April 2018, Kaduna)

Tiles are often used in recent graves for KTL workers buried near their houses in Kaduna (Figure 4.6). Since it is more difficult to mark these tiles, some do not include the name and date of death of the deceased although plaques are sometimes used to do so. While not mentioned by any of the KTL widows interviewed, more elaborate graves may be seen in the Kabala and Television Christian cemeteries (with even a few in the Barnawa Muslim cemetery).

Figure 4.6 Grave for Ishaya Netsi Musa, inside the family compound in Anguwan Gika, with the new style of patterned tiles with a cross, 15 May 2018, Kaduna (Photograph by E.P. Renne).

These large graves are covered with tiles and are enclosed with a low wall and a higher headstone.

These elaborate and expensive graves suggest a socioeconomic hierarchy that is represented by the types of grave finishes seen in Kaduna and in the hometowns of deceased KTL workers. Tiled graves with low walls outside family houses in Kaduna mark residents' ability to keep up with modern burial practices, while cement-covered graves reflect either earlier burial practices or recent reduced circumstances. Sand-covered graves, particularly in Christian cemeteries in Kaduna, are associated with poverty. Indeed, one small Christian cemetery, Anguwan Sule Cemetery, no longer exists, as one widow whose two children had been buried there explained: "There is no longer a cemetery at that place because people bought the land and built houses" (Interview: Filomena Vincent, 14 May 2018, Kaduna). Although there is no association of cemetery burial and poverty for Muslim burials, socioeconomic and religious differences are reinforced through "the work of the dead."

Social hierarchy of burial

The association of the physical qualities of graves—whether they are covered with sand, cement, or tiles, and whether they are with or without names and dates—with a particular socioeconomic status is mirrored by the assessment of where and how one is buried.

For Muslim KTL workers' families, burial in one of the Muslim cemeteries in Kaduna was expected and respectable. After washing the body, it was wrapped in a plain white cloth shroud (known as *alawayyo*), which is sewn to secure it.[8] Male family members and friends would then accompany the body to the cemetery, where a grave had been prepared. Nonetheless, families had alternatives to choose from in the type of grave that was dug. One type has two levels, with the body placed in the narrow lower level, then covered with earth. The second type, known as a Lahadi grave, is dug with a single rectangular level, but has a space dug on one of the long sides, where the body is slipped into place. According to one woman, the Prophet Mohammad's grave was dug like this.[9] While the land used in Muslim burial grounds in Kaduna is owned by the state government, families pay grave-diggers more for such a Lahadi grave, although the grave is unmarked once the body is buried. The use of low walls around a grave, however infrequent, also suggests such a distinction. There is one other distinction made among those buried in Muslim burial grounds such as the Barnawa Muslim cemetery, based on age but not gender. Adults are buried in one section, while children are buried in another.

For the families of deceased Christian KTL workers, the different options for where they bury their dead have distinctive implications both for a family's social status and its social identity. Of the Christian widows interviewed in 2018, the majority said that their husbands' bodies had been taken to their hometowns for burial in or near their family compounds. This practice was seen by many families as the proper place for the burial of family elders, whether they were living in Kaduna or in their hometowns. However, twenty-two widows who lived in houses that their husbands had built in Kaduna explained that their husbands preferred to be buried near their Kaduna houses, rather than in their hometowns.

Alternatively, a small number of Christian widows—ten to be exact—said that their husbands had been buried in Christian cemeteries in Kaduna (see Table 4.1). As has been mentioned, they did so because they did not own a house in Kaduna or could not afford to send their husbands' bodies to their hometowns. Their burial in Kaduna cemeteries, with graves often covered only with sand, indicated the lower social and economic standing of these widows and their families. Nonetheless, many widows had children who had died buried in any of a number of Kaduna cemeteries, mostly in the southern part of the city. Thus, colonial officials' interest in establishing cemeteries in Kaduna has had a mixed reception among Christian residents, which reflects their respective assessments of the importance of ties with one's extended family and of a modern, urban social identity as well as of their socioeconomic status.

Implications of cemetery burial in Kaduna

One might say that burial is part of "the work of the dead" in framing a particular form of modernity for the families of deceased KTL workers who have continued to reside in Kaduna after the closing of the Kaduna Textiles Ltd mill. Muslim burial grounds do not suggest the same decision—burial in a cemetery or at home—purported by Christian cemeteries; the families of deceased Muslim KTL workers did not bury their bodies near their family homes or compounds but rather in cemeteries. However, in Kaduna, Christian families prefer, if possible, to bury their dead near their homes, not in churchyards or cemeteries. This preference distinguishes them from other Christians living in urban centers in Nigeria such as Lagos and Ibadan, where Christian cemetery or churchyard burial is seen as the modern and proper form of Christian burial by many, as Olufunke Adeboye (2016: 6) explains:

> A Christian burial was devoid of all the sacrifices and rituals associated with "pagan" burials. It was also shorn of all the celebrations and festivities that characterized the latter. It was a solemn affair marked by Christian prayers and hymns. Finally, the dead person was interred in the church cemetery. This had a dual significance. First, it was to separate the Christian dead from "pagan" relations at home. Second, it was to unite the Christian dead with the community of other Christians, dead and alive, within the spiritual ambience of the church. The Christian dead, together with his new religious kin, thus awaited his resurrection from the dead. An important artifact of this new burial culture was the wooden coffin.

While coffins are indeed important for the Christian families of deceased KTL workers, as are Christian prayers and hymns sung at funerals, the practice of home burials has prevailed. This preference reflects the continued important of graves as markers of the ownership of family property. In Kaduna, one does not bury family members next to a rented house. The burial of deceased Christian KTL workers in Kaduna cemeteries does not convey the socioeconomic status of the families who bury their deceased next to houses that they own. Indeed, burial in a Kaduna cemetery—rather than a home burial either in Kaduna or in one's hometown—may be viewed as a sort of stigma, as one young man, the son of a deceased KTL worker, explained:

> There was one boy in my area, I know him but he's not my friend. We used to meet. There was a time I came back from football and I went outside again, that day we didn't cook food in our house. I saw him with my friends, they were eating something. I asked them to give me N50 so I could buy something to eat. He started shouting that he didn't have money and I shouted back to him because I didn't like him shouting at me. He said to me, "We have a house, you don't have a house, that's why your father was buried in the cemetery!" (because we don't have a house to bury him in). "Even the rent, you can't pay it now!" I went back to my house and cried and cried.
>
> (Interview: 23 July 2019, Kaduna)

Thus, while this young man's family was fulfilling the expectation that modern, urban burials in Kaduna would be conducted in one of the city's many cemeteries, the burial of his father there was a source of shame.

Hometown burials: Ideals and practice

However, despite the preference of many Christian families who buried deceased KTL workers in their hometowns, hometown burials did not always live up to the expected ideals of maintaining social connections with one's extended family and claims to family homes. After the closing of KTL mill, Kaduna has become an increasingly difficult place to call home, particularly without a house of one's own. Widows who farmed to earn money and provide food for their families often had to walk great distances from Kaduna to reach farmland that they rented for farming. Consequently, maintaining family ties with their husbands' hometown through their husbands' graves ideally provides an option for their return.

Nonetheless, the continuation of family ties was not always reciprocated in practice, as one widow described the burial of her husband and the consequences of his grave:

> He died on Sunday and we took him to his hometown on Thursday…We went to the church and prayed there before coming back to the house where he was buried, outside of the compound… We cemented the grave but when the children went back, they saw that the family was farming that place. We had written his name and his date of death on the cement, but they are farming there now.
> (Interview: Laraba Paul, 24 May 2018, Kaduna)

It is unlikely that Laraba Paul or her children will move back to her husband's hometown as their ties with his family have been dramatically severed.

Work of the living, work of the dead

The expansion of neighborhoods in the southern part of the city, with their associated cemeteries, reproduces the earlier colonial configuration of Kaduna by religion, ethnicity, economics, and work. Many of these neighborhoods are populated by families of textile mill workers, who were employed at any of the Kaduna textile mills and other industrial establishments in the area known as Kakuri.

Some Christian workers, through their extensive efforts, were able to acquire plots in these new neighborhoods and to build houses where they and their families live. Yet many of these workers who came from southern Kaduna and Middle Belt states continued to maintain connections with their hometowns. In both places, the practice of home burial has continued. Thus, the observation by the Acting District Officer B.S. Kennett in 1932 regarding the preference for home burial still holds: "The custom is very old and strongly held; and I do not see any immediate prospect of effecting any change" (Nigerian National Archives-Kaduna. 1944–1957).

In other words, the expanding layout of Kaduna has followed earlier British plans to some extent, while maintaining earlier ideas about family houses and continuity. It is somewhat ironic that while British missionaries brought

Christianity to southern Kaduna and Middle Belt communities, that Christians prefer house burials in their hometowns and in Kaduna as well. It is Muslims who bury their dead in cemeteries in Kaduna.

Nonetheless, both Christian and Muslim families of KTL workers who died around the time of the mill's closing and in subsequent years have expended considerable effort and resources in burying their dead. This work of the living for the dead constitutes as important religious obligation—that the dead must be properly buried and their deaths commemorated through prayer, although these practices reflect families' particular religious beliefs.

Conclusion

As has been frequently observed in this chapter, the dead work for the living in several ways. Their burial in hometowns maintains connections between urban and rural family members. Their burial in houses asserts claims to property in Kaduna. Their commemoration in funeral programs, that include their named photographs, their dates of birth and death, the times and days of funeral proceedings, and written prayers, also marked their employment at the Kaduna Textiles Ltd as waged laborers. As such, their lives represented a shift from a task-based conception of work to time-based industrial work associated with the clock and hourly income (Thompson 1967). As workers who were literate, who kept to time, who earned money, and fed and educated their children, they were involved in the shift to a particular form of industrial capitalism. Through the use of coffins, industrially-woven shrouds, roads and cars, purchased Kaduna house plots, rented mortuary space, tiled graves, death certificates, and written funeral programs, deceased KTL workers and their families address the question raised by Thomas Laqueur (2015: 12): "How did the dead help to make what we think of as the modern world?" While the "work of the dead" in Kaduna has reinforced changing perceptions about what it means to be a modern urban citizen of the capital of Kaduna State, both Christian and Muslim burials incorporate prayers and references to the will of God as part of funerary observances that distinguish them in a certain way from "the shift of the dead from divinity to history," as discussed by Laqueur (2015: 549) in the western context. The work of the dead, by involving the living in the cash economy, may have reduced kinship ties and fostered a preference for urban living but the importance of religious belief and home burials nonetheless persists.

While several Christian widows mentioned their disoriented state during their husbands' funerals, some mentioned later remembering their husbands through visits to their hometown gravesites and through flowers placed on their husbands' cemetery graves in Kaduna. Muslim widows did not attend burials but were secluded in their houses for 40 days. Yet both Christian and Muslim widows remembered their husbands in many ways, at times through instances when their husbands appeared to them in their dreams.

Notes

1. When asked why many Bajju people buried their family members in Kaduna cemeteries when they didn't own houses in Kaduna, I was told by one Bajju young man that Bajju people adapt to the place where they are living. "That's why there is no Bajju Local Government area" (P. Simon, 17 July 2019, Kaduna).
2. *Fate* (or *fatefate*; Bargery 1934: 313) is "a mushy food made with flour in which onions and…medicinal leaves are mixed."
3. She is referring to the rotating credit group known as *adashi*, which several widows contributed to in case of future needs.
4. For an example of traditional religious funerals in which masquerades played a part, see Renne 1995.
5. Laqueur (2015: 288) refers to this expansion of expensive graves and landscaping associated with modern cemetery burial as "the venue for the work of the dead that has made our modern world as a place to make money." While the hometown burials of Christian KTL workers often entailed great expense and indeed, were related to their new roles as salaried employees of the Kaduna Textile Ltd mill, being taken to one's hometown almost always meant being buried in the family house, not a cemetery.
6. For example, several men from the Gbagyi ethnic group were dressed in traditional clothing and caps.
7. The most recent fashion in tiled graves appears to be the use of multi-colored patterned tiles, as seen in Fig. 4.4.
8. The white cloth known as *harami* (in Hausa), worn by pilgrims during the period of *ihrām* when performing the pilgrimage at Mecca (Renne 2018), may also be used as a shroud.
9. I was also told that some, perhaps with guilty consciences, prefer the Lahadi grave because they believe that when the Angel comes to ask what the deceased has done on earth, the Angel will not be able to see the deceased to ask (Interview: Hassana Yusuf, 7 May 2018, Kaduna).

References

Adeboye, Olufunke. "Home Burials, Church Graveyards, and Public Cemeteries: Transformations in Ibadan Mortuary Practice, 1853–1960." *The Journal of Traditions & Beliefs* 2, no. 13 (2016). http://engagedscholarship.csuohio.edu/jtb/vol2/iss1/13.

Ahmadu-Suka, Maryam. "Save Our Souls, Widows of Unpaid Textile Workers Cry Out." *Daily Trust*, 24 July 2019. Accessed 27 July 2019. https://www.dailytrust.com.ng/save-our-souls-widows-of-unpaid-textile-workers-cry-out.htm.

Andrae, Gunilla, and Björn Beckman. *Union Power in the Nigerian Textile Industry*. New Brunswick, NJ: Transaction Publishers, 1999.

Bargery, G. *A Hausa-English and English-Hausa Dictionary*. 2nd ed. Zaria: Ahmadu Bello University Press, 1934 [1999].

Halevi, Leor. *Muhammad's Grave: Death Rites and the Making of Islamic Society*. New York: Columbia University Press, 2007.

Laqueur, Thomas. *The Work of the Dead: A Cultural History of Mortal Remains*. Princeton, NJ: Princeton University Press, 2015.

Nigerian National Archives-Kaduna. "Births, Deaths and Burial Ordinance, Chapter 47, Section 37." Kaduna: Nigerian National Archives, 1944–1957.

Renne, Elisha. *Cloth That Does Not Die: The Meaning of Cloth in Bunu Social Life*. Seattle, WA: University of Washington Press, 1995.

Renne, Elisha. *Veils, Turbans, and Islamic Reform in Northern Nigeria*. Bloomington, IN: Indiana University Press, 2018.

Thompson, E.P. "Time, Work-Discipline, and Industrial Capitalism." *Past & Present* 36, no. 1 (1967): 56–97.

5 Widows' dilemmas and experiences of hardship

Faith Mallam remembered her father as a hard-working person who would do whatever work needed to be done. One day her mother showed her one of his kaftans that she had saved. It was worn—"it wasn't a good one," his daughter remarked (Interview: 23 July 2019, Kaduna). Yet her mother kept her husband's kaftan which both reminded her of him and the sadness of his death, a sentiment expressed in Emily Fragos's poem, "The Sadness of Clothes" (2015):

> When someone dies, the clothes are so sad. They have outlived their usefulness and cannot get warm and full. You talk to the clothes and explain that he is not coming back.

For KTL widows, the shift from village life to urban life after their marriage to men who worked at the KTL mill was a significant change in terms of clothing, housing, and particularly food. One of the things that many widows liked about their new lives in Kaduna was access to many different foods, some of which they had not eaten before in their villages. Several widows mentioned their husbands' provision of these different types of food which they would purchase with the wages they earned through their work at KTL.

After the KTL mill closed in 2002, the sorts of foods that widows, their worker husbands, and their children had become accustomed to eat became too expensive. Some resorted to farming to grow food crops on plots in the outskirts of Kaduna, while others stopped eating many types of food and reduced the number of times they would eat in a day. And as the health of their husbands declined, some widows needed to prepare special foods for their husbands (see Chapter 5-Interlude, Portrait 1). Others needed to physically help them to eat as well as to find food in their straightened situations. Thus, when Ayuba Dandume was unable to feed himself, his wife both provided him with food and helped him to eat it before he died.

This chapter considers the situation of widows after their husbands' deaths, focusing on the ways that their experience of poverty is framed by their access to food. Several widows mentioned a severely reduced diet—mainly of corn meal porridge (*tuwo*), at times with leafy vegetable soup, with only one serving a day. For some, the means by which widows and their children have addressed this situation—referred to as food insecurity, *rashin abinci*—lack of food or as food poverty—relates to their earlier experiences of eating in their home villages and to subsistence farming. The return of some to farming suggests a sort of intermediate form of reverse migration, since many have remained in Kaduna but traveled some distance to the outskirts of the city to rent farm plots in order to grow food for themselves and their families. Some, however, have traveled back to their home villages, where they stay to farm and grow food, some for themselves and some that could be sold when they returned to Kaduna.

Several widows described going to farm near Kaduna with their husbands before their deaths. Their fond memories of working together suggest another aspect of food, namely the ways by which food—growing it, buying it, selling it, preparing it, and consuming it—comes to characterize nostalgic memories of the past (Holtzman 2006). The chapter considers these widows' memories in relation to their present situation in Kaduna characterized for many by poverty and hunger. It concludes with the ways that memories of the dead work to give widows strength to continue even in the absence of their husbands.

Poverty and hunger

Even before the Kaduna Textiles Ltd mill closed in December 2002, things were becoming increasingly difficult, with temporary shutdowns and reduced pay and production (Andrae and Beckman 1999). Women adapted to these constraints through their own work and changes in food consumption. Hunger became an increasing challenge after their husbands lost their jobs at KTL, although some men farmed or had other types of employment—e.g., as security guards, working until they were unable to do so. And while church participation and ethnic associations provided moral and physical support for their efforts, some women limited their participation in these activities due to lack of money for contributions at services and meetings. Yet for some women, these groups provided physical support in terms of food, clothing, and loans, particularly after their husbands were dismissed from the KTL mill.

When asked what problems they faced after their husbands lost their jobs at KTL, many widows mentioned two things—school fees for their children and getting food to eat. "Food poverty" has been an ongoing concern for families living in rural areas which are subject to the vagaries of rainfall (de Montclos et al. 2016; Pottier 1999; Rose and Charlton 2002), although years of famine may alternate with years of abundant harvests (Sen 1981). For widows living in urban Kaduna, they had become accustomed to food being available without such weather-related constraints:

> When I came to Kaduna…it was more than 50 years ago [in 1960] ago. But I know that Kaduna then, there were so many things to eat. But in our village, we only had *kuli-kuli* [ground peanut patties] and *dawa* [guinea corn]. It was in Kaduna that we came to know biscuits and sweets. And at

that time in the village, they didn't have Maggi they only had *kuntun stuk* [Gbagyi language for locust bean paste].

(Interview: Hannatu Gona, 25 July 2019, Kaduna)

The difficulties associated with food poverty were expressed by several KTL widows, whose situation is made worse by the loss of their husbands and the absence of their textile mill final remittances; several said that they no longer enjoyed living in the city. With limited cash to buy food, the shift to eating a very limited diet was a difficult shock for former KTL workers, wives, and their children as one widow, Cecilia Gabriel noted (see Chapter 5-Interlude, Portrait 3). Her husband, Gabriel Okoh, who had worked as a forklift driver at KTL, died in 2008, six years after the mill closed. The difficulty of getting to their farm on the outskirts of Kaduna, along with his dismay about his failure to provide sufficient food for his family contributed to his death, described as due to congestive heart failure on his death certificate. As one widow observed, "There are so many difficulties now, that is why we are farming—just like in my hometown" (Interview: Monica Daniel, 25 July 2019, Kaduna).

Return to farming

Many KTL workers who were discharged without their remittances returned to farming in areas outside of the city and to earlier methods of cooking, as one widow, Mary Joseph, described:

> After the factory closed, we started farming. We went back to a local village [near Kaduna] and started farming there. We built a house there and made the roof with grass. We farmed corn (*massara*) and guinea corn (*dawa*) but we couldn't afford to pay for our children's school fees. Some stopped in JSS, one stopped in JSS2. We used to eat corn and guinea corn, but when he was working we used to eat semovita, rice, and other things. But now we only eat *miya kakarshi* and *tuwo*. When he was working, I used to cook with a stove, but now I get firewood from the bush and cook with it. We have suffered backaches as a result of this farming.
>
> (Interview: 29 May 2018, Kaduna)

One former KTL worker, who was an assistant supervisor in the Weaving Department, went back to farming and has continued to farm:

> I went back to farming. There is nothing I can do, only farming. In Kaduna, I am doing farming near the NNPC—I'm growing rice, soy beans, and groundnuts. They don't allow us to farm maize and *dawa* (guinea corn) because they are tall. You have to go very far from Kaduna to farm those things now. Like Sabon Gaya and Rijana—but the situation of kidnapping now, people don't want to go far. The situation we are in now, even

when I planted rice this year, it was difficult to get fertilizer so I only harvested a small amount. That is what we are facing.
(Interview: Wuyah Adze, 24 July 2019, Kaduna)

Several former KTL workers, who have since died, walked to small farm plots where they grew food for their families, with the help of their wives. Later, some widows continued to go to these farms, at times with the help of their children:

> Because my children don't go to school now and they don't have any work to do, I called the children and told them that because their father and me, we used to farm before he died, they should get farms so we can be farming together. So, we started doing farming, corn and guinea corn.
>
> Since their father died, nobody from their father's family has come to see them or help us. I come back from the farm and will sell corn. If there is no corn, I will sell sugar cane. That is how I paid for the children's school fees. And if I need to, I will sell corn or guinea corn to feed them.
> (Interview: Hadiza Iream, 9 May 2018, Kaduna)

Other widows associated farming with scavenging for any remaining unharvested crops (see Chapter 5-Interlude, Portrait 4).

Memories of their husbands

Several widows had pleasant memories of their husbands, even when some described disputes: "I wish that he was still alive, even if we were fighting all the time" (Interview: Esther Jesuah, 9 May 2018, Kaduna), while others mentioned frequent fights and reconciliation. A few mentioned disagreements over church attendance and money. Others, such as Hadiza Luha, remembered her late husband's sense of humor:

> When my husband was alive…and when we were with his sisters, he used to crack jokes. He would say, "When I die you will be dancing and singing, *Keke ka e!*" [because they would inherit his riches]. So, some people would ask him if he had a house for himself. But when they realized that he didn't have a house or anything at all, they would just be laughing. He was a very funny person.
> (Interview: 29 May 2018, Kaduna)

Another widow, Laraba Paul, remembered her husband's teasing humor but with some unease:

> There was a time we were joking with each other. He called my name and said to me, "If I die, I know that KTL will provide a car to take me to my hometown. But you're not working. So, if you die, I don't know

who will take you to your hometown for burial." I told him that I didn't like what he was saying because he was talking about dying. "I'm just concerned about you, I'm just thinking about you," he said.

(Interview: 24 May 2018, Kaduna)

However, it was various aspects of food that many women frequently mentioned when they remembered their husbands:

> I can remember my husband because I really enjoyed living with him. We never fought. Whenever I was angry with him, he would just say, "Let me go out." When he came back home, I would calm down. Whenever I asked him to give me food, he would say, "Some women are fighting to get wrappers from their husbands, but you are fighting to get food." So, I said, "If I die because you didn't bring me food, people will blame you for letting me die and you will be ashamed." A day later, he brought a sack of rice for us. I will always remember that day.
>
> (Interview: Asabe Audu, 7 May 2018, Kaduna)

Some widows mentioned special gifts of food:

> Sometimes he used to buy things like meat and give it to me—and he said that I should just eat it alone. So, he would bring it to me when the children were asleep. If I was angry with him, I would refuse to eat it and would give it to the children [laughing]. I would wait until daybreak and give the meat to the children, then he would call my name and say, "You are not good!" Really, we had no problems together.
>
> (Interview: Laraba Paul, 24 May 2018, Kaduna)

> My husband and I, we lived in peace together. Whenever I pass men selling chicken, I think of my husband because he used to buy them for us. But now, no one will buy it.
>
> (Interview: Laraba Haruna Dalhatu, 1 May 2018, Kaduna)

Other widows remembered their husbands for their generosity:

> I remember my husband because we lived in peace and he would provide for us. When he was alive, I used to sell rice, beans. When he couldn't provide for us, he told me to cook the rice and beans. "When I have money, I will pay you back." When he had the money, he would give me a little more than I spent, around N7,000. He would say "I don't want your business to go down." That was why when I saw his corpse, I fainted.
>
> (Interview: Ruth Nuhu Saidu, 30 April 2018, Kaduna)

Similarly, Naomi Bulus remembered her husband's graciousness: "I will always remember my husband because we lived together in peace. And whenever I would give him food, he would say that I should sit beside him and eat with him" (Interview: Naomi Bulus, 29 May 2019, Kaduna).[1]

Other husbands helped their wives with their work. As one widow recalled, her husband helped with childcare when she went to the farm, while another remembered her husband's help with her food-selling business:

> We had problems when he lost his job because he couldn't do anything. It was me who was taking care of the house, that caused him to have high blood pressure. I used to make snacks—*dosa*, *kosai*, to take care of the house. I have a memory of my husband because he was very kind. He would wake up very early in the morning and would sweep my shop. And he would help me with my work, selling *kosai*, *doya*, and other things—such as peeling yams and sweet potatoes, he used to do that for me.
>
> (Interview: Elizabeth Kefas, 9 May 2018, Kaduna)

And one widow, Mercy Daniel, recalled her husband's apology for his earlier opposition to her food-selling business:

> I remember my husband because when he was alive, he refused to let me do any work. I even reported him to my mother. She called him and talked to him, then he allowed me to work. I started by selling sugar cane and *akara* (or *kosai*, bean flour fritters). I even started cooking and selling food to one farm house, to the laborers there. Later on, when he lost his job, he said, "You see, I refused to let you do this work—but now, you are helping us with this work. So you should forgive me." That is what I remember about him.
>
> (Interview: 10 May 2018, Kaduna)

Several widows remembered their husbands' farming efforts in order to provide food for their families. As has been mentioned, several widows went to farm with their husbands, which reflected both their intimacy and efforts to provide food for their families:

> We went up and down to see how we could solve our problems. Because at that time, our children stopped going to school because we didn't have money. So my husband and I would go to the farm together. We grew millet, guinea corn, corn, and groundnuts on the farm. But the farm was not our land so sometimes we gave them N5000 for rent and sometimes we would give them some of our crops.
>
> I would worry when we went to the farm before but now, I go there alone. Because the children don't want to go to the farm...I used to remember my husband because we would to go to the farm together. Even last year when I went to the farm, I began to cry, thinking of him.
>
> (Interview: Amina Dauda, 8 May 2018, Kaduna)

For some widows, these memories of farming even extended to their dreams:

> Sometimes my husband will come to me in my dreams. I saw him in my dream: there was a time I was going to my farm, I saw him going to the farm also. I asked him, "Are you going to the farm too?" He said, "Yes," and then he disappeared.
> (Interview: Hawa'u Luka, 15 May 2018, Kaduna)

Some widows' most poignant memories of their husbands are related to hunger and food poverty. Thus, Walida Ya'u remembered her husband's suffering and desperate hunger with much regret:

> I can remember my husband because he was humble and didn't like fighting. And I never went to the family house to complain about him. What I can remember and will never forget up until today, there was a time he was sick and he said he was hungry. And I only had fifty naira. I bought pap, twenty naira for him and thirty naira for us, but he was still complaining that he was hungry. Then he said to me, "Give me the N100 that you use in the morning for your yam to buy me something." But I said, "No, I have to have enough money to buy yam." And I have regretted not giving him the money to buy something to this day.
> (Interview: 7 May 2018, Kaduna)

Yet other widows had more fortunate memories, remembering the consolation that their husbands provided, even as they were close to death: "He used to say to me, if I went out to sell something, he was always sympathetic and said that God will reward me, even if he died, God will reward me" (Interview: Rakiya Ayuba, 15 May 2018, Kaduna).

Everyday exigencies

While food was and continues to be a major concern for KTL widows, there have been other everyday problems which they have had to face. Some involve selling at local markets, the complications of paying rent or maintaining deteriorating houses, their children's work, and their own health problems. For example, one widow, Laidu Benjamin, had been going to the farm and was selling cooked food until the time that she had an accident:

> There were many problems when he lost his job, we were suffering because we had no food to eat so I had to go out and sell *kosai* (bean flour fritters) and go to the farm for sugar cane. At that time, I went out to sell something to get something to eat because the children were not working.
>
> After my husband died, the first problem I faced was that if the children were sick, I had to go out and look for money. But we thank God, when they fell sick they got better. God is giving us grace again. But now I can't

go to the farm because I had an accident and burnt my hand. I bought some kerosene and it was mixed with petrol. I went to put it in the lantern and it blew up. So now I'm just selling groundnuts outside of the house.
(Interview: 15 May 2018, Kaduna)

Her inability to use her hands prevented her from making prepared food to sell or going to the farm, and subsequently she has been unable to raise sufficient funds for her children to continue their schooling. Such explosions caused by kerosene contaminated with gasoline, however, are not uncommon and have been reported for several years in different parts of Nigeria.[2] Laidu Benjamin was another victim of adulterated kerosene, a problem which has continued in Nigeria with several cases reported in 2019 (Eleweke 2019). As she put it: "Sometimes I used to stay quietly and remember my husband because if he was alive…the children would continue their schooling and they would have something in the future." Instead, the "cumulative disadvantage" of an incomplete education is likely to condemn them as well to a life of poverty, of low-paying jobs, and possibly drug use (Case and Deaton 2017, 2020).[3]

Widows have faced other everyday problems in terms of their work and their children. Several widows mentioned having sold soup ingredients, tomatoes, and other prepared foods in the past, although they no longer have money to sell these things: "Before I was selling *kunwa* (a type of cultured milk drink), but now I'm not doing it because I'm sick and…the ingredients are expensive" (Interview: Pauline Achoju, 15 May 2018, Kaduna). One widow had gone to her home village near Jos and set up a shop to sell corn, rice, and palm oil there. "But later, thieves broke into the shop and stole everything. So now I'm not doing anything…The food we eat now is whatever God gives us" (Interview: Cecilia Matthew, 29 May 2018, Kaduna).

Several widows said that they depended on their children for cash to buy food. For example, some children have gone to the Kaduna river bed to get sand to sell for construction and for making concrete blocks (Interview: Philomena Vincent, 14 May 2018, Kaduna). Other children, particularly daughters, help their mothers with selling foodstuff or firewood, while some do house work.

For widows who are renting rooms in Kaduna, the payment of rent is an on-going problem. One widow was threatened with eviction when the owners hired a lawyer and some families were simply forced to move:

> After my husband died, I faced a lot of problems. We were even sent away from the house we were renting. Even now, it's my father's house I'm living in. And I can spend a day without eating anything. Every week I go to Barnawa to wash cloths, they give me N3,000 that I use to feed the children.
> (Interview: Hauwa Garba, 9 May 2018, Kaduna)

Thus, aside from selling prepared food, as well as maize, and sugar cane, widows such as Hauwa Garba perform domestic work such as washing clothes and sweeping houses. The proceeds from their efforts are meager. But some widows have been fortunate to have family members, friends, and even recent acquaintances who have helped them:

> After my husband died, I faced problems finding food to eat for me and my daughter. Because sometimes she would make food for sale but couldn't sell it. So she would owe the woman from whom she'd borrowed money for its preparation and the woman would come and ask to be paid back. But then I met a woman who was working at the petrol refinery here in Kaduna, she was making *kunu tsamiya* [pap made with millet or guinea corn flour, flavored with tamarind] and I was helping her to sell it. She pays me N6,000 a month so my daughter is now attending the Federal College of Education.
>
> (Interview: Grace Bulus, 29 May 2018, Kaduna)

Nonetheless, that many widows and their children perform menial and/ or occasional work, employed by wealthy people in Kaduna, suggests how the process of deindustrialization has contributed to the growing inequality between former KTL workers (both alive and dead) and their families and the Kaduna elite. For when their husbands first came to Kaduna to work in the modern new textile mill, they aspired to a middle-class standard of living, with well-fed, well-dressed, and educated children, an ambition that is now beyond the reach of most. Their expectations of modernity have been thwarted with the closure of the Kaduna Textiles Ltd mill and the failure of the northern Nigerian governments to pay KTL workers or their survivors the remittances that are owed to them.

Work: rural/urban, food crops/cash

Thus, the lives of the widows of deceased KTL workers reflect the relatively short history of the sociocultural and economic process of industrialization and of deindustrialization in Kaduna, which include rural-urban migration, aspirations for their children's education, and changes in foodstuffs. Aspects of this process are most clearly seen in terms of housing, children's curtailed education, and families' changing relationships to food—its acquisition, consumption, and trade. Food is a particularly marked example of their participation in the industrialization of Kaduna and its decline.

Many widows, before their marriages and moves to Kaduna, lived in rural communities where food was acquired through subsistence agriculture. Through their families' access to land, women grew vegetables, corn, and sorghum, which provided the basis of their family diets, while men in their families grew corn, beans, millet, and sorghum, and at times, cash crops such as rice and ginger (*Daily Trust* 2019; Mahmud 2019; Richards 1990). When KTL widows married and moved to Kaduna, their access to food changed, as it was based on their husbands' work at the Kaduna Textiles Ltd mill, where they were paid cash wages. This shift from growing one's own food to exchanging cash for an array of food products—many of which they had not eaten before—was not entirely new. Village farmers during good years had excess crops to sell for cash which could be used for special food purchases such as sugar and tea. As several widows mentioned, however, the myriad food choices available in Kaduna were easily purchased rather than painstakingly (and, at times, precariously) grown, which was one of their cherished memories of Kaduna. But when the mill closed, their experiences associated with deindustrialization—unemployment, food poverty, and attenuation of their children's educations—contributed to a particular regime of food provision and consumption.

Yet rather than experiencing a complete reversal to their rural lives before moving to Kaduna, most widows remained in the city but began farming (or continued the farming they had practiced with their deceased husbands) in the outskirts of Kaduna. Some were able to provide food for their families, albeit with limited meals of ground corn porridge (*tuwo*) and vegetable soup (*miya ganiyi*). But some were also able to sell the corn and beans that they grew in order to buy other essentials and to pay for school fees. Being largely on their own, KTL widows were not subject to sociocultural restrictions on their activities or movements (Pottier 1999: 90), although those who farmed missed the support of their husbands in their endeavors. Thus, this situation represents a particular pattern of food poverty—not determined by village drought and famine but by urbanization and deindustrialization, the closing of the textile mills in Kaduna. As Johan Pottier (1999: 26) notes, "What people eat, what they grow, how they trade, who they turn to in need, are linked issues." The closing of the KTL mill rapidly reversed the foods that widows and their children associated with living in Kaduna and reorganized their work lives as they returned to farming, albeit for many, not in their hometowns. Their situation reflects the dynamics of food poverty in the context of urban migration and deindustrialization.

Several widows who had not eaten all day mentioned being helped with food by their neighbors. It is uncertain whether government services or special state or federal initiatives were or are available to provide widows living in Kaduna with a modicum of food security.[4] And while the "work of the dead" may be seen in the Coalition's list of their names which holds out the hope that KTL remittances will be paid to their widows, the absence of their husbands in helping these women with securing food for their themselves and their children represents an ongoing struggle for them. This situation was particularly difficult when they themselves were ill, as one widow explained: "What is troubling me now is sickness. I'm tired of this sickness and I tried hard to get medicine. I'm just tired of it" (Interview: Kande Peter, 21 May 2018, Kaduna).

The stories that widows tell

The point of conveying personal narratives is not, of course, *just* to tell stories. When we tell stories, it's not simply the content that is important, but the context in which we speak them. To whom do we tell our stories? Why? Toward what ends? And, most crucially, to what effect? Our stories are meant to intervene in the world, to persuade others, to give voice to feelings and events, to make our lives meaningful. In this way, stories are not a mere *reflection* of the material world; they are a dynamic part of it.

(Walley 2013: 14)

It is not surprising that widows such as Kande Peter are exhausted as a result of their efforts to support themselves and their children, particularly when they themselves are ill and have no one to care for them. Yet the memories of their husbands' deathbed blessings have provided comfort for others such as Maryam Markus, who recalled that: "On the day he died, he called me and said I should call the children. He told them, 'I leave you with your mother. I hope God will keep you alive and bless you.'"

The stories that these widows have told me about their lives, first in their hometowns, then coming to Kaduna, of their pride in their husbands' work and their children's education, of the distressing difficulties that they faced after their husbands lost their jobs at KTL, and their subsequent deaths, then their need to find work in Kaduna—farming, trading, or cleaning—or their return to their hometowns, document a particular process of industrialization and deindustrialization as well as rural-urban migration. Some widows have told their stories to reporters from the *Daily Trust* as part of Coalition efforts to publicize their struggles and to put pressure on the government to pay their late husbands' remittances. Thus, their stories, as Walley (2013: 14) suggests: "are not a mere *reflection* of the material world; they are a dynamic part of it." That their stories reflect the particularities of the historical context of deindustrialization in the fifth largest city in Nigeria makes them especially important. For their stories, while similar to those of other women—e.g., in the US, where husbands lost their jobs when textile mills in North Carolina and steel plants in East Chicago abruptly closed—are particular to northern Nigeria where the combination of textile mills opening and closing, along with rural-urban migration, took place within a very short period of time. Yet for all of these women—even if "the work of the dead" through the listing of their husbands' names on the Coalition documents results in the payment of their long-awaited termination remittances, the question remains about whether textile manufacturing will be revived in Kaduna and about the future employment of their children in the city in what may possibly be postindustrial times.

Conclusion

One widow, Jummai Daniel, recounted that her husband is alive in the sense that, "he is still living in my heart." Such comments reflect another aspect of "the work of the dead." For not only are their names part of the Coalition's list of unpaid textile workers and their hometown graves a reflection of connections between urban and rural family members, but they may also continue to live on in widows' minds and hearts. They are also remembered for the things they left behind, as Hassana Sylvester explained: "I only kept his caps—his clothes, all his relatives took them. But I kept that *kaɓe* style cap and other Yoruba style caps. I kept those caps so that his children can see them" (Interview: 15 January 2020, Kaduna).

The consequences of their husbands' loss of their jobs at the Kaduna Textile Ltd mill and their subsequent deaths are poignant reminders of absence. Similarly, the failure to pay their late husbands' termination remittances reflects the lack of political will to address the problems associated with deindustrialization—growing urban unemployment, poverty, and inequality. For even when widows and their children can find work in Kaduna, it is often either as petty traders selling sugar cane, mangoes, and groundnuts, or as security guards or house help—as sweepers, dish washers, and drivers—in the houses of the rich. Thus, even when KTL workers and their wives went to great efforts to support their children's educations, many children were unable to continue for lack of sufficient clothing and of funds for school and exam fees.

The payment of former KTL workers' remittances would help to remedy this situation. This money would also help widows whose inability to pay their rent or to make necessary home repairs has led to their precarious housing circumstances. And remittance payments would help to allay, although not alleviate, the food poverty experienced by many former KTL workers' families. Fortunately, some widows' church groups and neighbors have assisted them with food during times of dire need. Indeed, widows' frequent mention of food poverty and neighborly assistance underscores the social reciprocity reflected by such exchanges, as widows and their children might assist an impoverished neighbor in the future.

The recurrent reference to food by widows in remembering their husbands suggests the powerful relationship between conjugal relations and food consumption (Beidelman 1993: 211; Richards 1939). The shifting expectations of both husbands and wives as providers and recipients of food may be seen in their lives as rural farmers, as urban residents, and as urban resident-farmers. Thus, while many KTL workers lost their jobs and were unable to live up to the expectations of husbands' provision of food for their wives, their praise for the wives' efforts was reassuring for many.

Several widows also mentioned the help and encouragement that they received from their children. Some helped their mothers with farming, others provided them with food and cash when they could, while some provided emotional support. Yet other children were not so helpful. Some ignored their mothers' problems and some would not help or even visit them. However, these fatherless children of former KTL workers have problems of their own. Some are trying to complete their schooling while others are unemployed and constantly looking for work. As is the case elsewhere in the world where there are factory closures and high unemployment, some fill the time by taking drugs (Kumtung 2019; Obi 2018). These children's experiences of their fathers' death, their mothers' impoverishment, and their own difficulties are discussed in Chapter 6.

Notes

1 This invitation was not experienced by all widows, particularly those who ate separately from their husbands, both in Kaduna and in their home villages.
2 A 2011 news account, which described cases in Kano and Port Harcourt, indicated that the Nigerian National Petroleum Corporation had warned consumers about adulterated kerosene although it is difficult to distinguish it (Bello and Abdullahi 2011).
3 Case and Deaton (2017: 2), in their analysis of increasing deaths among middle-aged whites in the US, contend that "…*cumulative disadvantage* over life, in the labor market, in marriage and child outcomes, and in health, is triggered by progressively worsening labor market opportunities at the time of entry for whites with low levels of education." While many KTL widows have made every effort to support their children's continuing education, for children who have been unable to continue to do so for lack of funds, this situation is part of their "cumulative disadvantage" in an increasingly difficult job market.
4 Several Nigerian NGOs, such as Helpline Foundation for the Needy, Abuja, and political leaders such as Governor Ortom of Benue State, have organized distributions of food and cash to widows in recent years (Emmanuel 2019; Idris 2019). However, a federal program to offer widows assistance with food, health care, and school fees for their children has yet to be implemented.

References

Andrae, Gunilla, and Björn Beckman. 1999. *Union Power in the Nigerian Textile Industry*. New Brunswick, NJ: Transaction Publishers.

Beidelman, T.O. *Moral Imagination in Kaguru Modes of Thought*. Washington, DC: Smithsonian Institution Press, 1993.

Bello, Abdullahi, and Bahiru Abdullahi. "Multiple Kerosene Explosions Leave Scores Dead." *Weekly Trust*, 19 February 2011. Accessed 11 December 2019. https://www.dailytrust.com.ng/multiple-kerosene-explosions-leave-scores-dead.html.

Case, Anne, and Angus Deaton. "Mortality and Morbidity in the 21st Century, Conference Version." Brookings Papers on Economic Activity. Washington, DC: Brookings Institute, 17 March 2017.

Case, Anne, and Angus Deaton. *Deaths of Despair and the Future of Capitalism*. Princeton, NJ: Princeton University Press, 2020.

Daily Trust. "Kaduna Government to Export Ginger, Maize." *Daily Trust*, 31 October 2019. Accessed 31 October 2019. https://www.dailytrust.com.ng/kaduna-government-to-export-ginger-maize.html.

de Montclos, Marc-Antoine Pérouse, Elizabeth Minor, and Samrat Sinha, eds. *Violence, Statistics, and the Politics of Accounting for the Dead*. Heidelberg: Springer International Publishing, 2016.

Eleweke, Titus. "Kerosene Explosion Kills 11 Year-Old Girl in Anambra." *Daily Trust*, 3 April 2019. Accessed 11 December 2019. https://www.dailytrust.com.ng/kerosene-explosion-kills-11-year-old-girl-in-anambra.html.

Emmanuel, Hope Abah. "Ortom Plans Free Grains for 2300 Widows." *Daily Trust*, 8 December 2019. Accessed 11 December 2019. https://www.dailytrust.com.ng/ortom-plans-free-grains-for-2300-widows.html.

Fragos, Emily. "The Sadness of Clothes." In *Poem-a-Day*. Academy of American Poets, 21 July 2015. https://poets.org/poem/sadness-clothes.

Holtzman, Jon. "Food and Memory." *Annual Review of Anthropology* 35, no. 1 (2006): 361–378.

Idris, Shaba A. "Foundation Marks Widows' Day: Empowers 200 in Abuja." *Daily Trust*, 24 June 2019. Accessed 24 June 2019. http://www.dailytrust.com.ng/foundation-marks-widows-day-empowers-200-in-abuja.html.

Kumtung, Sylvia. "Drug Abuse: The Journey to Freedom." *Daily Trust*, 11 October, 2019. Accessed 11 October 2019. http://www.dailytrust.com.ng/drug-abuse-the-journey-to-freedom.html.

Mahmud, Idris. "As Planting Begins, Katsina Farmers Prioritize Cotton, Rice, Onions." *Daily Trust*, 16 June 2019. Accessed 16 June 2019. http:// www.dailytrust.com.ng/as-planting-begins-katsina-farmers-prioritize-cotton-rice-onions.html.

Obi, Solomon. "Poverty, Unemployment Causes of Drug Abuse." *Daily Trust*, 5 July 2018. Accessed 5 July 2018. www.dailytrust.com.ng.

Pottier, Johan. *Anthropology of Food: The Social Dynamics of Food Security*. Malden, MA: Blackwell Publishing, 1999.

Richards, Audrey. *Land, Labor and Diet in Northern Rhodesia*. London: Oxford University Press, 1939.

Richards, Paul. "Local Strategies for Coping with Hunger: Central Sierra Leone and Northern Nigeria Compared." *African Affairs* 89, no. 355 (1990): 265–275.

Rose, Donald, and Karen Charlton. "Prevalence of Household Food Poverty in South Africa: Results from a Large, Nationally Representative Survey." *Public Health Nutrition* 5, no. 3 (2002): 383–389.

Sen, Amartya. *Poverty and Famines: An Essay on Entitlement and Deprivation*. Oxford: Clarendon Press, 1981.

Walley, Christine. *Exit Zero: Family and Class in Postindustrial Chicago*. Chicago, IL: University of Chicago Press, 2013.

5 Interlude
Widows' portraits

Portrait 1

Widow: Jummai Daniel Interviewed: 1 May 2018
Ethncity: Limzo Religion: ECWA
Husband: Daniel Anche Died: 31 July 2017

My husband, Daniel Anche, died when he was 62 years old in Kaduna in the house here. He came to Kaduna in 1977. He was educated in accounting in Kaduna and he worked at KTL in the Accounts Department. Before he worked at KTL he worked as a storekeeper in Birnin Gwari LG.

After KTL closed, he worked as an agent; the problem he faced was that he was sick. My husband had diabetes and wanted his children to study and he didn't have money. It was me who was taking care of the house. I am selling tomatoes and soup ingredients and anything that can fetch me money so I can buy food. And I don't have much means to take care of the family and I have a son who is blind; he was blind a year after he was born. He wasn't able to school and I didn't have money.

My husband had diabetes before he died. If we had money, I would take him to Nasarawa Hospital for a check-up. I had to provide him with different food—like *acha* [seeds used as a cereal] and *tamba* [types of leafy vegetables]. A month before he died, he was admitted to Nasarawa Hospital. They discharged him after five days. And then we went to another hospital—in Sabo, Trinity Hospital. He was discharged after four days and we came back home. He was terribly sick and we didn't have a car to take him to the hospital, it was raining heavily and he died. We didn't have records but we had many medicines, I gave them to one nurse so that she could use them for other patients.

We buried him just outside our house here in Kaduna. His children, relatives, and I bought his coffin at Television Garage. It was the children and the church who helped with the funeral service and burial. The ethnic association didn't help us then because they helped us a lot when he was sick. We had a Christian burial, the pastor came to the house; they prayed and sang. After two days, praying and singing we went to the church with the pastor. We took the coffin to the church and they sang and prayed. Then we brought the coffin home and buried him. We didn't do anything for the grave because we don't have money now. Coalition and KTL workers came to the burial, they were crying since because of his death, he won't get his gratuity. KTL didn't help or the Coalition, just the church was helping with the burial.

I faced a lot of problems after my husband died. I have no one who can help me because his brother also died from diabetes. There is no one who can help me now. You see my blind son, he got admission to one school in Zaria. I collected money from some people to put him in school and I went to the Cooperative Bank to get a loan to pay them back. Now the bank is disturbing me about the loan. This thing is disturbing me too much; I don't have peace of mind.

I'm not crying because I saw you, I'm crying because I have no money. My blind son finished at the private school in Zaria and my first son finished his ATC-Kafanchan, but he's not working. My second daughter married and had two children but is no longer living with her husband and is living with me. My other son went to Abuja to look for a job—he is working, constructing new houses. He started going to Polytechnic-Kaduna but because of no money, he couldn't continue. My last son finished secondary school in Kajera but we have no money to send him to school to learn about computer processing.

I really enjoyed living with my husband, that is why he is still living in my heart. When he was alive, he was trying to do everything for us. It was his hard work that enabled him to build this house for us, he tried his best to see that his children had food and that his children studied.

****

Portrait 2

Ramatu Husseini Adamu   Interviewed: 8 May 2018
Ethnicity: Ebira   Religion: Tariqqa Muslim
Husband: Husseini Adamu   Died 2016

After KTL was closed, we had many problems, for example, lack of money and the children were going to school. And our relatives had no money to help us. But as I'm talking to you, five of our children finished school but they don't have work. When my husband, Husseini Adamu, was working at KTL, he made sure that he had food for us, even if he didn't have a kobo in the house. At that time, we ate different types of food, *tuwo shinkafa* (rice porridge) and many other things. But now we are facing problems because we hardly have food to eat. That is why I have high blood pressure now because I am facing so many problems. But if the children have work to do, they could help but they don't have work.

My last daughter finished Environmental Studies and she wants to go for her degree but we don't have the money. I even asked her to go and stay with her sister, she's the only one who is working. Then I can take care of the others.

My husband had malaria and we took him to the hospital but later on he had *shakuwa* (hiccoughs). We took him to Asibiti Dutse in Tudun Wada. He died there before a week's time. In the hospital they gave him medicine and drip but we don't have records from the hospital. But many KTL people came and visited us in the hospital because my husband was good to everyone.

My husband used to say that if you see wood at KTL, you shouldn't take it, it belongs to KTL. He used to say that he was an honest person; if KTL can get five people like him, maybe KTL would not be spoiled. When he was working at KTL, most of the workers would collect a loan from KTL. We and the children were telling him to collect the loan but he said he would not collect anything.

We buried him in Tudun Wada Cemetery. Because we are Muslim, everywhere is home, we don't take the body to the hometown. We stayed in our house in KTL Quarters and many people came to offer their condolences. They gave us lots of gifts: food, oil, semovita, even money. People were coming for a month for condolences. People stayed at the house for three days, praying. Then seven days later they went back to their houses. As I told you, some people came even after the seven days. I don't know whether they put a name on his grave since we women don't go to the cemetery and I didn't ask.

I'm facing many problems. If a person is alive, they will help you but if he's no longer alive, you won't see them. Sometimes I am taking pure water [sachets] and take them to a place where they sell bread to get money for food. Before I had a refrigerator outside the house and would sell pure water and other things but now if I use it…I can't afford to pay the NEPA electric bill, so now I'm finding it difficult to get food to eat.

My first two daughters are married, Amina and A'I. My last daughter finished Environmental Studies and Amina finished her NCE. Kabiru finished his youth service corps, he got a job as a new teacher but the place that they sent him is Paki (near Kano). They said he can't go because of the transport. Even now, Kabiru wants to go to see the place but we don't have the money to pay for transport. His sister wrote her exam but they couldn't find her name on the list.

One daughter died when she was 25 years old from typhoid fever, she died 11 years ago. She was giving polio vaccinations. And my other son, Ali died when he was eight, he had a fever. We went to St. Gerard's Hospital before he died. Halima died when she was five years old in our hometown, in her grandmother's house, from *kabir ruwa* (water) sickness. There was another child who died, he was two days old; he couldn't suckle.

I remember my husband because he always wanted to live in peace with everyone. We didn't fight. And he didn't want to see his children without education. He always wanted them educated. Even if they wanted to marry his daughters, he said, "No," because he wanted them to have an education. My husband was buried in Tudun Wada Cemetery; my children except for the one who died in our hometown were buried in Barnawa Cemetery.

****

Portrait 3

Cecilia Gabriel
Ethnicity: Idoma
Husband: Gabriel Okoh

Interviewed: 9 May 2018
Religion: Methodist
Died: 5 August 2008

When the factory closed, we suffered because my husband had no work. It was difficult to get food. Because of that, he started farming. But not for long because he died soon after. He died as a result of a fever, it started with a small fever, then later he was vomiting blood. We took him to Nasarawa Hospital for a week but it didn't change. We took him to Nursing Home, three days later he died at this hospital. The hospital staff asked whether he was smoking or taking alcohol. "Not now," I said, "but he used to take alcohol but then he stopped."

We took his body to his hometown and did Christian burial. When he died, it was KTL that gave us N10,000 to buy the coffin but it wasn't enough. The church helped us with the remainder. He was buried in his family house, near his brother's grave. We went with our pastor to his hometown. Friends and relatives came together and prayed for him—and we stayed in our hometown for seven days before coming back here. We cemented the grave but didn't put anything on it. KTL didn't attend but they did give us N10,000.

I faced a lot of problems. I used to go out hawking palm oil and *kunu* (gruel) to feed my children. But now I don't have money to buy those things, I only sell brooms now. My first son went to Lagos to get a job but found it difficult and came back, he has finished his secondary school. My second son finished at the polytechnic and got a manufacturing job in Owerri. But now the factory is closed. So I told him to come back and look for a job here but he said no. And he never sent even N5 to us. He said he didn't want to come back and said we should stay in different places. My two daughters both finished secondary school but no money to take their WAEC exams; they got married. The first one married a photographer. But last year, a thief broke into his shop and stole everything. And she was the one helping me. The other daughter married a mechanic but he didn't have work. He just left her and she has four children.

Before I had a funeral poster for my husband's burial but when I kept looking at it, my sister took it away and that's why I no longer have the poster. Whenever I don't have food to eat, I remember my husband. When he was alive, he used to help me with any little thing he had.

****

Portrait 4

Felicia Na'Allah Interviewed: 14 May 2018
Ethnicity: Kadara Religion: Roman Catholic
Husband: Na'Allah Kogi Died: 2006

My husband died 12 years ago. When he lost his job, he was sick up until the time he died. Sometimes his body would be swollen, then it would reduce, then swell up again until the time he died. We took him to Nursing Home Hospital, they didn't admit him, they only gave him medicine. He was suffering for two years, then he died.

We buried him in this house. It was his son-in-law who bought the coffin (I don't know how much it cost). Relatives and our neighbors helped a lot during the burial. We tiled the grave and wrote his name on it, but the grandchildren spoiled the name plate. It was a Christian burial, the body was taken to church and then they took him home and buried him. It was two days after he died that we buried him. KTL didn't attend the funeral and they didn't give us anything. The church gave us N10,000, the church women's association gave us corn and guinea corn. And I couldn't afford to buy these things because I am the only one paying school fees for the children.

The only work I do is go to the farm. After the farmers have harvested their crops, I go there and bring back anything that remains. I'm living with my last-born son, my two daughters have married. One of them finished primary school and the other finished secondary. They are working on the farm now. My eldest son is working in the aluminum industry, my last born is going to secondary school.

I lost one of my daughters, she died when she was four years old. Her name was Catherine. She had diarrhea and fever, we took her to Nasarawa Hospital and she died there. She was buried in Anguwan Sule cemetery but it's no longer there.

I had a joyful life with my husband. Even when we fought, we would reconcile and live together.

****

Portrait 5

Alisabetu Joseph
Ethnicity: Koro
Husband: Joseph Waziri Makadas

Interviewed: 14 May 2018
Religion: ECWA
Died: 22 February 2018

When he lost his job, the food we were eating was not same. At that time, the children couldn't continue their education because he had no work to do, they only finished secondary school.

He had hypertension and diabetes. We took him to Gwamna Awan Hospital, only for one day and he died in the hospital. His son said that he would collect the death certificate from the hospital so I don't have it. He is buried in the house here in Karatude. It was me, the children, and his relatives who bought the coffin, we bought it here in Kaduna. It was made by a carpenter who lives near our house. It cost N50,000 but he said that we should give him N45,000. We only cemented the grave—we will put tiles on it if God gives us the money. KTL workers who heard about his death came to offer their condolences but they didn't give us anything. The church gave us N3,000 and the church women's association gave us guinea corn (*dawa*). The Koro ethnic association helped us with N4,000.

I'm facing so many problems because I'm not feeling well. And it is me and the children who go up and down to find something so we can eat. I'm sweeping someone's house and he is paying me, that is the work that I'm doing. Some of my children are still with me but they have no work to do and some are still schooling. My second son got married and only finished his secondary school. He is doing electrical work and the other boy is learning tailoring. Two of my daughters finished their secondary school and my last daughter finished JSS2. I lost one of my children, he had a fever and we buried him in our home village. His name was Bitus. He died before he was one year old.

Now, when it is the rainy season, I remember my husband because he used to go to our village and farm for us and then bring us food. But this time, who will go to the village and farm for us?

****

Portrait 6

Angelina Simon   Interviewed: 28 May 2018
Ethnicity: Kulo   Religion: Baptist
Husband: Simon Ladan   Died 2008

When he didn't have work, we faced a lot of problems. When KTL closed, he said he could not become a security man, he didn't like the work. "What kind of work will you do?" I asked. "The children are not to be going to school? If you go farming, you can't get enough money. You have to work."

Because of that, he started working as a security guard. There is a difference between the time he was working and now. If you see my picture, you will see the difference. If you have work to do, the food you eat will be better than the food now. When he was working at KTL, we had yam, rice, pounded yam, fish, or meat with soup. After he lost his job, we have had *tuwo massara* (corn porridge) and sometimes we can't even get that. If we don't have soup ingredients, we will only eat *gari* (cassava flour) or *kunu* pap made with maize flour.

He had an accident—a vehicle knocked him down when he was riding his bicycle. We took him to St. Gerard's, but within one and a half hours, he died. At that time, I was confused and didn't ask for his papers. When his brothers heard about it, they came the next day and they took his body to their hometown. They buried him in the family house. It was a Christian burial and the person whose house he was guarding paid for the coffin—I don't know how they paid for transport.

They took him to church and then brought him back to the family house. They cemented the grave and put tiles on it. KTL didn't attend and they didn't give us anything. He died 10 years ago. The church gave us money and we made food in the village. Our Kulo ethnic association, the men's side gave me N6,000 and the women's side gave us corn and N2,000.

I remember my husband because we lived in peace together. No one ever heard us fighting and even when we were fighting, no one would know we were fighting, even our children wouldn't know. That was how we lived in peace and patience with one another.

I'm facing many problems now. When he was alive, I didn't have as many problems as I have now. You see, I'm sick, something is paining me in my chest. And my children are not going to school. My daughter didn't finish her school, another daughter got married, she has her degree. The [third] daughter didn't finish secondary school, she's now plaiting hair and now Buhari says we should not be doing this work because there's no money for it. My son is working with construction workers, he finished secondary school and has a diploma. My last daughter got admission to Kaduna State University but she can't go—no money.

I had four children who died—two boys and two girls. One of them was 10 years old when he fell in a toilet pit, he was playing around the pit and fell in, that caused his death. We took him to one government hospital near his school. They were supposed to give him an injection but they didn't do it—he died at home. We buried him in Anguwan Faima Cemetery in Kaduna. Deborah was six years old when she died, she had a convulsion and was buried in our home village. Eunach was sick, he died when he was three years old and was buried in Television Cemetery. The other girl was one and a half years old when she died.

6 Consequences for children, problems for families

> When you have no father, the whole house is ruined.
>
> Philip Simon, son of deceased KTL worker

> The Kano state governor Umar Ganduje on Father's Day [told] fathers what to do about their families and drug addiction. "I urge all fathers to continue looking after their families, to continue to monitor the discipline of their children," he said.
>
> *Daily Trust*, 17 June 2019

After their husbands' deaths, many widows mentioned their difficulties in providing for their children. Many children had to stop their education for lack of school fees and even money to buy the required clothing. Some widows were unable to buy sufficient food to feed their children, resorting to the practice of one meal a day—often consisting of a starchy dish of *tuwo massara* (corn meal porridge). For as Jummai Dauda recalled:

> The children, they didn't have it easy when their father died. Because even now, my youngest son used to remember when his father would trek to get N50 to give to him to buy biscuits and yogurt. He will say to me, "If my father was alive, he would bring me biscuits and yogurt and take me to school." And when he would say that, I would be very unhappy and sad.
>
> (Interview: 14 May 2018, Kaduna)

Yet children had various responses to their fathers' deaths—some left school for lack of fees but also went to work to help support their mothers and siblings. Some, especially girls, married, while others farmed plots on the outskirts of Kaduna. A very few went back to farm in their home villages. This chapter examines their experiences—of family and friends, of school and work, and of drug use and treatment, mainly among those who remained in Kaduna. It begins with these sons and daughters' memories of their fathers and how they experienced the deaths of their fathers after they lost their jobs at the KTL mill. While some children were quite young when their fathers died, others participated in their funerals and burials, as they explained. The chapter continues with their discussions of their present-day situations, which vary depending on their mothers' and extended families' circumstances as well as their own actions. For children who have become involved in drugs and the drug trade, the association of drug use—particularly marijuana, Tramadol, and codeine—with unemployment and lack of opportunities with the closure of many of the textile mills in Kaduna reflects a global connection between deindustrialization and drug use among the young (McLean 2016). How some young people have become involved in these activities is discussed by KTL widows and their children, who also have thought about how this situation might be remedied by government efforts. The chapter concludes with a discussion of the consequences of deindustrialization in Kaduna, Nigeria, for the lives of children and their mothers after the loss of their fathers, a situation also experienced by families of former mill workers in "Rust Belt" areas of the US. It considers the similarities in their experiences of suffering and shared support as well as underscoring the distinctive historical contexts and future prospects for areas affected by deindustrialization in different parts of the world (Cowie and Heathcott 2003).

Memories of fathers

In Kaduna, some children who were very young when their fathers died have only vague memories of their fathers. According to his mother, Monday David was only two years old when his father died. "I don't remember him because I was young but my mother showed me his grave in our hometown and she showed me where he worked—Kaduna Textiles Limited."

Others who were older when their fathers died have very specific memories of their fathers, which they continue to remember:

> There was a day that I went to a football match, when I came back I saw my father sitting in the house. I met him there and told him I was hungry. He told me that he only had N30, the last money he had but if I was hungry, I should take it and buy something with it. "I can live without anything," he said. So, I went and bought *kosai* in the street, I was there when somebody ran to me and told me that my father went to the bathroom and didn't come out. I quickly ran to the house and went into the bathroom and put his trousers on. I then brought him out of the bathroom. When he came out, he was not himself so I called my senior sister to tell her that our father was sick. She was in school then but she quickly came back home. Then we got a *keke* Napep [a motorized tricycle] and took him to the hospital. My father walked to the *keke* Napep but when he got to the hospital and was put in bed, he couldn't move his hand or one side of his body. I stayed with him that night and the next day, my mother came and stayed with him in the hospital. The next day she went

back home so that she could cook for us. She had already finished making *tuwo* and was about to cook the soup when my sister called and told her that our father had died.

I remember the N30 he gave me, I will always remember it. And he always told me, whatever we have, if someone is seeking help, we should always help him. We should not be proud if we have money, we should always help people.

(Interview: Benedict Taru Yashim, 23 July 2019, Kaduna; Figures 6.1 and 6.2).

Along with providing money for food, the generosity of their fathers was remembered by some children for other things as well. For example, Martha John recalled a cloth she was given: "When he was alive, I was schooling and whatever I asked for, he would give it to me. He used to buy cloth for me. There is one cloth that he bought for me, I'm still using it. It is a white gown"

Figure 6.1 Benedict Taru Yashim, who remembers his father's generosity, 23 July 2019, Kaduna (Photograph by E.P. Renne).

Figure 6.2 Former KTL worker, Taru Yashim, received a Certificate of Long Service after he had worked in the Weaving Department for 20 years, 15 May 2018, Kaduna (Photograph by E.P. Renne).

(Interview: 23 July 2019, Kaduna). One son, Bartholomew Samson, remembered his father for a very special gift:

> I remember my father because when I was schooling, he did something that I will never forget. There was a time I came back from school, he gave me a paper. He said that it was the gift he would give me. That paper said that he had bought a plot [of land] for me, it was a receipt for the plot. I still have the plot and hope to build on it.
> (Interview: 23 July 2019, Kaduna)

Others remembered their fathers for their insistence on pursuing an education. Patience Florence thought of her father "as a very special person who made us go to school, that we should like school, that school was everything. And I benefitted from him for this" (Interview: 17 July 2019, Kaduna). Similarly, Philip Simon's father made a special effort for him because of the family's situation:

> He didn't allow me to go to public school, I went to private school for primary and secondary up until the time he died, when I was in my 200 level at the University of Abuja. After he died, everything has stopped. My schooling has stopped. That is why I came back home to Kaduna to start some business in sound engineering…But he tried for my education. Whatever I become now, it's because of my father.
> (Interview: 17 July 2019, Kaduna)

Many fathers made every effort to foster their children's education, possibly because their own education helped them to get employment at the Kaduna Textiles Ltd mill where literacy was one of the criteria for being hired. More recently, the completion of secondary education and the passing of the WAEC exam are necessary in order to obtain government employment. Thus, fathers paid for WAEC exams fees, although their efforts did not always work out as planned:

> My father's death affected my own education because he said that he was going to pay my WAEC exam fee because I was supposed to write my exam two years ago, not this year. My father gave me the money for my exam but he got sick so we had to use the money to buy medicine.
> (Interview: Benedict Taru Yashim, 23 July 2019, Kaduna)

While Benedict Yashim plans on taking his WAEC exam, others, such as Julius Markus, decided to go for vocational education: "It was because of my father's death that I didn't write my WAEC exam. Now I am learning how to be a mechanic (for *akada*) to get money" (Interview: 17 July 2019, Kaduna).

Education and work

The fact that so many former KTL workers attempted to see that their children were educated, even after they had lost their mill jobs, reflects the hierarchy of labor in Kaduna. Many widows and their children thought of work in terms of white-collar jobs, particularly as government employment. Thus, when I asked some children about the work that they did, some would say that they had no jobs, even if they were selling things in Kaduna or farming just outside the city. What they meant was that they didn't have government work, perhaps because one does not receive a regular paycheck or wear office attire. As one son put it, "Now I am married but I'm not working, I'm selling *kullu zafi* [hot millet flour drink]" or as another son described it, "my mother's relatives, they don't have government work so they are just managing," probably as farmers (Interview: Godwin Usuman, 23 July 2019, Kaduna).

Options for sons

Yet several sons have continued with farming, some because it was the work that their fathers had trained them to do:

> I used to remember my father by his name, Gona [*gona* means farmer in Hausa]. That was the work he left for us—farming. I remember going to the farm with my father. If you are not hard-working, if you are lazy, he used to go with a cane so if he saw you were not hardworking, he was beat you with the cane. Even now, when I go to the farm with the children, I bring a cane and do the same thing—what my father taught me. We don't have a change in our food because we are farming and our dress hasn't changed because we are earning money from farming… When he died, I stopped my education and I continued with the work he left us—farming.
>
> (Interview: Habila Gona, 23 July 2019, Kaduna)

Another son, Christian Kabila, went to his family's hometown to farm after his father's death: "A year after I finished my secondary school…I started farming to help my family. That is why I decided to stay in my home village to farm ginger" (Interview: 25 January 2017, Kaduna). A few older sons also moved back to their family's hometowns to farm on family land: "My oldest son is now in the village, he is farming there and has a wife and children to take care of" (Interview: Lami Iliya, 14 May 2018, Kaduna). Yet some sons only reluctantly farmed as day work outside of Kaduna: "After my father died, I had to go to work—I had to go to somebody's farm and work for him so he could pay me" (Interview: Monday David, 23 July 2019, Kaduna).

Besides farming, sons had several options for work although it was not always the type of work they wanted to do. For example, day jobs as laborers were seen as particularly unattractive, even though they could provide a reasonable income, as Martha John explained:

> One of my neighbors who drank *giya* [alcoholic beverage], he fell down and wounded himself. He even wrote his WAEC exams like me. Because he didn't have work to do, people said he should go and look for a job like a laborer. But he was feeling big, he was above that kind of work, he can't do it.
> (Interview: 23 July 2019, Kaduna)

Yet some sons did mention working as laborers or builders on construction sites. Others found work as drivers, mechanics, printers, security men, or gardeners. Occasionally, such jobs led to other opportunities; one son, who worked as a gardener for an army officer, was later sponsored by this man to continue his postgraduate education.

Those with postgraduate education have also found work as primary school teachers, as pastors, and as lawyers. Others were not so fortunate, having lost their jobs due to absenteeism, as one widow, Rahila Goro, explained: "One of my sons, he was working for a television company, but he lost his job because he was taking care of his father. Now he is washing clothes for people" (Interview: 28 May 2018, Kaduna).

Options for daughters

Several daughters who married live with their husbands. Some live with their mothers, where they take care of their children and some help their mothers in selling cooked food. Some who have not married stay with their mothers, while others are attending school in order to further their education. One widow described the work of her three daughters, all of whom are married:

> My first daughter is teaching in secondary school, my second daughter is working in the Local Government Secretariat, and my other daughter follows me to the farm to help me and she also helps me with selling our crops [maize and ground nuts] in order to feed her children.
> (Interview: Fatu Tom, 30 April 2018, Kaduna)

One daughter opened a hair salon, while other daughters do housework:

> My daughters are going to people's houses to get cleaning jobs…They go to wash dishes in people's houses and sometimes, when they finish washing, the people will give them cloth or food. There are three girls and they all finished secondary school.
> (Interview: Saidi Ishaya, 15 May 2018, Kaduna)

Options in general: better staying in Kaduna

Despite the limited options for work, many children chose to remain in Kaduna rather than return to their families' rural hometowns. For some, they saw Kaduna as their hometown because they were born there. Indeed, several mentioned their inability to farm, either because did not know how or did not want to do such work, to explain their decision to stay in Kaduna:

> The reason we don't go to our hometown, it's because we can do something in Kaduna and get a little money. Because if I go back to my hometown, I don't know how to farm. So, no, I will not go back to my hometown because in Kaduna, it may be possible that the government in the future can open a company and then we can get a job there. But when we go back to our hometown, we will not get that opportunity, we will only farm.
>
> (Interview: Julius Markus, 17 July 2019, Kaduna)

> We went to check the farm and on the way we "harvested" my shirt. So we'll see. But seriously, I don't want farming for now…But I may go back to my hometown if the local government can find me a job, I can go back there—a government or contract job.
>
> (Interview: Peter Daniel, 23 July 2019, Kaduna)

What Peter Daniel jokingly meant was that he tried farming and made enough money to buy the shirt he was wearing. Like him, many KTL workers' children saw more opportunities for finding paying jobs in the city:

> Here in Kaduna, we used to do small-small business so I want to stay in Kaduna. By the grace of God, I will never go back to my hometown. Because I have nothing to do there, because I have my life in Kaduna and have nothing there. When we go to my village, we would see how difficult it was to live there. It is not easy when we saw how they lived.
>
> (Interview: Ruth Galau, 17 July 2019, Kaduna)

Another reason for these children staying in Kaduna is that having been born in Kaduna, their ties with their rural family members have weakened:

> Now I have a family so it's better to stay where you were born because you're familiar with the place. I can't go back to my hometown because I don't know what I will start doing there. And we don't receive any help from our relatives.
>
> (Interview: David Vincent, 23 July 2019, Kaduna)

The rural-urban migration of their parents and their children's subsequent birth in Kaduna has led many to see themselves as city people, who do not want to move to remote rural villages. Alternatively, rural family members still living in their hometowns may be resentful of their urban relations' expectations about living comfortably, unable to cope with the rigors of a farming life. Indeed, even those who continue to farm outside of Kaduna prefer to stay there rather than return to their families' hometown:

> No, I will not go back to my hometown because I was born here in Karatude. I was born here and will continue to farm near the Kaduna-Abuja Rd. It was not the same with my father—as he was born in Lukulu, along Abuja Rd. if you pass Dutse.
> (Interview; Habila Goma, 23 July 2019, Kaduna)

Yet while there has been a reduction in kin ties for some families, for others these ties persist. For example, after Abubakar Inuwa lost his job when the KTL mill closed, it became increasingly difficult for him to care for his family, as his wife explained:

> We had so many problems, that time I was pregnant with my son who died recently. Because of that, my husband said we should go back to my hometown [Katsina] because we didn't have enough food to eat if we stayed in Kaduna. There were so many times he'd go out to get us something to eat but he couldn't get us anything. I was making caps (*hula*) to help but because I was pregnant, he said I should go back home with our five children.
> (Interview: Saudi Abubakar, 9 May 2018, Kaduna)

When her husband was later recalled to work at KTL as a groundskeeper, he told his wife to return to Kaduna with the children. Yet she has maintained her family connections for her emotional, social, and economic security.

Difficulties of living in Kaduna

Despite the reluctance of many children to return to their family hometowns, living in Kaduna has been a challenge for many of them since the textile mills closed, their fathers have died, and they have not completed their secondary school education. Several children mentioned that if the Kaduna Textile Ltd mill reopened, they would like to work there although this remains an indefinite prospect. Other children have received training for work, but without a certificate, they cannot move forward:

> Before my father died, I was learning how to work from a friend of my sister—video editing. We didn't pay him the fee he charged, so he said whenever my father received his gratuity, we can pay him. I finished

learning from him but we couldn't get the money. But he said it was ok but he wouldn't give me my certificate until we paid the money.
(Interview: Benedict Taru Yashim, 23 July 2019, Kaduna)

Another son who had started a photography studio later closed the shop for a lack of customers, while one daughter had a tailoring shop that burnt down. Another daughter was working in a school but lost her job when they needed to reduce the number of workers. Some simply could not find work: "There was a Sunday when my father called me and asked why I didn't want to go for a job. So I said to him, 'I can't get a job—that's why I don't go for a job'" (Interview: Fidelus Clifford, 17 July 2019, Kaduna). For those without funds for certificates, for WAEC exams, for vocational training, for buying items to sell in the market, or for renting plots for farming, involvement in drugs is another option.

Drug use and the deindustrialization of Kaduna

> As he walked along a familiar feeling came over him, the sadness of youth swinging free, having nothing and nobody, and nowhere to go.
> Eileen Chang, *Naked Earth*

That drug use among young people in Kaduna, and in Nigeria more generally, has increased dramatically in recent years is evident in news reports and from the observations of KTL widows and their children themselves.[1] Part of the problem is drug availability, as the Director General of the NAFDAC, Professor Adeyeye noted: "Many youths are dying of drug overdose because it is very easy for them to access addictive drugs" (Muhammad 2018). For example, shipments of two of the most commonly used drugs by young people in Kaduna—Tramadol and codeine cough syrup—have been reported as intercepted by National Drug Law Enforcement Agency personnel in recent years: "[Tramadol] tablets worth N19,000 were intercepted after being concealed inside LG Plasma TV cartons in a trailer along [the] Kano Eastern bye-pass," while they also "impounded a trailer in [the] Dutsenreme area of Funtua [in Kaduna State] loaded with 24,000 bottles... of cough syrup with codeine" (Muhammad 2018). In September 2019, three men were arrested in Kaduna for suspected drug dealing; they were found with Tramadol, Axzol 5, Valinex 5, and Diazapam on their person (*Daily Trust* 2019b).[2]

However, while this easy supply helps to explain their use, there are also socioeconomic factors which have contributed to drug behavior in Kaduna. For as has been discussed in the US context, deindustrialization—e.g., the closure of steel mills in the Midwest and eastern Pennsylvania—has contributed to drug use and drug overdoses (McLean 2016). Drug use associated with the closing of the textile mills in Kaduna represents another aspect of this deindustrialization story, with young people's educations and expectations of employment ending when their fathers lost their jobs at mills such as Kaduna Textiles Ltd. Indeed, when asked about why many young people whom they knew were using drugs, some suggested that drugs provided relief from their problems:

> The reason some are involved in drugs, they say that they have so many problems. They say that when they take the drugs, they would have relief and forget their problems. They don't have work to do, they don't have money to face their problems and some who have children, they don't have money to buy food for their children, pay rent, pay their children's school fees. So when they take drugs, it reduces their problems. If they have something to do—work—it will help.
> (Interview: Godwin Usuman, 23 July 2019, Kaduna)

Others mentioned the lack of education or of work opportunities as reasons for their behavior:

> Some children involve themselves in drugs because they are not educated. Some, it is because of bad background, their parents don't tell them the right things. Another is the influence of friends because sometimes they see their friends taking drugs so they want to take drugs too. Because they think that when you are taking drugs, you are a Big Boy. But I used to tell myself, friends can't make me do what I don't want to do except what my heart tells me to do. So we can reduce this thing, if they have counselling or some work to do. Because the school doesn't help now because you can finish the school but they don't have work to do. If they can get vocational education it can help them. Also the environment—if the environment in which they live is surrounded by all these youth, they will involve themselves. A good environment will help you to go to school and you won't have a problem.
> (Interview: Benedict Taru Yashim, 23 July 2019, Kaduna)

Some also attributed drug use to a lack of character and an inability to maintain a proper lifestyle, which was exacerbated by the loss of one's father: "The reason why some are involved in drugs, it's when a child is brought up without a father, because the mother sometimes cannot control them. Unless the child has committed themselves to the church" (Interview: Mashim Daniel, 17 July 2019, Kaduna).

Several children mentioned the need for government support for vocational education that would train young people for practical jobs rather than academic careers (Ighakpe 2019). Indeed, the assumption that a university degree would lead to white-collar employment was not always justified, as one KTL widow, Roselynn Ugbonji, explained: "My senior son, he has just gone to do menial job—he is a graduate of sociology—going to carry loads. You see, it's disheartening but it's work" (Interview: 10 May 2018, Kaduna). Thus, many believe that vocational education, which includes basic computer skills, photography, video editing, baking, hair styling, carpentry, and plumbing, are more likely to lead to employment for former KTL workers' children.

Using drugs

Two men in their early thirties—children of former KTL workers who have since died—explained how they became involved in drug use and the means which could encourage them to stop. For both, taking drugs became a way of handling their problems—of not having sufficient food to eat, of not having work, of not having "peace of mind," as one man put it:

> Lack of peace of mind makes people to engage in drugs…I was really sad—because I had nothing, no food or work or house, because our house was destroyed, it was burnt during the 2002 crisis [after Goodluck Jonathan was elected]…If I find something to do, I think that I can quit taking drugs. Doing nothing led me to get involved in drugs, but if you have something doing and food to eat, it will make me to help myself and my family. Then I can try my best to stop taking drugs.
>
> (Interview: 14 January 2020, Kaduna)

He became involved in drugs when some men saw him sitting by the road and asked him to join them. They gave him odd jobs to do, buying cigarettes and water for them as well as washing their clothes. While he was looking for food to eat, one of the men gave him marijuana (*wiwi*) "because he said it would help me to forget my problems." He took it and the man continued to give him this drug: "He always gave me *wiwi* to take because I washed his clothes and did so many things. I was just a houseboy for him." Later, he began to take *kwiya* [capsules]: "The type of *kwiya* I'm taking is Tramol [Tramadol]—250ml capsules." Because he takes drugs in his family house, his mother is aware of his drug use and regularly advises him and prays for him to stop.[3] Since he is learning to repair generators, if he succeeds in obtaining employment in this line of work, it is possible that he will stop taking drugs, as he has said.

The other man started taking drugs 10 years ago, when he was in his early twenties:

> I started taking drugs 10 years ago,[4] I started with *wiwi* [marijuana] then *cigare* [cigarettes] and then I started taking drugs [*kwiya*-capsules]. I started taking drugs after my father died. Because at the back of our house, they sell drugs there. I used to see people taking them, so after my father died, I went there and so many people were buying it there, so I bought it and started taking it. At that time, I didn't know how to take it but I forced myself to take it. And I bought it with my own money.
>
> (Interview: 14 January 2020, Kaduna)

As he is working part-time as a driver on an occasional basis, he takes drugs to "be strong," as he put it:

> I'm getting drugs now where I am working. Sometimes I do drive so I am getting it early at the bus stop because at the bus stop there are many people selling it in baskets there. I buy it and take it so I will be strong. I take Tramdol, Exol, *wiwi*, *cigare*, *giya* [bottled beer], and cough syrup—Totalyne…We sometimes call *wiwi* Moroccan or Indian hemp; [codeine] syrup we are calling it drip; Ezol we are calling it *iya'yen wasu*; *cigare* [cigarettes] we call dry stick.

What he would really like to do is to have a car to drive on a permanent basis—so that he could transport people from Kaduna to Abuja and back. And "because on the highway, you can meet security people and if you are taking drugs, they won't allow you to take those you are driving, they will make you stop."

Whether permanent employment with adequate pay will actually lead both of these men to stop or reduce their use of drugs, the remedy of work was suggested by many. Yet none mentioned or knew of drug remediation programs in Kaduna, although such programs are available through hospital psychiatric wards in major hospitals in Kaduna.[5] However, in Kaduna, there has been no separate state office for drug use prevention and treatment until recently. In 2016, the Kaduna State Bureau for Substance Abuse Prevention and Treatment (KADBUSA) was established to address the problem of drug use, initially with offices in Kaduna State Ministry of Health (see Ahmadu-Suka and Shuiabu 2017). In August 2019, Dr. Joseph Maigari was appointed Director-General of the new bureau, and three months later, the KADBUSA headquarters opened its own office in Kaduna.

As the Bureau's name suggests, its objectives include both prevention and treatment. Previously, the focus had been on stopping drug supplies through the National Drug Law Enforcement Agency efforts, which are ongoing. Using numerous billboards (seen throughout Kaduna; Figure 6.3), radio jingles, community outreach, educational activities, and the involvement of political and religious leaders, KADBUSA hopes to reduce drug demand. Dr. Maigari also mentioned the establishment of large remediation centers dedicated to helping drug users to quit and to provide them with vocational training (Interview: 22 January 2020, Kaduna). As he noted, "The problem of drug dependence is that you will need to take more and more drugs" in order to achieve what one drug user referred to as "peace of mind."

Yet some children were able to reduce their dependence on drugs without remediation assistance. For example, one widow described her son's drug problem and his subsequent recovery:

> After my husband died, I started facing problems because my son starting taking drugs. I spent a lot of money at the police station to get him back home because he used to steal to buy drugs. With the money I spent in the police station, I could have bought a plot [of land]. People said I should

Figure 6.3 Kaduna State Bureau for Substance Abuse Prevention and Treatment (KADBUSA) signboard, which reads: "Message From: KADBUSA, Children and Adults, You Should Avoid Taking Drugs," 15 January 2020, Kaduna (Photograph by E.P. Renne).

just leave him because he was the only person who was giving me that problem. But I couldn't leave him there—I would rather stay with him in the prison. But God saw my problem and He helped me. Now my son is married with two children and he doesn't do drugs like before, only cigarettes and he doesn't steal now. Even the drugs, he doesn't go out to take them, he only does it at home.

(Interview: Titi Joseph, 29 May 2018, Kaduna)

Her support for her son, despite his continued arrests, convinced him to reduce his drug use although his mother observed that he still uses them, but not as before.

Other widows were not so fortunate as was the case for one mother whose son's death was attributed to cancer and drugs: "He was more than 20 years, he was getting thin...he died 7 years ago...He had cancer and he was taking drugs—which made the sickness worse. He finished his secondary school [but] that time he was drinking *gogoro*" (Interview: Saratu Simon, 24 May 2018, Kaduna). This son's brother, however, had a more detailed description of his death associated with drugs:

One of my brothers died as a result of taking drugs. Because we have no father who will look after us and who will help us...As I said, my brother had cancer from taking drugs. Because he was mature when my father died, but still he lived under my father. My father was the one who provided for him, food and other things. When my father died and he didn't get these things, he started taking drugs—many heavy, heavy drugs. That is why he had cancer. Up until time, he didn't have any blood in his body.

(Interview: Philip Simon, 17 July 2019, Kaduna)

Some widows who mentioned that their sons who were taking drugs knew precisely what they were taking: "My youngest son, he's now on drugs, he's taking codeine and other illegal drugs (*kwiya*, capsules)" (Interview: Amina Dauda, 8 May 2018, Kaduna). She was particularly distressed because he refused to accompany her to the farm and she was unable to interest him in apprenticeship training or continuing his education as his sister was doing.

Yet many widows were fortunate in the support—both emotional and financial—that their children have provided for them:

I don't have problems with my children, except when I can't pay school fees, they used to worry me and I worry too. As I told you, my first daughter is in Kaduna State NCE [National College of Education], my second son is about to finish but we don't have money for his school fees. That is why he will continue going next year and if I have money, he will write his exams.

The other two are in secondary school and the young one is in primary. I don't have any problems with my children; they used to sympathize with me and my situation. When they see me sitting alone, they come and talk to me and say that I should be patient. And if they are not in school, they will help with my business.

(Interview: Maryam Markus, 30 April 2018, Kaduna)

Several children have also helped their mothers with providing money for their siblings' school fees:

My father and I, we went to the farm together and I still farm—I remember him then. After he died, that was the time I started working as a builder in order to help my siblings, that is why I didn't go back to school.

(Interview: Timothy Tom, 17 July 2019, Kaduna)

Construction work, farming, food sales, and house cleaning, not industrial labor, are the main ways that children can earn money for themselves and their families.

Family responses to deindustrialization

The situation in Kakuri and the other areas of Kaduna near the textile mills is not unlike other parts of the world where textile mills and other industrial plants have closed down. In Kannapolis, North Carolina, for example, the Pillowtex textile mill closed its doors in July 2003, leaving around 4,800 people without decent-paying jobs to which they had become accustomed.

Commenting on the shutdown, Robert Freeman [a union organizer] noted in August that:

> "I have friends who have lost their job and are now dealing with foreclosures, having their cars taken away, and telling their kids they can't pay for college this fall."
>
> (Minchin 2013: 285)

Many children in Kannapolis, however, did not expect to go to college. Some completed their high school education but many dropped out of high school with the intention of working at the Pillowtex mill (Minchin 2013: 285). While dropping out of secondary school was not a preferred strategy for the children of KTL workers, many had to abandon their education after their fathers died. Some, like the children of Pillowtex workers, hoped to follow their fathers' work at the textile mill in Kaduna, although this was not a likely prospect. Similarly, textile workers and their families at the Pillowtex mill lost their access to affordable health care when the plant closed, just as KTL workers and their families lost access to the company clinic and coverage for health care.[6] Thus, the closure of the mill's clinic and the lack of company health care for his dying father meant that the money which had been set aside for Benedict Taru Yashim to take his WAEC exam was used to purchase medicine for his father.

The experiences of children and widows after the closure of the Kaduna Textile Ltd mill and the subsequent deaths of their fathers and husbands were also not unlike the experiences of families in East Chicago, where many of the steel mills unexpectedly closed in the early 1980s. Christine Walley described her family's difficulties associated with the ways that deindustrialization undermined people's expectations of a better, middle-class life:

> Although a large part of my father died with the steel mills, his physical death came in 2005, twenty-five years after Wisconsin Steel abruptly expelled its workers. His death not only marked a passage of generations within my own family—my son would have no firsthand experience of his grandfather—it also marked a change of generations in societal terms. Those like my father, who had come to adulthood anticipating the promises of an expanding middle class rather than the expanding social

inequalities of the late twentieth and early twenty-first centuries, seemed increasingly like dinosaurs on the verge of disappearing.

(Walley 2013: 153)

Like the widows who had been brought to Kaduna from their rural hometowns by their husbands who had been hired to work at the Kaduna Textiles Ltd mill when it opened, they came with the expectation of improving their lives and the lives of their children—with better food, housing, and education. Yet when the KTL mill closed, many men—as suggested by Coalition's list of deceased textile workers—seemed to lose heart, as did Christine Walley's father, as she notes: "a large part of my father died with the steel mills." The consequences of the closure of these mills and the socioeconomic inequality that ensued has meant that many of the children of deceased KTL workers, unable to complete their educations, have had to take low-paying work, building or cleaning the houses of the wealthy residents of Kaduna. Some have addressed their downward mobility through drugs, as has been documented in deindustrialized communities elsewhere in the world (McLean 2016). And as several children of deceased KTL workers, such as Peter Daniel, observed:

> Poverty is the cause of drugs. It's a very big disease, it kills, very quickly. Empowerment will solve this problem. If we train them and then give them a little work they can start—wealthy people and even Government can help."
>
> (Interview: 23 July 2019, Kaduna)

This assessment is similar to comments made by drug users in McKeesport, Pennsylvania—another area of steel mill deindustrialization: "Reflecting upon the area epidemic, interviewees forged a consistent connection between overdose, drug use, and poverty…[and] the dearth of legitimate employment opportunities was a theme reiterated across multiple interviewees" (McLean 2016: 24). In Kaduna, while not all children of deceased KTL workers responded by taking drugs, the difficulties that they and their mothers face have required a reevaluation of their expectations of city-living. Rather than the middle-class life style which their parents aspired to after having migrated from their rural hometowns, necessity required many of them to accustom themselves to precarious means of livelihood and urban poverty.

In other words, the consequences of closure of the textile mills and the deindustrialization in Kaduna has contributed to growing economic inequality in Nigeria, as it has in many other places in the world. Yet as Walley (2013: 7) has argued:

> Acknowledging the impacts of deindustrialization does not mean indulging in an act of nostalgia, but rather the need to take part in a hard-nosed

critical exploration of where we have come from as a nation and where we are heading.

While she is referring to residents of the US communities where mills have closed down, Nigerians, particularly those whose lives have changed as a consequence of rural to urban migration and whose children have been born in urban centers such as Kaduna, need to consider new directions as well.

Conclusion

The memories of their fathers—when they were working at the Kaduna Textiles Ltd mill and after the mill closed—underscore the loss that these men's deaths represent for their children. Yet they also represent, at least for some, a moral bearing that continues to guide them in their current lives: the need to be generous to those in need, the importance of hard work for family farming, and the value of education.

There are similarities with factory closures in the West, such as problems with loss of income, severing of health benefits, depression, and death of unemployed workers, but there are differences as well. In the case of Kaduna Textile Ltd mill workers, many had recently migrated to Kaduna from small villages in southern Kaduna and Middle Belt states. This rural-urban transition affected the lives of these men and particularly their children who were born in Kaduna and hence, were not inclined to move back to their families' rural hometowns. Several children mentioned that they have not learned to farm and also that family members in their hometowns would not help them, suggesting the way that rural-urban migration has reduced extended family connections. Several children stated that they had no expectations of help from their rural relatives. Yet for those with more affluent urban family ties, such as those with families in Jos, the capital city of Plateau State, the situation may be somewhat different, as Fidelus Clifford explained:

> After my father died, I stopped going to school. Now I am working to get money to help my siblings to finish their education, it was only me who didn't finish my education. My brother finished at the University of Jos—my mother's brother was the one who helped my brother finish his university education…And now my brother has a good job but he said I shouldn't follow him until he knows how the work goes…But I think in the future, we will go back to Jos. Even my mother's relatives and sister don't want her to stay in Kaduna.
>
> (Interview: 17 July 2019, Kaduna)

The impact of deindustrialization on these children's lives and on the world in which they grew up to expect—getting an education and perhaps working in one of Kaduna's textile mills or getting further training and obtaining a white-collar job, these expectations were largely destroyed after the KTL mill closed and their fathers died. Some continue to hope that by the Coalition's naming of the dead that KTL will pay their fathers' gratuities—so that they may obtain training certificates or pay WAEC exam fees or buy a plot of land to farm near Kaduna. Others hope that the textile industry will be revived in Kaduna, so that they can work in mills like their fathers. Most will remain in Kaduna, rather than returning to their families' hometowns, although for many, it is uncertain precisely what they will do in the future. Indeed, what the future holds for them and for families elsewhere in the world whose lives have been turned topsy-turvy by the closure of large manufacturing plants is the subject of the following, final, chapter.

Notes

1 The BBC documentary, *Sweet, Sweet Codeine: Nigeria's Cough Syrup Crisis*, aired in 2018, discusses the pervasive use of codeine cough syrup. The film shows the ways that the syrup, which was manufactured by companies in Ilorin, was illicitly distributed to drug dealers and then sold to young people.
2 The most commonly used substances were codeine (85%), alcohol (75%), cannabis (70%), Tramadol (65%), rohypnol (65%), and tobacco (50%). (Abasiubong et al. 2014; Adekeye et al. 2017).
3 Because he is a Muslim, he had considered going to one of the Islamic Rehabilitation Centres in the Rigasa area of Kaduna. However, his mother advised against it and he did not go.
    The wisdom of this decision was recently seen in the scandal in September 2019, which led to the closing of the Rigasa Islamic Rehabilitation Centre in Kaduna where some children and young adults were said to have been beaten and kept in chains (Yaba 2019). Many had been brought to this centre by their parents who were no longer able to control them—often relating to their use of drugs: "The name of the centre is Niggas Rehabilitation and Skills Acquisition and Training Centre with the motto: The sad end of drug abuse. Alhaji Muduru was nicknamed Malam Nigga, meaning that he is a teacher of drug addicts" (Muhammad 2015). A similar type of centre run by a *mallam* for Muslim women is depicted in the popular Kannywood film, *'Yar Mayé* (Abdoul-Salam 2015).
    However, since most of the children of former KTL workers are Christians, they would not be sent to these centres since they are run by Muslim religious leaders.
4 Several men included cigarettes and alcohol as forms of abused substances, although they are also referred to as drugs.
5 In Sokoto State, the National Drug Law Enforcement Agency (NDLEA) has partnered with the Federal Neuro Psychiatric Hospital-Kware to attend to drug rehabilitation. According to Yakubu Kibo, the NDLEA Commander, in Sokoto: "Fifty drug addicts were counselled with 20 of them rehabilitated during the period under review." This rehabilitation will support a decline in demand as he observed: "Many of our young ones are already languishing in various prisons across the country because of drugs issue. The supply reduction and the demand reduction should be given equal importance" (Muhammad 2020).
    Several hospitals in Nigeria have psychiatric units which care for those suffering from substance abuse (Adamson et al. 2010; Oni et al. 2017). There have been several studies conducted on drug use, often by university and medical students (Adekeye et al. 2017; Abasiubong et al. 2014).

6 In a somewhat ironic twist, some former Pillowtex workers were able to access free health care in a local clinic run by a Nigerian medical doctor living in Kannapolis, North Carolina:

> Particularly notable was the role of Kenny Tokunboh, a Nigerian-born doctor who offered free medical care to Pillowtex employees after the plant closed. Using complimentary samples from pharmaceutical companies, Tokunboh was able to treat Morris and many others. "I did medicine to help," explained the modest director of Kannapolis's Grace Medical Clinic. "You want people to continue to have their dignity." By 2008, Tokunboh estimated that he had seen between 1,500 and 2,000 former Pillowtex employees, and that he had lost count of the number who had broken down in tears in his office (Minchin 2013: 292).

References

Abasiubong, F., J.A. Udobang, A.O. Idong, S.B. Udoh, and H.E. Jombo. "Patterns of Psychoactive Substance Use in the Northern Region of Nigeria." *African Journal of Drug & Addiction Studies* 13 (2014): 107–115.

Abdoul-Salam, Moussa, director. 2015. *'Yar Mayé*. Kano: Al-Umma Productions.

Adamson, T.A., P.O. Onifade, and A. Ogunwale. "Trends in Socio-Demographic and Drug Abuse Variables in Patients with Alcohol and Drug Use Disorders in a Nigerian Treatment Facility." *West African Journal of Medicine* 29, no. 1 (2010): 12–18.

Adekeye, Olujide, Jonathan Odukoya, Olufunke Chenube, David Igbokwe, Angie Igbinoba, and Elizabeth Olowookere. "Subjective Experiences and Meaning Associated with Drug Use and Addiction in Nigeria: A Mixed Method Approach." *Global Journal of Health Science* 9, no. 8 (2017): 57–65.

Ahmadu-Suka, Maryam, and Faruk Shuiabu. "Drug Abuse: Kaduna Strategises Against Menace." *Daily Trust*, 20 December 2017. Accessed 31 January 2018. https://www.dailytrust.com.ng/drug-abuse-kaduna-strategises-against-menace.html.

BBC Africa Eye. *Sweet, Sweet Codeine: Nigeria's Cough Syrup Crisis*, directed by Charlie Northcutt, 2018. Accessed 21 February 2020. https://www.youtube.com/watch?v=-I_Lche2otU.

Chang, Eileen. *Naked Earth*. Hong Kong: Union Press, 1956.

Cowie, Jefferson, and Joseph Heathcott. *Beyond the Ruins: The Meanings of Deindustrialization*. Ithaca: ILR Press, 2003.

Daily Trust. "Fathers' Day: Ganduje Urges Fathers to Fight Drugs." *Daily Trust*, 17 June 2019a. Accessed 18 June 2019. https://www.dailytrust.com.ng/fathers-day-ganduje-urges-fathers-to-fight-drugs-video.html.

Daily Trust. "NSCDC Arrests 3 Suspected Drug Dealers in Kaduna." *Daily Trust*, 24 September 2019b. Accessed 24 September 2019. https://www.dailytrust.com.ng/nscdc-arrests-3-suspected-drug-dealers-in-kaduna.html.

Ighakpe, Daniel. "Need for Vocational Education Training." *Daily Trust*, 3 July 2019. Accessed 5 July 2019. https://www.dailytrust.com.ng/need-for-vocational-education-training.html.

McLean, Katherine. "'There's Nothing Here': Deindustrialization as Risk Environment for Overdose." *International Journal of Drug Policy* 29 (2016): 19–26.

Minchin, Timothy. *Empty Mills: The Fight Against Imports and the Decline of the U.S. Textile Industry*. Lanham, MD: Rowman & Littlefield Publishers Inc, 2013.

Muhammad, Ibraheem Hamza. "How I Reformed Over 1000 Drug Addicts in Kaduna—Malam Nigga." *Daily Trust*, 4 January 2015. Accessed 4 January 2015. https://www

.dailytrust.com.ng/how-i-reformed-over-1000-drug-addicts-in Kaduna-malam-nigga.html.

Muhammad, Bala. "Drugs: Arewa Must Defend Itself!" *Daily Trust*, 7 April 2018. Accessed 7 April 2018. www.dailytrust.com.ng/drugs-arewa-must-defend-itself-3.html.

Muhammad, Rakiya. "7,296 Youths Empowered in Sokoto." *Daily Trust*, 29 January 2020, 27.

Oni, O., A. Erinfolami, A. Olagunju, and O. Ogunnubi. "Pattern of Comorbidity, Problem Among Drug Users Undergoing Inpatient Rehabilitation at a Tertiary Hospital in Nigeria." *Annals of Medical & Health Sciences Research* 7 (2017): 173–179.

Walley, Christine. *Exit Zero: Family and Class in Postindustrial Chicago*. Chicago, IL: University of Chicago Press, 2013.

Yaba, Mohammed Ibrahim. "Another Kaduna Rehab Centre Busted." *Daily Trust*, 20 October 2019. Accessed 20 October 2019. https://www.dailytrust.com.ng/another-kaduna-rehab-centre-bursted.html.

Conclusion
Death, deindustrialization, and time

"We felt that society was dragging anchor and in danger of going adrift. Whether it would drift nobody could say, but all feared the rocks."
Edward Bellamy, *Looking Backward, 2000–1887*

This volume focuses on the consequences of deindustrialization on the lives of former factory workers at the Kaduna Textile Ltd (KTL) mill in the Kakuri area of Kaduna and the "work of the dead" in ameliorating these changes. As such it addresses the question, "How is deindustrialization experienced differently by people in varied places, times, and circumstances?" (Cowie and Heathcott 2003: 5). As many of the workers at KTL came from rural towns and villages to the south of the city of Kaduna, their experience reflects many changes: from rural to urban living, from agricultural to industrial labor, and to new conceptions of time and work. Their experience has been complicated by the failure of the government to pay negotiated remittances owed to KTL workers following the company's closure, which was not the case for most other Kaduna textile mills. Consequently, KTL workers, as members of the National Union of Textile Garment and Tailoring Workers of Nigeria, sought to pressure the company to release these funds in order to ease the difficulties of finding alternative sources of income and of paying for food and health care as well as supporting their families. As their entitlements were not forthcoming and former workers were dying, the Coalition of Closed Unpaid Textile Workers Association Nigeria was established in 2005 to maintain a list of textile mill workers who had died since KTL's closing. Fifteen years later, their remittances have still not been paid and the list of the dead has grown as more have died and been buried in family compounds in their home villages as well as in family houses or cemeteries in Kaduna. Nor has textile manufacturing at the Kaduna Textiles Ltd mill been revived.

Several writers, both within Nigeria and abroad, have noted the difficulties of operating industrial textile mills where a tradition of large-scale manufacturing is hardlly over 50 years old. Facilities and trained personnel for the manufacture of new spare parts do not exist, they must be imported. This situation is due, in part, to poor government planning but also due to more pressing needs in terms of health and education. Furthermore, as Kaduna was only formally established as the capital of the Protectorate of Northern Nigeria in 1917, the provision of electricity only came sometime later. Presently, with growing demand, a deteriorating infrastructure, and a failing privatization scheme, electricity is irregularly available (Sunday 2019). Thus, countries in Europe, the Americas, and Asia have had an advantage in this regard. Even African countries, such as Ghana, where the provision of a steady supply of electricity is in place, have had difficulties competing with lower-priced Chinese textile imports, which are produced with the latest equipment and with various efficiencies of scale and manufacture.[1]

Some scholars have argued that the fragility of Nigerian industries was undermined by the sort of neoliberal reforms that the Structural Adjustment Program represents (Akinrinade and Ogen 2008).[2] More recent trade agreements, such as the ending of World Trade Organization Multifibre Arrangement in 1994 and the implementation of GATT rules in 2005 which lifted trade restrictions on global textile exports and imports, have also affected Nigerian textile production.[3] In a way, textile manufacturing and distribution practices in Nigeria have come full circle, approaching the situation in the early 1950s when Nigerians obtained their manufactured textiles from England (and to a lesser extent, from France and Japan) and when European agents working for foreign marketing firms distributed textiles to Nigerian traders. With the decline of Kaduna textile manufacturing, imported textiles once again dominate the market, although they are from China, not England. However, before the deindustrialization of the Kaduna textile industry took place, a particular history of industrialization occurred.

A period of transition

> The attempt to provide simple models for one single, supposedly-neutral, technologically-determined, process known as "industrialization"…is also suspect…[For] there has never been any single type of "the transition". The stress of the transition falls upon the whole culture: resistance to change and assent to change arise from the whole culture. And this culture includes the systems of power, property-relations, religious institutions, etc., inattention to which merely flattens phenomena and trivializes analysis…What we are examining here are not only changes in manufacturing technique which demand greater synchronization of labour and a greater exactitude in time-routines in *any* society; but also these changes as they were lived through in the society of nascent industrial capitalism.
>
> (Thompson 1967: 80).

KTL workers and their families have lived through many changes in their lives associated with the industrialization of Kaduna, beginning in the late 1950s. Many moved to Kaduna from rural villages to the south of the city. They became accustomed to particular time regimens, to new sources and types of food, and to new social organizations—such as the National Union of Textile Garment and Tailoring Workers of Nigeria and ethnic associations. Despite these processes of urbanization, many returned to their village homes for family affairs and ultimately for burial. Yet what Thompson has noted regarding the sociocultural specificities of industrialization is also relevant to the process of deindustrialization, which began in Kaduna in the early 21st century. While some former KTL workers and some KTL widows have returned to farming on the outskirts of Kaduna, this modified version of urban-rural migration has little appeal to many of their children who were born and raised in Kaduna. For as Orwell (1937 [1958]: 200) has observed, "No human being ever wants to do anything in a more cumbrous way than is necessary." Buying a variety of foodstuff from the market with income from a salaried job is the preference of these children, not the slowness and tedium of farm work.

Yet it is important to realize that while the challenges faced during such transitional periods may be different, they are not new, as Bellamy (1887 [1951]: 36) noted more than a hundred years ago:

> You must, at least, have realized that the widespread industrial and social troubles, and the underlying dissatisfaction of all classes with the inequalities of society, and the general misery of mankind, were portents of great changes of some sort.

In the novel, *Looking Backward*, Bellamy describes a utopian society where these "great changes" included the ending of private ownership, government provision of food to the needy, and where the problem of socioeconomic inequality has been addressed.[4] Precisely how these "great changes of some sort" will play out with respect to the textile industry in northern Nigeria is unclear, for it is not private ownership, but government ownership by the 19 Northern Nigerian states that has contributed to the ongoing problems of former KTL workers, widows, and their children.

Establishing small-to-medium scale industries

Yet aside from the uncertain possibilities of reviving textile manufacturing at Kaduna Textiles Ltd, there have been numerous discussions of the possibility of renovating the site to include several related medium-sized textile operations such as the manufacture of military and workers' uniforms.[5] Indeed, in Kano, some medium-sized textile businesses have been able to continue manufacturing, as Sa'idu Adhama, the owner of Adhama Textiles, which has been in operation since 1979, explains:

> Textile industry, the best we can do as far as I learned in the 70s, was upper medium [size operations]. Anything above upper medium had [a limited] lifespan…Industries—in the northern part of the country, some of these units can operate with solar, you don't have to the national grid to operate

the sewing department, you don't have to the national grid to operate the printing department, you don't have to the national grid to give you your light…In small to medium industries, you can operate with solar. So, you see, the issue of electricity is 75% taken care of.

(Interview: 27 January 2020, Kano)[6]

Aside from the manufacture of textiles, Adhama mentioned other small to medium-sized businesses, such as soap and sanitary napkin manufacturing, that could be profitably run in Kano, were the initial capital and government administrative support available.

In addition to the promotion of small to medium-sized enterprises (SMEs), the Nigerian and several state governments as well as private industrial firms have been actively involved in job-training programs. For example, the Dangote Group collaborated with the Kano State Government to build the Aliko Dangote Ultra Modern Skills Acquisition Centre just south of Kano. One area of training will focus on cement use and construction (Ibrahim 2019). Other programs, such as the National Directorate of Employment program in Zamfara State, will train over 400 unemployed young people in the state in tailoring, knitting, confectionary, GSM repairs, and computer use (Umar 2020). Training in the repair of GSM [cell phones] and use of computers is particularly appropriate as another aspect of this transitional era is the dominance of digital technology. Indeed, computer literacy is one of the programs offered by vocational training programs in several northern Nigerian states. For the children of KTL workers who can afford digital phones and are computer-literate are more likely to pursue this line of work, even if they may not receive a regular salary. Other types of training include tailoring, hair-dressing, and barbering, while work in the informal economy, such as drivers and food-sellers, has continued.

In addition, the Nigerian government's programs for agricultural training and produce processing have also provided opportunities for some, despite the disinterest in farming expressed by many KTL workers' children. For example, the government's promotion of rice farming (and the closure of borders for rice imports from neighboring countries) has led to a surge in rice production and processing, as may be seen in many small rice mills in Kura, in Kano State (Adebayo and Al-Kassim 2015). There, young people who have left their family farms have returned to reclaim their patrimony in order to participate in this thriving rice economy. As the chairman of the Rice Producers Association of Kura explained, such support for agricultural production has social as well as economic benefits:

> If government can assist farmers, a lot of people will have means of sustenance for their families and we will have less street urchins causing havoc across the states, because everyone will have a legitimate business to do. Poverty and ignorance are the two major causes of most of the problems in this country. If people are learned in their respective fields and have

capital, no matter how little, to run their businesses, they would be unwilling to be involved in violence.

(Adebayo and Al-Kassim 2015)

Most recently, the Central Bank of Nigeria has announced a program to provide financial support for small-scale farmers throughout Nigeria and "apart from funding, the bank will also provide the farmers with high yielding seedlings and extension services to ensure that they succeed" (Owuamanam 2020). Similarly, in Kaduna, the ground-breaking ceremony for the Tomato Jos Farming and Processing business in the Igabi Local Government Area (just east of Kaduna) represents the partnership of government and private citizens, in this case between the Kaduna State Government and private firms. According to the company's general manager: "The current employment of the company is about 2,000 people and they are mainly sourced from the surrounding communities, adding that 'once [the] processing plant is completed, more than 5,000 people will be employed'" (*Daily Trust* 2020: 22).[7] Plans for expanding ginger cultivation in southern Kaduna State for export have also been reported (*Daily Trust* 2019a).

There is a difference, however, between planning projects and their actual implementation and completion. For example, one plan discussed for reviving the Kaduna Textile Ltd mill in Kaduna, based on an assessment made by the Swiss consulting firm, GHERZI, in 2016, exemplifies such "development on paper." To date, nothing has been done to follow up on the firm's recommendation of renovating a portion of the mill for the manufacture of polypropylene bags at the KTL site (GHERZI 2016b).[8] Yet the discussion of the need to support medium-sized industries that can more efficiently produce jute bags and polypropylene bags as well as textiles and clothing is an important first step. Furthermore, if these plans move forward, they will constitute a new era of textile production in northern Nigeria. For when considering textile manufacturing in northern Nigeria in the early 21st century, factories in Kaduna, such as the Chellco Textile Industries Ltd—a blanket factory in Kaduna (Bashir 2013)—and the Adhama Textiles factory in Kano, that continue manufacturing are smaller and more specialized operations.

The digitization of textile-production processes has also contributed to this downsizing and specialization of textile production. Indeed, smaller operations that are attuned to local demand may be the way that textile manufacturing in Nigeria will continue. For with the liberalization of imported textiles, Chinese textile companies and trading firms with overseas offices in Kano and Lagos now distribute to Nigerian wholesale brokers who sell textiles to Nigerian traders. Perhaps new efforts to revitalize Kaduna textile manufacturing with small to medium manufacturing firms will succeed, following the past example of the origin of Kaduna Textiles Ltd, which represented the collaboration of Nigerian political leaders, government agencies, and foreign manufacturing partners (Maiwada and Renne 2013). Perhaps political leaders, such as Ahmadu Bello, will emerge who will bring about a new era of small to medium textile manufacturing in Kaduna.[9]

Revitalization of cotton farming

While there have been numerous studies of the textile industry in Nigeria and recommendations for its revival,[10] one related initiative is being implemented by the federal government. This program involves the introduction of two varieties of high-yielding genetically-modified BT cotton and the distribution of hybrid cotton seed to farmers (Sa'idu 2018). In late 2019, Mr. Anibe Achimugu, the national president of the National Cotton Association of Nigeria, observed that "We are praying that farmers would be encouraged with the yield you can see; and of course, the quality of the cotton would encourage the textile industry, the spinners, even the ginners, to be able to sustain the businesses" (Daily Trust 2019b). The availability of locally grown cotton for the remaining textile mills in the country will perhaps encourage the renovation of portions of older mills in Kaduna such as KTL and UNTL (Renne 2019). This situation raises the question of whether textile production for domestic markets by national textile industries using local labor and raw materials is a worthy social as well as an economic goal.

Local philanthropy and personal acts of kindness

Nigerian newspapers regularly carry stories about wealthy patrons and astute politicians who provide financial support and food aid to those who have experienced various sorts of disasters. For example, on 7 February 2020, a fire at the Government Girls' Secondary School—Kawo in Kaduna destroyed dormitory buildings, leaving students and some staff without clothing, bedding, or books. Senator Uba Sani immediately donated one million naira to them to enable them to carry on with their studies and teaching (Ahmadu-Suka 2020).

Yet while there have been several stories about NGOs and groups which have provided food and clothing to widows, such as the Nigerian Army Officers Wives Association, which donated "rice, cooking oil, spaghetti and [cloth] wrappers" to widows throughout Nigeria (Hunkuyi 2020), none of the KTL widows interviewed had received aid from such groups. Rather, many Christian widows mentioned the distribution of foodstuff (e.g., rice, corn, and Maggi bouillon cubes) by their churches during the Christmas season. However, in some Kaduna neighborhoods where several widows live, individual women have taken responsibility for looking out for their neighbors in need, as Hassana Sylvester explained:

> There was one woman who helped widows in our area, Maraba Rido. She was living in the neighborhood and was working for the government during Governor Yakowa's time. She brought rice and distributed it to widows—it was her own initiative, not government—she was a widow herself. But two years ago, she moved to another area so she's not distributing food again.
>
> (Interview: 15 January 2020, Kaduna)[11]

In another case, a former KTL supervisor, Haruna Joshua, witnessed the sort of individual generosity that sometimes occurs:

> I saw an old man—he was KTL staff—last year at the First Bank. He was inside the bank and was crying. So I asked him why he was crying. He said that he had a loan, that he couldn't pay the loan to the bank and now the loan has multiplied two times. So now they already had buyers for his house. They called him to bring his papers, that he will have to sell the house the following day.
>
> Then one very large young man who was standing behind me said to me, "I don't hear English but what is this man saying?" I explained to him. So he said, "Let's go to the manager." So myself, the owner of the house, and that young man went and he asked the manager, "The loan—how much is the money?" "N1.2 million," the manager said. That young man paid the amount.
>
> So you see? God is working, He used me. I didn't ask that young man and he didn't pay me anything! If I had known I would have cried. Maybe he would have likely given something to me! So, I came out empty. On the way out, they gave the old man his papers. So you see, if depends on God only.
>
> (Interview: 10 May 2018, Kaduna)

These examples of individual generosity, along with the giving of food and clothing to the needy by wealthy individuals and political leaders, are commendable. However, without regular government programs that provide food for the unemployed and destitute, their actions cannot stop the flood of hunger and food poverty experienced by many in northern Nigeria. And of course, the payment by state-owned companies such as Kaduna Textiles Ltd of agreed-upon benefits such as worker remittances after factory closures, is another aspect of government responsibility.

Deindustrialization and poverty, corruption, and mortality

The closure of the Kaduna Textile Ltd mill and many other textile mills in Nigeria is related to the decline of textile manufacturing in the UK and in the US. What appears to be happening in Nigeria is being experienced in various ways elsewhere in the world, although within a particular historical and cultural context. This situation raises the larger global issue of mill closures and deindustrialization more generally (Freeman 2018; Minchin 2013). For as Walley (2013) has discussed, mill closures—be they steel mills or textile mills—have had a profound effect on unemployed workers and their families. "Deindustrialization is a process, a historical transformation that marks not just a quantitative and qualitative change in employment, but a fundamental change in the social fabric on a par with industrialization itself" (Cowie and Heathcott 2003: 6).

In Nigeria, some continue to speak of the importance of industrializing the country in order to bring it into the realm of modern, developed economies. For example, Haraguchi et al. (2017: 293) have argued that despite "premature deindustrialization" in many developing countries, the manufacturing sector in some countries, such as China, has supported the country's economic development for the period from 1970 to 1990 (Haraguchi et al. 2017: 306-307). Yet it was precisely the upsurge in Chinese textile manufacturing and exports during this period that contributed to the decline in textile manufacturing in Nigeria. While there are discussions to involve Chinese companies in textile manufacturing in Nigeria, they have yet to be implemented.[12] However, other forms of industrial production have continued or have commenced, such as the production of tomato-based goods in Nigeria by the Jos Tomato Jos Farming and Processing business (*Daily Trust* 2020). But rather than pursuing the construction or revival of huge manufacturing plants, new forms of production need to be imagined and pursued. For as Freeman (2018: xv) has noted:

> Understanding the history of giant factories can help us to think about what kind of future we want...Today, as we may well be witnessing the historic apogee of the giant factory, economic and ecological conditions suggest that we need to rethink the meaning of modernity and whether or not it should continue to be equated with ever more material production in vast, hierarchically organized industrial facilities of the kind that were the bane and the glory of the past.

Thus, many Northern Nigerian business leaders, such as Sa'idu Adhama see industrial development in the medium-sized industries as the way forward. This position does not deny the benefits of industrialization—such as the support for local value chains and employment for countries such as Nigeria—but rather considers the importance of more efficient and environmentally sound manufacturing practices.

Indeed, Orwell (1937 [1958]: 204), in his discussion of textile manufacturing in the UK, noted the allure of mechanization: "Wherever you look you will see some slick machine-made article triumphing over the old-fashioned article." Yet as Livingston (2019) has observed in her discussion of "self-devouring growth," such mechanization can entail detrimental and destructive consequences for families and society. For example, the expanded building of roads for the use of cars and trucks which distribute manufactured goods throughout the country has also contributed to many road-related deaths and injuries.[13] Several KTL widows have experienced the consequences of road accidents which have affected their husbands or children. Most recently, Alisabatu Babu mourned for her son, who was killed in a motor accident on his way back to Kaduna from Zaria:

> I have a problem because my son who died recently, they buried him close to my husband's grave in our house in Kaduna. Seeing his grave makes

me cry all the time. I told them not to bury him in the house but they refused. Because he was the one child—I spent all my money to educate him, the other children didn't go to school. He was the only one who was educated and he had just received his degree from the Pastor's School in the Wusasa area of Zaria.

(Interview: 22 January 2020, Kaduna)

Yet one cannot expect Nigerians to deny themselves the use of cars when those in the West are hardly divesting themselves of travelling by road in cars and buses or of using roads to transport locally manufactured and imported products. While efforts are being made to develop more extensive public transport and encourage the use of bicycles in cities in the West, for long distance travel and trade, the use of cars and trucks on large interstate highways is still preferred by many.

Poverty and roads

Hence it is not surprising that many Nigerian federal and state political leaders are using development funds to build roads. Thus, in early 2020, when the US government announced the return of 308 million dollars (US) to Nigeria, stolen money which had been placed in overseas accounts by the former president of Nigeria, Sani Abacha, the Buhari administration announced that the funds would be used in "expediting the construction of the three major infrastructure projects across Nigeria—namely Lagos–Ibadan expressway, Abuja–Kano expressway and the second Niger bridge" (Odeyemi 2020).[14] Yet as Sen (1998) and others have suggested, presuming that these funds can be genuinely monitored, they might be better spent on a national government program to provide food subsidies for widows and children as well as primary health care. In addition, primary and secondary education for students throughout the country will enable them to take up new forms of employment, such as information and communication technology and electrical installation (Muhammad 2020). Dr. Akinwumi Adesina, the president of the African Development Bank, similarly has observed that "growth without food for the poor will worsen the poverty level on the continent," while education for young people is also critically important: "Only by developing our workforce will we make a dent in poverty, close the income gap between rich and poor, and adopt new technologies to create jobs in knowledge-intensive sectors" (Hanan Morsy, ABD, cited by Akinmutimi 2020). For while the expansion of railroad transportation is environmentally sound, train fares are beyond the reach of many who must travel by road. Such roads, no matter how well-paved, are frequented by robbers and kidnappers in many parts of the country, which reflects the consequences of unemployment and desperate poverty. Indeed, the social problems associated with unemployment and poverty have been frequently discussed in Nigeria, in part, as they have been linked with continuing insecurity—robbery and kidnapping—in many parts of the country (Oke 2020).

Corruption and insecurity

One might also add that this insecurity is an outcome of corruption on several levels. On the local level, kidnappers may bribe police not to pursue investigations of particular cases. Police officers may also be directly involved in such incidents.[15] At the state and national levels, several politicians and business people have been convicted of the misuse of government funds, which end up in their own bank accounts or as palatial houses (Oxfam 2017).[16] And, as the Country Representative for the MacArthur Foundation, Dr. Kole Shettima, has noted: "Nigerian politicians wasted over N60 trillion budgeted for the country's development from 1999 to 2018" (Jimoh 2020). Some of these development funds also end up in overseas bank accounts, as was the case with the enormous sums of money held in banks in Switzerland, France, the UK, the Isle of Jersey, and the US (Azu 2019). Yet even when these funds have been returned to the Nigerian government, they may be embezzled again, thus repeating the cycle of corruption.[17] It is not surprising then that some see this form of indirect violence as legitimating their own, more overtly violent means, of acquiring resources.[18] How these types of theft can be stopped is a major challenge. But if the country is to move forward, a means must be found to keep political corruption in check if the problems of insecurity are to be solved.[19]

Urbanization and mortality

This study also provides clarification as to why high rates of mortality exist in urban areas in many parts of sub-Saharan Africa, such as Nigeria, associated with industrialization as the study of Demographic Health Survey data from 18 sub-Saharan African countries suggests. While the study by Günther and Harttgen (2012) does not include Nigeria, the situation they document suggests the conditions in Kaduna, as they have noted:

> High rates of urbanization combined with limited progress in some developing countries have led to a growing concern deteriorating health conditions and increasing mortality rates in urban areas. Some observers see a pattern that may repeat the nineteenth-century of today's industrialized countries…where rapid and unplanned urban high population densities and insufficient environmental and health in combination with large wealth inequalities, led to an "urban penalty".
>
> (Günther and Harttgen 2012: 469)

According to their analysis:

> On average, we find adult mortality rates of 14.1 percent in urban areas and 12.4 percent in rural areas. This means that for adults the negative impact of an urban disease environment overshadows the positive effects

of the usually higher material well-being and superior health infrastructure available in urban areas.

(Günther and Harttgen 2012: 470)

While Kaduna may indeed have a better health infrastructure than the villages from which many KTL workers and their widows came, once the mill closed, they no longer had access to the KTL clinic nor the means for prolonged hospital stays in Kaduna. This situation may be seen in the tragic consequences experienced by the family of James Agene (Figure C.1).

James Agene died on 15 August 2009, almost seven years after KTL closed; his name is number 78 on the Coalition of Closed Unpaid Textile Workers Association Nigeria list. I interviewed his wife, Josephine James, on 30 April 2018, outside her rooms in the Television area of Kaduna.[20] Her description of her husband's illness before he died reflects the family's impoverished state and their difficulties in obtaining health care in Kaduna once the KTL had closed:

> The sickness he developed was hypertension, so we took him to the hospital. But before that, we gave him traditional medicine but it didn't work. So, we took him to Nasarawa Hospital; the day we took him to the hospital was the day he died. Before we thought it was typhoid but we didn't have money for the medicine. I remember my husband when he was sick, I was sympathizing with him because we didn't have money to treat him.

During the interview, Josephine James was seated on a long bench, in the center of the house courtyard, where several young people had gathered. Two of her sons were with her, including her eldest son, Ezekiel Levinus (Figure C.2), who was disabled.

The following year, I was told that Josephine James had died and had been buried, as was her husband, in the Television Cemetery (Figure C.3). They were not taken to their home village in southern Kaduna State due to a lack

Figure C.1 Photograph of the former KTL worker, James Agene, who died in August 2009, Kaduna (Photograph of photograph by E.P. Renne).

146 Conclusion

Figure C.2 Ezekiel Levinus was interviewed on 17 July 2019. He died in February 2020, a second generation of KTI deaths, 17 July 2019, Kaduna (Photograph by E.P. Renne).

Figure C.3 Television Cemetery, where James Agene and members of his family are buried, 9 May 2018, Kaduna (Photograph by E.P. Renne).

of funds; rather they were buried in a large public cemetery in Kaduna—as earlier colonial officials would have approved. Later, in July 2019, I interviewed her eldest son, Ezekiel, who explained his situation after the death of his mother:

> My mother's relatives took us back to our hometown, but I ran away back to Kaduna. Because I can't farm, I'm not in good health. Because I was born in Kaduna and lived in Kaduna, that is the reason I want to stay here.
> (Interview: 17 July 2019, Kaduna)

However, with neither family support nor the physical capacity or educational training to find work in Kaduna, Ezekiel was suffering: "I'm not schooling and I don't even have enough clothes. Even food, unless somebody helps us...and some of my friends would run away when they see me, because they think I will ask them for something."

Ezekiel Levinus died in February 2020. I was told that his condition had worsened, mainly due to lack of food. He was also buried in Television Cemetery. For Ezekiel, the modicum of assistance from his family required that he remain in his mother's home village, something that he was unwilling to do. Yet his younger brother, Collin, did return there and supported himself making *fanke* (a small pancake-like cake). Thus, continued family connections may be maintained by some, but not all, KTL children. Their return to their parents' homes villages may be reinforced by the presence of the graves of their grandparents, and for some, the graves of their parents, underscoring the continuing importance of the work of the dead in Nigeria.

Conclusion

This volume represents a memorial for the men who worked at KTL who have died since the closing of the Kaduna Textiles Ltd mill without being paid their entitlements, many of whom had their names included on the list compiled by the Coalition of Closed Unpaid Textile Workers Association Nigeria. This listing of names, along with their graves, funeral programs, and death certificates constitute "the work of the dead" in redressing some of the failures of their government and their society. As one of the widows of these men described their continued meetings with the Coalition:

> We are coming together to talk about the ways we can get our husbands' remittances in order to get something to help ourselves and our children. But here in Nigeria, they make us feel like we are not part of Nigeria, we have no dignity, we have no respect.
> (Interview: Fatu Tom, 22 January 2020, Kaduna)

Stories such as those told by the widow, Josephine James, and her eldest son, Ezekiel, of their husband and father, James Agene, underscore the disrespect of many wealthy individuals for the impoverished members of their communities. The food and health care which the Agene family lacked are the minimum requirements needed for a decent life. The deaths of many former KTL workers reflect this situation as does the scarcity of paying factory jobs. While there is talk of reviving the textile industry in Kaduna, government funds for improving the power grid and for providing new equipment as well as controlling customs duties on imported textiles are yet to be put in place.

However, those affected by the closing of the Kaduna Textile Ltd mill and the deindustrialization of the Nigerian textile industry are not alone. This situation has occurred in other parts of the world—even in the relatively wealthy

US where the hopes for healthy, educated, and well-fed lives have gone astray.[21] As Walley (2013: 14) has observed, it is important to document the consequences of the decline of industrial production:

> Thinking through these kinds of stories and the challenges to them, from an era in which deindustrialization still seemed unfathomable to an era in which it may seem inevitable, can help us make sense of a past that we need to understand both to comprehend the roots of our country's expanded inequality and to create alternative paths for the future.[22]

The stories of KTL widows and their children underscore the conditions of their shattered lives and reflect the growing disparity in wealth—with ever greater inequality—in Nigeria. Whether this situation may be lessened through the reduction of corruption and whether government programs for widespread food, health care, and education can be implemented remain to be seen.

Nonetheless, many Nigerians are considering the creation of alternative paths to well-being. Through the numerous programs proposed for increasing youth employment—training and support for small and medium enterprises, agricultural programs, and more efficient and environmentally sound smaller-scale industries, the possibilities for a new deindustrialized era are being imagined and may be pursued. For as the sayings often painted on the back of trucks traveling the highways between Kaduna and Kano suggest: "*Lokacin ne*—It's Time."

Notes

1 Rose Skelton (2012), in the article, "Ghana: Motifs for Survival," examines the difficulties of preventing Chinese-manufactured textiles from being sold in Ghana and strategies for protecting Ghanaian textile manufacturing.
2 For a discussion of the failure of structural adjustment programs to limit unofficial transborder trade which also affects industries such as textile manufacturing, see Meagher (2003).
3 See Muhammad (2019) on the consequences of the WTO agreement.
4 While Bellamy's vision of the future referred to the situation in the United States, his aspirations for a more humane and just society has been supported by others—even if such aspirations have not been achieved in the 21st century.
5 The Swiss consulting firm, GHERZI, assessed the possibilities of establishing a garment factory to produce workforce uniforms as part of a revival scheme for the Kaduna Textile Ltd site (GHERZI 2016a). The following year, "In August 2017, the Turkish textile firm SUR entered into an agreement with the [New Nigeria Development Corporation] to renovate the textile manufacturing company, Kaduna Textiles Limited. Initially, the company was to refurbish the mill with updated equipment to produce military uniforms, then it was expected that other garments would also be manufactured…While parties involved planned to move forward on this project, the SUR management's insistence that a large prepaid contract for uniforms from the Ministry of Defence be provided led to the abandonment of the project" (Waziri et al. 2020: 108).
6 The reliance on solar power, however, is not without its own problems. In Kaduna and Anambra states, for example, two rural communities with stand-alone solar projects "still suffer outages over the poor condition of the facilities" (Iloani 2019). Solar equipment

needs regular cleaning and maintenance, something which may have been lacking at these sites.

7   The private firms include Arlan, a Danish mill processing company, and the Miyetti Allah Cattle Breeders Association. Earlier, in March 2019, the Dangote tomato processing plant began production (Giginya 2019).

8   The report mentions that during Phase I of the project, 14,166 square meters would be required for its operations (GHERZI 2016b), which is a fraction of the size of the KTL complex.

9   It is worth noting that Kaduna Textile Ltd's partner, David Whitehead & Sons, is no longer manufacturing textiles either, as it did in the past. Bernard Laverty and his wife, present co-owners of David Whitehead & Sons, bought the capital of David Whitehead & Sons in 1996 and operate the business from an office in Parbold, Lancashire (Bernard Laverty, Parbold, Lancashire, 27 February 2012, interview by Jaclyn Kline).

10 These include the United Nations Industrial Development Organization (UNIDO) technical report, "Diagnostic Appraisal For Rehabilitation of Kaduna Textiles Ltd" (1988); and the UNIDO/Federal Ministry of Commerce and Industry, Nigeria report, "Update of the Textile and Garment Industry Sector Study-Nigeria" (2009).

11 Another woman, Malama Halima, a divorced woman living in the Makere neighborhood of Kaduna, started an organization known as Ta'alimu for widows and their children as well as for disabled and impoverished people living in Makere. Widows who participate in this organization normally meet on Fridays and she sometimes brings cloth wrappers, as well as rice, corn, salt, and Maggi bouillon cubes for them to distribute. During Ramadan, she brings corn, millet, and sugar.

12 In 2019, the Kaduna State Government signed a Memorandum of Understanding with the Institute of New Structural Economics, Peking University, concerning the revival of the textile industry in Kaduna. However, the difficulties in carrying out plans for the earlier agreement with the Turkish textile manufacturer, SUR, has discouraged other investors.

13 Only 10 days into January 2020, thirty people were reported to have died and 58 were injured in road accidents in Nigeria (Sule and Adeniyi 2020).

14 This money, referred to as "Abacha loot," was amassed in overseas accounts in the US that were frozen by the US government. After negotiating a return of these funds, the US State Department "requires Nigeria to repay any funds lost as a result of any new corruption or fraud" (Olaniyi 2020).

15 For example, Jibrin Ibrahim (2020) was told about a very wealthy man, whose mother was a recent kidnapping victim, who was ordered to bring clean naira bills for ransom money. He obtained clean bills but also alerted banks to look for specific serial numbers. Shortly after his mother was released, officers at one bank called to say that they had two men—a police inspector and a military officer—who had attempted to deposit the bills. The ransom money was returned.

16 In 2018, fifty individuals with assets surpassing N50 million were prohibited by the Nigerian government from traveling abroad "pending the determination of their cases" (Mudashir 2018).

17 Although there is a law which requires the Federal Government to document how the repatriated funds have been spent, no such documentation has been revealed. Hence the Socio-Economic Rights and Accountability Project (SERAP) leaders are demanding that the government provide detailed information on moneys already received and also provide documentation of the spending of the "Abacha loot" (Bamgboye 2020).

18 For example, there have been recurring thefts of textile mill equipment, wiring, and even roofing materials at the KTL mill and other mills in the Kakuri area. In January 2020, a request was made by the acting KTL manager to the military police group known as Operation Yaki (*yaƙi* means war in Hausa) to provide armed personnel to protect the KTL site. An agreement for security was subsequently reached.

19 Since members of the Nigerian legislature are not made to pay taxes, requiring them to pay income tax might be one way of regulating graft—at least to some extent.

20 The older neighborhood known as Television consists of unpaved streets and impoverished housing.
21 Anne Case and Angus Deaton (2020) discuss the related problems of unemployment experienced by working-class whites in the US, who without college degrees, have been relegated to low-paying and insecure service work. The high death rate of among this particular group of Americans, referred to as "deaths of distress" by Case and Deaton, reflects drug use, alcoholism, and suicide.
22 Walley (2013: 168) notes that "what is at stake is not simply particular kinds of jobs—industrial work is not something to romanticize—but whether such jobs can foster a society that pays living wages and that supports families and communities."

References

Adebayo, Ismail, and Murjanatu Al-Kassim. "How We Started Rice Production in Kura." *Daily Trust*, 28 November 2015. Accessed 14 February 2020. https://www.dailytrust.com.ng/how-we-started-rice-production-in-kura.html.

Ahmadu-Suka, Maryam. "Senator Donates Money to College Fire Victims." *Daily Trust*, 13 February 2020. Accessed 19 February 2020. https://www.dailytrust.com.ng/senator-donates-money-to-college-fire-victims.html.

Akinmutimi, Tola. "GDP Growth Without Food Meaningless—Adesina." *Daily Trust*, 4 February 2020, 15.

Akinrinade, Sola, and Olukoya Ogen. "Globalization and De-Industrialization: South-South Neo-Liberalism and the Collapse of the Nigerian Textile Industry." *Global South* 2, no. 2 (2008): 159–170.

Azu, John Chuks. "What We're Doing About Abacha's $300m, by FG." *Daily Trust*, 6 June 2019. Accessed 6 June 2019. https://www.dailytrust.com.ng/what-were-doing-about-abachas-300m-by-fg.html.

Bamgboye, Adelanwa. "SERAP Gives FG 7 Day Ultimatum to Disclose How Recovered Abacha Loot Was Expended Since 1999." *Daily Trust*, 16 February 2020. Accessed 17 February 2020. https://www.dailytrust.com.ng/serap-gives-fg-7-day-ultimatum-to-disclose-how-recovered-abacha-loot-was-expended-since-1999.html.

Bashir, Misbahu. "How We've Controlled Blanket Market for 35 Years—Chellco." *Daily Trust*, 22 December 2013. https://www.dailytrust.com.ng.

Bellamy, Edward. *Looking Backward, 2000–1887*. New York: The Modern Library, 1887 [1951].

Case, Anne, and Angus Deaton. *Deaths of Despair and the Future of Capitalism*. Princeton, NJ: Princeton University Press, 2020.

Cowie, Jefferson, and Joseph Heathcott. *Beyond the Ruins: The Meanings of Deindustrialization*. Ithaca, NY: ILR Press, 2003.

Daily Trust. "Kaduna Government to Export Ginger, Maize." *Daily Trust*, 31 October 2019a. Accessed 31 October 2019. https://www.dailytrust.com.ng/kaduna-government-to-export-ginger-maize.html.

Daily Trust. "Bt Cotton Revolution." *Daily Trust*, 22 December 2019b. Accessed 23 December 2019. https://www.dailytrust.com.ng/bt-cotton-revolution.html.

Daily Trust. "Kaduna Hosts Another Ground Breaking." *Daily Trust*, 27 January 2020, 22.

Freeman, Joshua. *Behemoth: A History of the Factory and the Making of the Modern World*. New York: W. W. Norton & Company, 2018.

GHERZI. *Techno-Economic Feasibility Study to Set Up a Garment Manufacturing Project in Nigeria, for Kaduna Textiles Ltd.* Zurich, Switzerland: GHERZI, 2016a.

GHERZI. *Techno-Economic Feasibility Study to Set Up a PP Tape Woven Sack Manufacturing Project in Nigeria, for Kaduna Textiles Ltd.* Zurich, Switzerland: GHERZI, 2016b.

Giginya, Ibrahim Musa. "Dangote Tomato Begins Production." *Daily Trust*, 7 March 2019. Accessed 19 February 2020. https://www.dailytrust.com.ng/dangote-tomato-begins-production.html.

Günther, Isabel, and Kenneth Harttgen. "Deadly Cities? Spatial Inequalities in Mortality in Sub-Saharan Africa." *Population & Development Review* 38, no. 3 (2012): 469–486.

Haraguchi, N., C. Chin Cheng, and E. Smeets. "The Importance of Manufacturing in Economic Development: Has This Changed?" *World Development* 93 (2017): 293–315.

Hunkuyi, Magali. "Army Wives Association Trains 5000 Women on Entrepreneurship." *Daily Trust*, 7 February 2020. Accessed 7 February 2020. https://www.dailytrust.com.ng/army-wives-association-trains-5000-women-on-entrepreneurship.html.

Ibrahim, Yusha'u. "Dangote, Kano Govt Collaborate on Youth Empowerment." *Daily Trust*, 1 December 2019. https://www.dailytrust.com.ng/dangote-kano-govt-collaborate-on-youth-empowerment.html.

Ibrahim, Jibrin. "Borno and Nigeria's Growing Distance from the President." *Daily Trust*, 14 February 2020, 56.

Iloani, Francis. "Despite N240m Solar Power Grids Communities in Kaduna, 5 Others Suffer Outages." *Daily Trust*, 9 December 2019. Accessed 26 February 2020. https://www.dailytrust.com.ng/despite-n240m-solar-power-grids-communities-in-kaduna-5-others-suffer-outages.html.

Jimoh, Abbas. "Nigeria Wasted N60trn in 17 Years – MacArthur Foundation." *Daily Trust*, 17 January 2020, 19.

Livingston, Julie. *Self-Devouring Growth: A Planetary Parable as Told from Southern Africa.* Durham: Duke University Press, 2019.

Maiwada, Salihu, and Elisha Renne. "The Kaduna Textile Industry and the Decline of Textile Manufacturing in Northern Nigeria, 1955–2010." *Textile History* 44, no. 2 (2013): 171–196.

Meagher, Kate. "A Back Door to Globalisation? Structural Adjustment, Globalisation & Transborder Trade in West Africa." *Review of African Political Economy* 30, no. 95 (2003): 57–75.

Minchin, Timothy. *Empty Mills: The Fight Against Imports and the Decline of the U.S. Textile Industry.* Lanham, MD: Rowman & Littlefield Publishers Inc, 2013.

Mudashir, Ismail. "Corruption: FG bans 50 High Profile Persons from Traveling." *Daily Trust*, 13 October 2018. Accessed 14 October 2018. www.dailytrust.com.ng.

Muhammad, Murtala. "Trade Liberalisation and Deindustrialization of the Textile Industry in Nigeria (1997–2000)." *Journal of Advances in Social Science & Humanities* 5, no. 6 (2019): 834–856.

Muhammad, Rakiya. "7,296 Youths Empowered in Sokoto." *Daily Trust*, 29 January 2020. Accessed 29 January 2020. https://www.dailytrust.com.ng/7296-youths-empowered-in-sokoto.html.

Odeyemi, Joshua. "US, Nigeria Sign Agreement on Abacha Loot Return." *Daily Trust*, 4 February 2020. Accessed 4 February 2020. https://www.dailytrust.com.ng/us-nigeria-sign-agreement-on-abacha-loot-return.html.

Oke, Jeremiah. "UI Professor Identifies Cause of Prevailing Insecurity." *Daily Trust*, 6 February 2020, 21.

Olaniyi, Muldeen. "US to Nigeria: You'll Repay Abacha Loot If Re-Stolen." *Daily Trust*, 5 February 2020, 6.

Orwell, George. *The Road to Wigan Pier*. New York: Houghton-Mifflin Harcourt, 1937 [1958].

Owuamanam, Jude. "CBN to Create 10 Million Jobs in 5 Years." *Daily Trust*, 21 February 2020. Accessed 22 February 2020. https://www.dailytrust.com.ng/cbn-to-create-10-million-jobs-in-5-years.html.

Oxfam International. *Inequality in Nigeria: Exploring the Drivers*. Oxford: Oxfam, 2017.

Renne, Elisha. "United Nigerian Textiles Limited and Chinese-Nigeria Textile Manufacturing Collaboration in Kaduna, Nigeria." *Africa* 89, no. 4 (2019): 696–717.

Sa'idu, Isa. "Our GMO Cotton Is Targeting Textile Revival – IAR." *Daily Trust*, 19 August 2018. Accessed 19 August 2018. www.dailytrust.com.ng.

Sen, Amartya. "Mortality as an Indicator of Economic Success or Failure." *Economic Journal* 108, no. 446 (1998): 1–25.

Skelton, Rose. "Ghana: Motifs for Survival." *The Africa Report*, 3 January 2012. Accessed 26 February 2020. https://www.theafricareport.com/7855/ghana-motifs-for-survival/.

Sule, Daniel, and Taiwo Adeniyi. "Tragic Deaths, Killings, Abductions Foul Early 2020." *Daily Trust*, 11 January 2020, 6.

Sunday, Simon Echewofun. "Power Supply Still Poor Operations Unstable 6 Years After Privatization." *Daily Trust*, 1 November 2019. Accessed 1 November 2019. https://www.dailytrust.com.ng/power-supply-still-poor-operations-unstable-6-years-after-privatisation.html.

Thompson, E.P. "Time, Work-Discipline, and Industrial Capitalism." *Past & Present* 36, no. 1 (1967): 56–97.

Umar, Shehu. "NDE Trains 420 Zamfara Youths on Various Trades." *Daily Trust*, 29 January 2020. Accessed 30 January 2020. https://www.dailytrust.com.ng/nde-trains-420-zamfara-youths-on-various-trades.html.

United Nations Industrial Development Organization. *Diagnostic Appraisal for Rehabilitation of Kaduna Textiles Ltd*. Vienna: UNIDO, 1988.

United Nations Industrial Development Organization. *Update of the Textile and Garment Industry Sector Study Nigeria (Prepared by GHERZI)*. Vienna: UNIDO, 2009.

Walley, Christine. *Exit Zero: Family and Class in Postindustrial Chicago*. Chicago, IL: University of Chicago Press, 2013.

Waziri, M., S. Maiwada, and E. Renne. "Kaduna Textile Industry, Trade, and the Coming of Chinese Textiles." In *Textile Ascendancies: Aesthetics, Production, and Trade in Northern Nigeria*, edited by E. Renne, and S. Maiwada, 87–114. Ann Arbor, MI: University of Michigan Press, 2020.

Index

Page numbers in **bold** denote tables, those in *italic* denote figures.

Adhama, Sa'idu 11; Adhama Textiles 137, 139; on small to medium-size industries 137–138, 142; solar power 137–138
Aremu, Issa (General Secretary, NUTGTWN) 11

Bellamy, Edward (*Looking Backward*) 1, 137, 148n4
Bello, Ahmadu (former Premier of the Northern Region, Nigeria): assassination of 43; establishment of Ahmadu Bello University, Zaria 44; meetings with David Whitehead & Sons personnel 39; promotion of industrialization in Northern Nigeria 39, 44, 54, 139; *see also* David Whitehead & Sons
Births, Deaths and Burial Ordinance 14n2
British colonial policy: anti-manufacturing policy 39, 41; rail service 20, 21, 30; raw cotton exports 21, 33n4, 39; road-building 20, 31; support of British trading firms 39–41, 61; textile imports 21; *see also* cemeteries
British colonial rule in Kaduna: administrative offices 21; mercantile business firms 21, 41; military barracks 21; segregated residential areas 19, 23, 31; support for textile manufacturing in Kaduna 39
British textile mill closures in UK 54–55, 56n11, 141; imported textiles 54; insufficient labor 54; reduced production capacity 54; social services for unemployed workers 55
Buhari, Muhammadu, President of Nigeria 30; administration 143
burial **77**; deceased Kaduna Textiles Ltd workers 3, 26, 71, 74–90, 91n5, 107, 110, 111, 114, 137; expenses 26, 79, 82, 87; house in hometown 5, 26, 74–81, 89; house in Kaduna 5, 26, 74, 79; and modernity 82–83, 86, 88, 90, 91n5; social hierarchy 58, 79, 86–88; *see also* cemeteries; Christian funerals; Muslim funerals
byssinosis ("brown lung" disease) 60, 71n3; associated with cotton textile manufacturing 60, 64; attributed to breathing cotton dust 64, 65; lack of KTL diagnostic facilities 64; use of masks 64–65; symptoms 64

cemeteries: Christian 20, 33n1, 34n10; and colonial "sanitation syndrome" 26; establishment in Kaduna 20; in Ibadan and Lagos 87–88; and hyenas 27; and medical officer of health-Kaduna 27; Muslim 20, 27; planning 27; "pocket handkerchief" burial sites 27; "the public health argument" 26, 34n8; regulations and upkeep 26–27
cemeteries, Kaduna 74; African Christian Cemetery *28*; Anguwan Faima Cemetery 114; Anguwan Romi 28; Anguwan Sule Cemetery 86, 112; Barnawa Cemetery 20, *75*, 85, 87, 109; Kaduna Civil Cemetery 20, 26; Sabon Gari Cemetery 27; Television Cemetery 28, 85, 114, 145, *146*, 147; Tudun Wada Cemetery 20, 85
Central Bank of Nigeria 12; cotton-growing loans 12, 139; currency exchange restrictions for textile importers 12; seedlings and extension services 139
Chellco Textile Industries Ltd—Kaduna 139

154 *Index*

children of deceased Kaduna Textiles Ltd workers: assisting mothers 5, 99, 103, 120, 128; cash support for mothers 99, 115, 128; cemetery burial 28, 79, 86, 87, 109, 112, 114; "cumulative disadvantage" 14n4, 99; death 109, 112, 113, 114, 142, *146*–147; disrupted education 5, 94, 97, 99–103, 114–115, 130; drug use 3, 14n5, 103, 116, 123–128, 130; farming 95, 97, 115, 119; hometown village burial 109, 113, 114; hopes for revival of textile industry 102, 122, 132; insufficient food 92–94, 115; married 3, 107, 109, 111, 112, 113, 114, 115, 119, 120, 127; separation from mothers 110; "sibling chain of assistance" 5, 55n3, 119, 131;
stories 148
children of deceased Kaduna Textiles Ltd workers, employment 3, 107; computer, video 122, 138; construction work 107, 128; driver 103, 126, 138; farming 112, 119, 120, 122, 128; food sales 99, 119, 128, 138, 147; gardener 120; hair stylist 114, 138; housework 103, 120, 128; laborer 120; lawyer 120; mechanic 118, 120; office work 120; pastor 120; printer 120; security 103, 120; tailoring 138; teacher 120
children of deceased Kaduna Textiles Ltd workers, memories of deceased fathers: clothing 103, 117; generosity 116; grave site 116; hard work 119; importance of education 118; land plot 117; payment of exam fees 118
children of deceased Kaduna Textiles Ltd workers, preference for Kaduna 31, 71, 121, 131, 133; birthplace 53, 120, 122; family's rural–urban migration 122, 131; job opportunities 121; reduced rural extended family connections 53, 89, 122, 147; urban identity 122
children of deceased Kaduna Textiles Ltd workers, situation of: blind 107; sickness 109, 112, 113; unemployed 98, 103, 110, 113, 123
Chinese textile imports 14n10, 136, 139, 142, 148n1; *see also* Kaduna Textiles Ltd mill, reasons for closure
Christian funerals: burial 4, 78, 80–81, 82, 88, 107, 110, 111, 114; church assistance 75, 79, 80, 83–84, 93, 107, 110, 112–114; church service 78–79, 82, 110, 111, 114; ethnic association assistance 78–80, 84, 93, 113–114; family members wearing white *84*; food 78, 79, 83, 91n2, 112, 114; pastor to house 81, 107, 110; prayers 81, 88–90, 107, 110, 113; program, posters 1, 5, 75, 80, 82, *83*, 90, 111, 147; women's association assistance 26, 78–79, 83, 84, 112, 113; wake-keeping 78, 81
Christianity 75, 79, 81–83 88, 107, 110, 111, 114
Coalition of Closed Unpaid Textile Workers Association Nigeria 2–3; coffin 84–85; demonstrations 8, 84–85, 102; establishment 2, 8, 135; failure by government to pay dismissed worker remittances 3, 8; lists of deceased dismissed textile workers, Kaduna 2, 6, 8, 13, 58, 60, 101, 130, 145; objectives 3, 8–9, 132; "work of the dead" 2, 3, 102, 147; *see also* unpaid Kaduna Textiles Ltd remittances
coffins 12, 75, 78–81, 83, 90; carpenter made 78, 82, 113; KTL contribution 110; purchased near Television garage—Kaduna *81*, *82*, 107
corruption: Abacha embezzlement 52, 56n9, 143, 149n14, 149n17; bribery of police 144, 149n15; illegal imported textiles 10, 147; indirect violence legitimating overt violence 144; misuse of government funds 144; and overseas bank accounts 56n9, 143, 144, 149n14; politicians' use of development funds 56n9, 144; reduction of 148, 149n14, 149n17
cotton farming, revitalization of 12, 140; high-yielding BT cotton seed to farmers 140
"cumulative disadvantage" 14n4, 99, 104n3

David Whitehead & Sons, Ltd 14n4, *28*, 37, 99, 104n3, 149n9; agreement with northern Nigerian officials, Rawtenstall, Lancashire, UK 1955 39; Overseas Liaison Office 39; *see also* Ahmadu Bello
deindustrialization 3; different experiences 135; distinctive histories 54, 102, 116, 129, 136, 145; "premature" 142; process 100–102; and social changes 6, 103, 141
deindustrialization, Kaduna 54, 102; and drug use 116, 123, 130; family response 129–130, 132; hunger 3, 5, 31, 38, 59, 93, 98, 141; increased socioeconomic

Index 155

inequality 13, 32, 100, 103, 130; and Nigerian citizenship 13; postindustrial time 102; poverty 3, 103, 141; of textile manufacturing 137, 148; and unemployment 3, 6, 9, 101, 103; worker mortality 9, 141; *see also* "food poverty"
deindustrialization, US 102, 123, 130; drug use 116, 130; East Chicago steel mill closures 102, 129; North Carolina 102; "Rust Belt" 116; *see also* Pillowtex
Department of Development and Welfare, Textile Training Centres, Nigeria 55n5
"development on paper" 139; GHERZI 2016 report for Kaduna Textiles Ltd 139; polypropylene bag production 139
Dickens, Charles (*Hard Times*) 1
digital technology: computer literacy 138; GSM phones 138; and textile manufacturing 139
documents, deceased KTL mill workers: death certificates 1, 5, 9, 13, 58, 60, 65, 66, 67–70, 90, 147; family photographs 5; funeral programs 1, 5, 90, 147; hospital records 58, 69; ID cards 4, 5, 7, 13, 58, 83; *see also* Coalition of Closed Unpaid Textile Workers Association Nigeria
dress 83, 100, 119; burial 83, 91n6; caps 5, 103; kaftan 92; uniforms 11–12, 14n11, 43, 137, 148n5
drug treatment programs in Kaduna: hospital psychiatric wards 126; remediation centers 126, 132n3; Rigasa Islamic Rehabilitation Centre 132n3; *see also* KADBUSA
drug use in Kaduna 3, 115, 125–126; availability 123; capsules (*kwiya*) 125, 128; cigarettes 125, 126, 132n2; codeine cough syrup 116, 123, 126, 128, 132n1, 132n2; and death 127–128; drug dealers in Kaduna 123; marijuana (*wiwi*) 116, 125–126; mothers' knowledge of 125–128, 132n3; reduced dependence 126–127; rohypnol (sedative) 132n2; and smuggling 123; and theft 126; Tramadol 6, 14n5, 116, 123, 125, 132n2; '*Yar Mayé* (Nigerian film) 132n3
drug use in Kaduna, reasons for: lack of character 124; lack of vocational education 99, 124; loss of father 124; "peace of mind" 125, 126; poverty 125; unemployment 71, 116

education, higher in Kaduna: and employment 124, 131; Kaduna Polytechnic 10, 29, 44, 46, 107; Kaduna State University 29, 114
education, Islamic 44, 55n4
education, vocational 124–126, 138; *see also* job-training programs
education, western: basic literacy 42, 118; Christian missionaries 4, 42; clock-based time 4, 47, 50; Methodist schools 47; "push" of western education 37; secondary school 42, 107, 110–114, 118–120, 122, 127–129, 143; Sudanese Interior Mission 4, 42, 47; time discipline 46–47, 56n6; *see also* Sudanese Interior Mission
El-Rufai, Nasir (Governor of Kaduna State) 30
employment in Kaduna after mill closure: construction 114, 120, 128, 130; drivers 103, 120, 126, 138; farming 31, 53, 60, 67, 71, 74, 89, 92–95, 97, 101–103, 110, 119, 128, 137; food sales 99, 100, 128, 138; housework 99, 102, 120, 128, 130; sand collection 14n3, 99; security guards 10, 93, 103, 114; trading 102, 119; washing clothes 99, 120, 125; water sachet sales 84, 109
employment at Kaduna Textiles Ltd: Accounts Department 106; clerical 41; cotton ginning 65; finishing 41; managerial position 9, 10, 17, 41, 43, 50, 52, 54, 59, 62, 149; operations 46; personnel manager 45–46; printing 41; Spinning Department 10, 41, 52, 65; Weaving Department 7, 31, 41, 45, 94, *117*
ethnic associations 26, 34n7, 93, 107, 137; funeral contribution 34n7, 75, 76, 78–80, 83, 84, 113–114; meetings 76, 93; rotating credit group (*adashi*) 80, 91n3
ethnic groups 4, 6–7, 14n6, 23–25, 32, 42, 54, 74, 75, **77**; Atakar 7, 14n6; Atyap 7, 14n6; Bajju 74, 91n1; Ebira 108; Hausa (language) 14n6, 67, 83, 91, 119, 149n18; Idoma 45–46, 110; Igala 42, 76; Igbo 22–23, 43; Jaba [Ham] 7, 14n6, 79; Kadara 111; Kagoro 7, 14n6; Kataf [Atyap] 7, 14n6; Koro 112–113; Kulo 113; Limzo 106; Yoruba14n1, 22, 23, 103
ethnicity 5, 13, 20, 21, 29, 31–32, 45, 74, 76, **77**, 89, 106, 108, 110, 111, 112, 113

Falaye, Olusola (Kaduna Textiles Ltd clinic doctor) 64
farm crops: corn (maize) 94, 95, 97, 100, 101, 120; ginger 5, 100, 119; ground nuts 94, 97; guinea corn (*dawa*) 94, 95, 97; millet 97, 100; rice 94–95, 100, 138; sorghum 100; soy beans 94
farming: Central Bank of Nigeria small-scale program 12, 139; cotton production 12, 140; and famine 93; fertilizer 95; ginger in family hometown 5, 119; in hometown villages 100; plots on outskirts of Kaduna 31, 92–94, 101, 115, 137; rejection of farm work 121, 146; rice production, Kano State 138; scavenging unharvested crops 95, 112; subsistence 93, 100; Tomato Jos Farming and Processing business, Kaduna State 139, 142
food: buying 93; and conjugal relations 96; consuming 93; growing 93; hunger 5, 31, 38, 59, 93, 98, 141; and memories of husbands 93, 96, 98; preparing 93; selling 23, 50, 93, 96, 97–99, 103, 107, 119, 120; *see also* food in Kaduna; food in village; "food poverty"
food after mill closure: food insecurity (*rashin abinci*) 93, 122; limited diets 92, 94, 101; neighbors' assistance 103; reduced number of meals 92; special foods for sick husbands 107
foods eaten: acha seed 107; biscuits 93, 115; bouillon cubes (Maggi) 25, 70, 94, 140, 149n11; corn meal porridge (*tuwo masara*) 92, 101, 114, 115; fish 114; ground cassava (*gari*) 114; leafy vegetable (*tamba*) 107; meat 25, 70, 96; palm oil 70, 72n7; porridge (*tuwo*) 25, 83, 94, 117; rice 25, 70, 94, 114; rice porridge (*tuwo shinkafa*) 108; sorghum porridge 71; vegetable leaf soup (*miya ganiyi*) 101; yam 98, 114; yogurt 115; *see also* rural–urban migration, health consequences
"food poverty" 5, 93, 94, 98, 101, 141; deindustrialization 101; drought and famine 93, 101; unemployment 103; urbanization 101
Foucault, Michel (*The Birth of the Clinic*) 71n1

Gankon, Sylvester 6, 9, 10, 42, 62
government mismanagement and textile mill closures, Kaduna 10–11

graves: cement-covered 1, 75, 85, 86, 113; name plate 111; sand 75, 85–87; tiled 75, 78, 80, 85, *86*, 90, 91n7, 111, 113, 114; tombstones 1, 75, 85, 86

Hartley, Gordon (David Whitehead & Sons Ltd) 40–41
Hertz, Robert (*Death and Right Hand*) 6
hierarchy of labor, Kaduna: construction site work 114, 120; definition of work 119; farming 103, 119; food sales 119; government employment 119; laborers 120; trading 102; white-collar jobs 119
hospitals, Kaduna: ABUTH-Kaduna 67–68; Al-Barka Hospital 64; Asibiti Dutse 108; Gwamna Awan Hospital 65, 66, 67, 78, 112; Nasarawa Hospital 107, 110, 112, 145; Nursing Home Hospital 110, 111; St. Gerard's Catholic Hospital 53, 62, 65, 68, 109, 114; Trinity Hospital 107; Yusuf DanTsoho Hospital 67

industrial capitalism in Kaduna 43, 48, 55, 90, 136; collapse 52, 54, 102, 142; growth 23, 31, 54; post-capitalist industrial time 53, 54, 102; public capitalism 55
industrial time-keeping 4; clocks 38, 48, 49, 50, 51; clocking cards (punch cards) 38, 43, 47, 48, 53; sirens 38, 47; wristwatches 43, 47, 48, *49*, 50
industrialization: and assessment of time 55; criterion of success 142; decline of large textile mills 54, 129; and developed economies 142; different types of transition 54, 102, 136–137; expectations of better life 100, 130; health care 46, 51, 59–60, 61–65, 67, 68, 69–70, 129, 133n6, 144, 145; historical experiences of 102; labor organization 3; manufacturing techniques 142; middle-class lives 100, 129, 130; and modernity 90, 100; wages 53, 59, 92, 100–101, 150n22; work regimen 38, 47, 53, 55
inequality 14; access to food and health care 137, 143, 147, 148; deindustrialization 13, 32, 103, 130, 148; disrespect of wealthy individuals for the impoverished 147; infrastructure 32; irregular provision of electricity 29, 33, 136; unemployment 13, 29, 30, 32, 33
insecurity 20; corruption 29, 144; ethnic conflict 30, 71; kidnapping 12, 31, 143;

Index   157

neighborhood segregation 30; poverty 143; religious conflict 30; robbery 143, 144; unemployment 12, 71, 138–139; violence 12, 25, 29, 31

job-training programs: Aliko Dangote Ultra Modern Skills Acquisition Centre, Kano 138; National Directorate of Employment-Zamfara State 138

Joshua, Haruna (Kaduna Textiles Ltd mill worker) 12, 43, 45–48, 51, 59, 65, 141

Kaduna city: capital of Kaduna State 1, 90; cemeteries 3, 28; centenary celebrations 20, 30, 33; colonial capital of the Protectorate of Northern Nigeria 3, 20, 23, 33n2, 136; colonial origins 3, 20; house ownership 5, 23, 26, 74, 76, 78–79, 86–90, 95, 107, 141, 142–143; industrial areas 3, 31, 89; infrastructure 11, 22, 29, 32, 33, 136, 145; population 22, 29, 34n11; preliminary colonial segregated residential plan, 1913 19–20; rail service 20, 21, 23, 34n5; residential areas 3, 4, 19, 20, 21, 30–32, 89, 140; Township Ordinance, 1917 21; train station, 1927 20

Kaduna Exhibition—"Made in Nigeria" 1959: attendance by Ahmadu Bello and Harold Macmillan 41; cotton field to cotton cloth exhibits 41; highlighting Kaduna Textile Limited 41

Kaduna, first impressions of widows 20, 24; "another country" 25; electric light 24, 25; food availability and variety 25; lack of sociality 25; pipeborne water 25; trains 24

Kaduna neighborhoods: GRA 19, 32; Kaduna South 8, 23, 29, 30, 31, 81; Kakuri 4, 8, 10, 19, 23, 24, 31, 48, 89, 129, 135, 149n18; Kawo 19, 32, 140; Sabon Gari 19, 23, 24, 28, 31, 32; Tudun Wada 19, 27, 30, 31, 32, 67, 108

Kaduna State 1, 4, 7, 23, 30, 32, 42, 44, 79, 80, 90, 123, 139, 145

Kaduna State Bureau for Substance Abuse Prevention and Treatment (KADBUSA) 126, 127; drug prevention 126; treatment 126; vocational training 126

Kaduna Textiles Limited (KTL): Board of Directors 59, 60–62; burial expenses 5, 65, 110; free hospital care 51, 59, 62, 64; free medicines 59; mill clinics 51, 59–61, 62, 63–65; Quarter housing 10, 80, 109; social services 59, 60; subsidized canteen food 59, 62; Welfare Centre 48, 51

Kaduna Textiles Ltd clinics: attendance lists 60, [63]; employee clinic 62, 64; part of hiring process 62; prescribed drugs 62; transfers to local hospitals 62, 64; work incentives 38, 62; worker attendance 63

Kaduna Textiles Ltd clinic, workers' diagnoses 63; aches/pains 63; cor pulmonale 64; coryza (cold) 63; cough 63; diabetes (*ciwo suga*) 63; enteritis 63; fever 64; hypertension (*hawan jini*) 63, 65; ischaemia 64; malaria 64, 108; plasma (blood disorders) 63; stress 65; typhoid 64; *see also* byssinosis

Kaduna Textiles Ltd employment: "certificates of long service" 38, 50; condition of hands 45; education 4, 7, 10, 23, 37, 38, 42, 44, 46–47, 118; *Employee's Handbook* 37, 38, 47, 48; family connections 37, 43, 44; gifts of cloth wrappers 50–51, 56n8; hiring process 37, 43, 45–46, 59, 62; number of employees 41–42; pay levels 38, 59; primary school certificates 45; promotion 38; training 37–39, 46, 47; *see also* employment at Kaduna Textiles Ltd

Kaduna Textiles Ltd mill: closure in 2002 1, 5, 9, 10, 11, 20, 29, 32, 52; establishment 23; opening in 1957 4, 23; products 40–41; transfer of Northern Nigerian Textile Mill ownership to KTL 41; *see also* David Whitehead & Sons Ltd

Kaduna Textiles Ltd mill buildings: construction by Taylor Woodrow (West Africa) Ltd 39–40; equipment installed 40; foundation stone ceremony 40; Welfare Centre for films 48, 51

Kaduna Textiles Ltd mill closure consequences: decline in quality of life 59; different food 92; end of burial support 5, 82, 110; end of education stipends 59; farming 93, 94–95, 101; insufficient food 5, 59, 92–94, 98, 101, 103; lack of health care 59; return to hometown villages 71, 74, 93, 102, 147

Kaduna Textiles Ltd mill closure, reasons for 37; compared with British textile mill closure 54–55; expense of black oil for power generation 52; fall in international oil prices 51; irregular electricity 51,

52, 136; lower-priced Chinese textile imports 136, 139, 142; obsolete equipment 51, 52; structural adjustment program and currency devaluation 51–52, 136
Kaduna Textiles Ltd mill final years: compulsory leave 52, 65; labor protest 52; pay reductions 52, 65, 93; temporary shut-downs 52, 93; work-force reductions by attrition 52
Kaduna Textiles Ltd mill revival: jute bags 139; medium-sized textile operations 137, 149n8; polypropylene bags 139, 149n8; uniforms 11, 12, 137, 148n5; see also SUR International Investments (Turkey)
Kaduna Textiles Ltd unpaid remittances 1, 3, 8, 9, 11, 13, 31, 58–59, 60, 71, 84, 94, 100–103, 135, 141, 147
Kaduna Textiles Ltd widows of dismissed textile mill workers: church groups 75, 78, 83, 84, 103, 112, 113; demonstrations in Kaduna 8–9, 84–85; ethnicity **77**; extended family assistance 31, 122; hometowns 25, 26, 31, 74; husbands' deaths from cardiovascular and pulmonary diseases 60, 66, 67; husbands' health problems 55, 67, 97; problems 8, 25, 93, 98, 99, 100, 107, 108, 109, 110, 113, 114, 115, 126–127, 128; questioning benefits of modern, urban living 25, 31; reconsideration of farming 74, 95, 97, 98, 101, 137; religion 10, 24, 74, 76, 79, 80–81, 84, 87, 90, 107, 109, 110, 111, 113, 114; verbal autopsies 58, 60, 65, 67, 70; work 103, 109, 110, 113, 122
Kaduna Textiles Ltd widows' health 108, 113, 114; adulterated kerosene explosions 99, 104n2; lack of medicine 101
Kaduna Textiles Ltd widows' memories of husbands: assistance with work 97; built house in Kaduna 107; children's education 109; deathbed blessings 98, 102; disagreements and reconciliation 95, 112, 114; dreams 98; farming 97, 98; food 93, 96–97, 98, 113; funeral poster 111; generosity 96; graciousness 96–97; praise for efforts 97; regrets 98; sense of humor 95
Kaduna Textiles Ltd workers' deaths: cardiovascular arrest 66, 67; diabetes mellitus 67, 107, 112; fever 110; gastroenteritis 66; hypertension 65, 112; liver-related disease 60; low glucose blood level 67; malaria 108; road-related accident 60, 68–9, 70, 72n5, 114; *shakuwa* (hiccoughs) 108; swollen body 111; vomiting blood 110; witchcraft 65
Kaduna textile mills: Arewa Textiles 8, 11, 29, 56n5, 81; Finetex 8; Kaduna Textile Limited (KTL) 11, 29, 140; Norspin 29; Nortex 8, 29; Northern Nigerian Textile Mill 41; United Nigerian Textiles Ltd (UNTL) 29, 140

Laqueur, Thomas (*The Work of the Dead*) 1, 13, 34n8, 34n10, 90, 91n5
Livingston, Julie (*Self-Devouring Growth*) 142
Lugard, Frederick (former British colonial administrator) 3, 19–22, 31, 33n2
Lugard Hall 22

Maigari, Joseph, Director-General, KADBUSA 126
Max Lock & Partners report 27–28, 32, 34n9; non-implementation of recommendations 28
mercantile firms: John Holt 40; Kano Merchants Trading Company 41; Paterson Zochonis 40; sale of British manufactured textiles through European firms 41; sale of KTL textiles through Nigerian firms 41; UAC (United Africa Company) 40, 61
Middle Belt states 4, 6, 13, 19, 20, 41, 44, 54, 56n10, 74, 81, 89–90, 131; Benue 4, 23, 46, 104n4; Kogi 4, 10, 23, 42, 44, 76; Nasarawa 4; Plateau 4, 24, 42, 43, 45, 131
migration to Kaduna: education and urban employment 37, 54; expectations of urban living 103, 130; from Middle Belt states 4, 6, 19, 23, 42, 44, 54; modified 93, 137; return visits to hometowns 20, 89, 90; reverse migration 31, 93, 101, 107, 119; rural–urban 75, 102, 131; RWAFF land allocation 23; from southern Kaduna State 4, 6, 7, 23, 42, 44, 54; textile mill employment 6, 41–45; urbanization process 100, 137; see also rural–urban migration, health consequences
mortality data: death certificates 1, 5, 9, 13, 58, 60, 65, *66*, 67–70, 90, 147; hospital

records 58, 69; lack of standardization 58, 60, 66, 68, 69; verbal autopsies 58, 60, 65, 67, 70
Muslim funerals: burial 5, 76, 86–88, 109; cemeteries 76, 84, 86, 87, 109; condolences 76, 77, 109; food 84, 109; gifts 109; graves 5, 75, 86–87; prayers 77, 109; widows' 40-day seclusion 76, 84, 90

national development, government programs 143
National Drug Law Enforcement Agency (NDLEA) 123, 126; drug rehabilitation partnership with Federal Neuro Psychiatric Hospital-Kware 132n5; obstruct drug supplies 126
National Union of Textile, Garment and Tailoring Workers of Nigeria (NUTGTWN) 9, 11, 135, 137
New Nigeria Development Corporation 9, 11, 148
Nigerian Civil War, 1967–1970 28, 43
Nigerian Independence, 1960 19, 23, 31, 33, 41
Northern Nigeria 1, 13, 21, 39, 44, 51, 54, 56n10, 68, 102, 137, 139, 141
Northern Nigerian Textile Mill: company transferred to KTL in 1974 41; production of printed cotton textiles 41
Northern Region Development Corporation 37, 39, 148
Northern Region Marketing Board 39
"Northernization Policy" 23

obituaries 14n1
Orwell, George (*The Road to Wigan Pier*) 137, 142; "allure of mechanization" 142

philanthropy: churches in Kaduna— Christmas food to widows 140; individual donations of food 140, 149n11; individual donations of money 141; Nigerian Army Officers Wives Association, food to widows and orphans 140
Pillowtex textile mill, North Carolina mill closure: incomplete education 129; Kenny Tokunboh, director of Grace Medical Clinic 133n6; loss of affordable health care 129; unemployment 129
political violence in Kaduna 12, 25, 29, 30–31; introduction of Shari'a law 12, 30; kidnapping 12; Miss World pageant 20; post-presidential 2011 election 12, 30
portraits, photograph: children of deceased textile mill workers *117, 145*; widows of dismissed KTL textile mill workers *106, 108, 110, 111, 112, 113*
Protectorate of Northern Nigeria 3, 20, 23, 31, 136; *see also* Kaduna city

railway between Lagos, Kaduna, and Kano 20–21
religion 5, 20, 21, 29, 31–32, 74, 89; Ansar-ud-Deen 23; Baptist 113; ECWA 80, 106, 112; Methodist 47, 110; Muslim-Tariqqa 108; Roman Catholic 4, 13, 111; *see also* burial; cemeteries
rice production: closure of borders to rice imports 138; return to farming 94–95; rice mills in Kura, Kano State 138–139
roads *see* Kaduna city, infrastructure; transportation development projects
road-related accidents: congested city streets 68; high-speed driving 68; importance of qualitative accounts 60; and minimal traffic regulation 68; pedestrian deaths 68; road traffic accidents (RTA), 69, 71, 72n5; road traffic deaths 60, 68–70, 142
Royal West African Frontier Force (RWAFF): barracks in Kaduna 21; post-World War II land allocation 23; rail transport 21
rural–urban migration, health consequences: cardiovascular disease 70; colorectal cancer 70; diabetes 70; food and changing diet 70; hypertension 70; obesity 70

Sen, Amartya: famine and poverty 93; government programs 143; "positional objectivity" 72n4; quality of life and longevity 9, 59, 70
Simdik, Wordam (president, Coalition of Closed Unpaid Textile Workers Association Nigeria) 2
Small to Medium-Sized Enterprises (SME) 137–138, 139, 148; environmentally sound manufacturing 142, 148; and new forms of production 139, 142; *see also* education, vocational
Sokoto Caliphate 54, 56n10; Muslim rule 54; slavery 54; southern Kaduna ethnic groups 14n6, 54; subsequent Christian conversion 54

160 Index

stories of mill closures 101–102; documentation of deindustrialization 102; "dynamic part of material world" 102; Nigerian newspaper reports 102, 140
Structural Adjustment Program 29, 65, 136, 148n2; currency devaluation 29, 65; deteriorating conditions of KTL mill 29; KTL workers' compulsory leave 65
sub-Saharan Africa mortality 58, 144
Sudanese Interior Mission (SIM): churches 42; "classes for religious instruction" only 42; Middle belt and southern Kaduna state 42; missionaries 4, 42
SUR International Investments (Turkey): focus on military uniforms 11, 12, 148n5; refurbish KTL mill and update equipment 11; request for prepaid contract from Nigerian government 12
Sweet, Sweet Codeine: Nigeria's Cough Syrup Crisis (BBC documentary) 132n1
The Sympathetic Undertaker ('Biyi Bandele-Thomas) 7, 12–13, 24

textile imports to Nigeria: Central Bank of Nigeria forex restrictions 12; Chinese trading firm offices in Lagos and Kano 14n10, 139; customs duties 10, 147; manufactured in China in 21st century 136; manufactured in UK 21, 40, 136; *see also* mercantile firms
textile manufacturing decline: in Nigeria 54–55; in UK 54–55, 56n11, 149n9; in US 129
textile mills in Kaduna *see* Kaduna textile mills
textile mills in UK 21, 54, 55
textile mill workers, mortality data: British textile workers 9, 14n8; Coalition of Closed Unpaid Textile Workers Association Nigeria 1, 2–3, 8–9, 13, 58, 60, 130, 135, 147; hospital records 58, 70, 69–70; 107, 109, 114; politics of mortality 14n12
Thompson, E.P. (*The Making of the English Working Class*): industrial capitalism 38; industrialization 136–137; school 46–47, 56n6; time 38, 46, 56n7
time: attention to 47, 82, 83, 90, 139; clock-based 4; employers' time 38; equation of time and money 13, 38, 48, 52, 53; "free" 52, 53, 55, 103; punctuality 37, 43, 47, 48, 53, 55, 83, 90, 136; "time thrift" 46; wasting 38, 47, 61; and work 13, 38, 47, 51, 135; *see also* industrial time-keeping
transportation development projects, 21st century, Nigeria 143–144

unemployment: compared with Boko Haram 12; and deindustrialization 3, 6, 9, 29, 101, 103; and drug use 71, 103, 116; as indirect violence 12; and inequality 13, 30, 32–33; and insecurity 143; youth 6, 71; *see also* drug use in Kaduna
UNIDO textile reports, Nigeria 149n10
urbanization and mortality 144–145

vital statistics: demographic analysis 58; difficulties of determining causes of adult deaths, Northern Nigeria 58; and longitudinal studies 71n2

Walley, Christine (*Exit Zero*): deindustrialization in US 129, 130, 141; reevaluation of future directions 130–131, 148, 150n22; stories 102
"work of the dead" in Northern Nigeria: burial and religious belief 75, 76, 86, 90; cemeteries and social identity 5, 147; Coalition of Closed Unpaid Textile Workers deceased worker list 2, 101, 102; family connections and home village graves 6, 89, 90, 102, 147; graves and claims to houses, property 6, 10, 74, 88, 90; maintain past traditions 76; and modernity 87, 90, 91n5; naming 1, 6, 13, 85, 132; payment of termination remittances 2, 101, 102, 132, 147; *see also* Laqueur, Thomas
World Trade Organization: GATT rules (2005) 14n10, 136; Multifibre Agreement (1994) 136
World War II 22–23

youth: drug use 71, 99, 103, 116, 126; ethnic and religious conflict 30, 71; inequality 71; insecurity 31, 71, 143; interrupted education 14n4, 99, 104n3, 112, 115, 122, 130; unemployment 6, 71; vocational education 124, 126, 138
Yusuf, Shaibu 42